Mari

PLAYS THREE

Marina Carr's plays have been translated into many
languages and are produced around the world. A member
of Aosdána, she lectures in the School of English at Dublin
City University and lives in Dublin with her husband
and four children.

MARINA CARR

Plays Three

Sixteen Possible Glimpses
Phaedra Backwards
The Map of Argentina
Hecuba
Indigo

Introduced by the author

FABER & FABER

This collection first published in 2015 by Faber and Faber Ltd
74–77 Great Russell Street, London WC1B 3DA

Typeset by Country Setting, Kingsdown, Kent CT14 8ES
Printed in England by CPI Group (UK) Ltd, Croydon CR0 4YY

A CIP record for this book is available from the British Library

ISBN 978–0–571–32881–9

4 6 8 10 9 7 5 3

For Dermot, William, Daniel, Rosa and Juliette

Contents

Introduction

A few thoughts on this new collection.

Sixteen Possible Glimpses came out of my reading of the work and the life of Anton Pavlovich Chekhov. What can be said about Chekhov except he was here for a mere forty four years and that he left an enormous legacy after him, both in what he wrote and in how he lived.

Sixteen Possible Glimpses is an attempt to capture, imagine and riff on those fleeting moments that make up his life and work. He has been an enormous influence on me as he has on many writers before me and no doubt on many to come.

It was directed by my good friend Wayne Jordan.

Phaedra Backwards is a retelling of the Phaedra myth. I wanted to go back into her family and see how that had shaped her, so it deals as much with the Minotaur and Pasiphae as it does with Phaedra. It takes elements, motifs and images from everywhere and runs with them.

It was commissioned by the McCarter Theater and directed by Emily Mann, a brilliant woman.

The Map of Argentina is a meditation on love and what happens when it is denied and betrayed or pursued and hunted down. There seems to be no right answer to this conundrum. There is always fallout. There are always consequences and happiness ever proves a maddening and elusive quantity.

It was commissioned by the Abbey Theatre under the auspices of Fiach Mac Conghaile, another good friend.

So far it has had a staged reading, directed with great aplomb by the wonderful Fiona Shaw.

It has yet to be produced.

Hecuba. I always thought Hecuba got an extremely bad press. Rightly or wrongly I never agreed with the verdict on her. This play is an attempt to reexamine and, in part, redeem a great and tragic queen. History, as they say, is written by the winners. Sometimes I think myths are too and the fragile Greek state circa 500 BC needed to get certain myths in stone to bolster their sense of themselves and validate their savage conquests. It was easy to trash her. She was dead. She was Trojan. She was a woman. No doubt she was as flawed as the rest of us but to turn a flaw to a monstrosity smacks to me of expedience. This is my attempt to show her in another light, how she suffered, what she might have felt and how she may have reacted.

It was commissioned by the RSC, an institution that has been very supportive of my work down the years and for that they will always have my gratitude.

Indigo was also commissioned by the RSC. It came out of many great and crazy conversations I had with the actor, writer and director Mikel Murfi. I attended a workshop he gave at the RSC on fairies, demons, ghouls and every sort of fantastic creature you could imagine out of folklore and myth. *Indigo* is my response to both Mikel's ideas and the fabulous actors and creative team who were part of that workshop.

So there you have it. Another collection. I didn't think it would take so long to get together. But Time races and Life has many claims. Huge thanks and appreciation to all who have helped me this far along the road.

Marina Carr, July 2015

SIXTEEN POSSIBLE GLIMPSES

Sixteen Possible Glimpses was first performed on the Peacock stage of the Abbey Theatre, Dublin, on 30 September 2011. The cast, in alphabetical order, was as follows:

Alexander Malcolm Adams
Olga Cathy Belton
Suvorin Michael James Ford
Kolya (*student*) Gavin Fullam
Black Monk / Dr Schworer Will Irvine
Pavel Mark Lambert
Tolstoy Gary Lilburn
Kolya (*brother*) Aaron Monaghan
Lika Deirdre Mullins
Masha Caitríona Ní Mhurchú
Yevgenia Bríd Ní Neachtain
Chekhov Patrick O'Kane

Director Wayne Jordan
Lighting Designer Sinead McKenna
Voice Director Andrea Ainsworth
Movement Director Sue Mythen
Composer Sam Jackson
Design Assistant Cáit Corkery
Audio-Visual Design Hugh O'Conor

Characters

Anton Pavlovich Chekhov
writer, doctor

Masha
his sister, teacher

Yevgenia Moroza
his mother

Pavel
his father

Kolya
his brother, painter.

Alexander
called Sasha, his brother, writer, journalist

Suvorin
friend, newspaper magnate, writer

Lika
young woman, opera singer

Olga
his wife, actress

Tolstoy
writer

Kolya
young Russian in Badenweiler

Black Monk
supernatural figure

Dr Schworer

Old Man

Waiter 1

Waiter 2

Servant

Setting

The set must encompass a hotel room, a train station, two restaurants, several gardens and interiors. I suggest a bare space with a table and chairs.

A backdrop that spans the length and width of the stage. On this backdrop Russian paintings of the period, magnified. A different painting for each scene. These paintings along with lighting will be paramount in creating the many different atmospheres in the play. (Levitan's paintings are stunning, he was also a close friend of Chekhov's. Also look at Chagall and designs for Diaghilev's ballets.)

Music. Also hugely important. From Russian church music to folk to Gypsy to piano. All to create mood and tone.

Act One

Badenweiler. The balcony of a room in the Hotel Sommer.
   Darkness.
   We hear the laboured breathing of Anton Pavlovich.
Let us listen to this fight for breath a while.
   Lights up.
   We see Anton Pavlovich standing in the stifling heat.
Quartet music from below. A fan whirrs.
   Suddenly the Black Monk is there. A tall, gaunt figure
in black robes and cowl. We never see his face. He
stands there till Anton Pavlovich registers him.

Anton So you tracked me down?

Black Monk What is distance to me, or time for that
matter?

Anton You take unfair advantage. Don't have the energy
to stave you off any more.

Black Monk It's not a war, Anton Pavlovich.

Anton Believe me from this vantage point it is. I'm only
forty-four.

Black Monk You think eternity cares whether you're
nine or ninety?

Anton Go away. You don't exist. I must've finally lost it.

Black Monk Oh, but I do exist. Don't be afraid. I've
watched you since you were a boy, came out of a
thousand-year sleep to watch you live. There isn't a thing
about you I don't know so don't be afraid. Eternity has

9

always had its claim on you. Why should that surprise you?

Anton Doesn't surprise me. It shames me.

Black Monk Why does it shame you?

Anton I'd have liked more of eternity here.

Black Monk And so you're not prepared?

Anton Give me five more years.

A knock on the door. The Black Monk disappears.

Come in, it's open.

Enter Kolya, a student.

Kolya Was wondering if you needed anything.

Anton Could you pass me that glass of water please?

Kolya does. Anton can barely hold the glass. His hand trembles as he drinks.

Kolya You don't want to lie down?

Anton Better to keep moving.

Kolya Yes . . . but . . . it's hot, isn't it?

Anton Unbearable. Isn't there a cooler room?

Kolya The whole place is a furnace, maybe at the back, I'll ask them again.

Anton Thank you.

Kolya Those reporters from home are still in the lobby. They keep asking about you.

Anton Don't let them near me.

Kolya Certainly not.

Anton And don't give them any information about me.

Kolya God no.

Anton You're Moscow, aren't you?

Kolya Yeah, and you're from the south.

Anton A lazy southerner. And what brings you to Badenweiler? You don't look sick.

Kolya No, the brother. My mother sent me to keep him company only he doesn't want my company. Are you hungry?

Anton No.

Kolya Just your wife said to take care of your lunch order.

Anton You're very kind. Kolya, isn't it?

Kolya Yeah.

Anton I had a brother Kolya. He was a painter. A very gifted painter. Could have been better than Levitan.

Kolya 'Had'?

Anton Drink . . . women . . . the dreaded bacilli.

Kolya Oh, I'm sorry.

Anton Yeah, the same as me . . . For years I wouldn't name my disease, thought to confuse it, thought if I didn't acknowledge it, it would go away . . . I nursed Kolya at the end, carried him from room to room like a child, the wild eyes of him. Then I couldn't watch any more. I'm waiting for a train and a telegram comes. Three words. Kolya is dead.

Kolya Keats nursed his brother too.

Anton That's right. Tom, wasn't it? The brother?

Kolya And Keats was a doctor too.

Anton And Keats was one of God's own.

Kolya What do you mean?

Anton He came with it all, just had to transcribe it.

Kolya Many would say the same about you.

Anton They're wrong. As usual. Every word, every line has been a struggle for me. Do you have a few minutes to spare?

Kolya I've all the minutes, nothing to do here.

Anton Yeah, the women are hogs, have you seen the state of them in the dining room, lashing into the grub, sweat pouring off them, will you write a letter for me? There's paper there. What date is it?

Kolya June thirtieth.

Anton Okay? Mariya Chekhova, Autka, Yalta, Rus. Got that?

Kolya Yeah.

Anton 'Masha, why haven't you written? Where are you? We're still at the Hotel Sommer and will be a while yet as I've had a bit of a setback. I'm high as fifty kites thanks to the morphine. The food is gorgeous but my ruined stomach can't take it so I watch Olga eat. The people here have the fattest arses I've ever come across and so satisfied with themselves that I'm glad I don't have to wander the streets looking at them. I miss my garden. How is my new cedar? And how is Mamasha? Is she sparing the ink too? Olga got her teeth fixed and bought me a new suit you could wrap four times round me. The poor fool thinks she's married to a giant. Be well, be happy, be good to the poor, look after my old

mother and don't be alarmed this is not my handwriting.
I'll be fine in a few days.' Let me sign it.

Kolya If I run down now I'll catch the post. Need
anything from the shops?

Anton No.

Kolya I'll be able to tell my grandchildren that I wrote a
letter for Chekhov.

Exit Kolya.

Anton Long, long ago, once upon a time, the end.

Lights.

SCENE TWO

*St Petersburg. Train station. A military band off. A choir.
Noise and bustle from a huge crowd. Trains. Whistles.
Smoke. Din.*
  *Enter Olga Knipper in travelling clothes. She powders
her face and puts on lipstick as she is followed by an old
man wheeling a coffin on a trolley.*

Man It's light. Is it a child, mam?

Olga What?

Man Lost a child myself, mam.

Olga (*looking around*) What are you on about?

Man It's when they hammer the lid on.

Olga (*shouts*) Masha! Masha!

Man The worst.

Olga Masha, over here!

Hugs her dramatically.

Masha Oh Olga, Olga, what did you do to him?

Olga And they've a full military band playing for him. All these people. And the choir. They don't usually have military bands for writers, do they?

Masha The band is for a general that died in Manchuria. What on earth happened to him? I told you not to take him abroad. You never listen. (*Shouts off.*) That's my mother! Let her through! For God's sake, where's she going now? Let her through!

Olga None of these people are for Anton? None of them? Just you?

Masha They're all waiting in Moscow.

Olga But I wired them! I wired all the newspapers. The damn train. They threw him into a carriage with 'Oysters' written on it at the border. They had him on ice.

Masha (*shouts*) Sasha! Here! Over here!

Olga Don't be surprised if you find fish scales all over the coffin.

Enter Alexei Suvorin on a walking stick.

Suvorin Is this Anton Pavlovich?

Olga Yes it is. (*Kisses him.*) Alexei. Yes that's all that's left of him now. And the cork flew out of the champagne as he died.

Masha You gave him champagne?

Olga I didn't give it to him.

Masha Over here! For God's sake, she's deaf as . . . He's not allowed to drink. You know that!

Olga It was the doctor, some doctor thing, they give champagne to one another at the end. And the cork just flew out of the bottle, and a big black moth flapping at the window and fog slithering into the room.

Suvorin He was angry with me, don't know what I did to him, think he was just tired of me. I bored him, he was very easily bored, but I loved him like a son. More.

He strokes the coffin.

Masha This is what happens when I'm not around. This is all your fault! Dragging him halfway round the world. I hope he didn't suffer.

Olga Of course he suffered. You think it's easy to die? It's not like on stage when they take their last breath. It's awful. Awful. The panic in his face, minutes going by, thinking it's over and then this terrible sound. How are we going to get out of here?

Suvorin I wrote to him the other day and didn't post it, said to myself, I'll give him a dose of his own medicine. Can I be of any assistance?

Masha We better wait till the general goes.

Olga Is he being buried today? He should be, the heat, the smell, do you get it?

Masha What smell . . . What are you . . .

Olga He has to be buried today. He has to. I'm a wreck. I haven't slept for a week.

Masha What did he talk about at the end?

Olga He was raving, muttering about I don't know what, sharks, neckties, the Japanese and at the very last, he did call my name. Twice.

Masha Twice? Did he mention me?

Olga I don't think he did. Should he have?

Masha You standing there so smug with your corpse. You're only the handmaiden of death. Don't forget that. You don't own him. You meant nothing to him. You dare bring him home like this and you don't even have the decency to tell me what he said.

Olga You're just out of control.

Masha Keep your information. Keep it! You show up here blathering about fish scales and moths. You have a nerve. You're talking about my brother! My brother.

Enter Yevgenia Moroza. She kneels at the coffin. She is followed by Alexander (Sasha).

Yev (*stroking the coffin*) That's three of my children you've taken from me . . . and I dreamt about you the other night. You were eating sunflower seeds, a chubby little fella with no shoes, the way you went round as a boy, always chewing on something.

Alexander Tolstoy sent a telegram.

Masha and Olga go for it. Olga gets it.

He's sick himself or he'd meet the train in Moscow. Let's get out of here. Come on, Mamasha.

Suvorin If you'll allow me I think I can get us through the paperwork fairly quickly. Come this way.

And they exit with coffin.

Masha Show me Tolstoy's telegram.

Olga Later. Later. I'm ready to collapse.

Masha It belongs with his papers.

Olga Which means it belongs to you now. (*Shoves it at her.*) Take it then. You're one of those people, no matter what you take it'll never be enough.

And they are off by now.

Lights.

SCENE THREE

The garden of a dacha at Lintvariov's estate outside Moscow.
   Enter Lika, a beautiful blonde in her early twenties. She smokes, drinks a glass of champagne.
   Piano music off.
   Enter Anton, radiant, in the prime of his youth and beauty. He comes up behind her, kisses her.

Anton And how is my nightingale?

Lika You're a complete flirt.

Anton Would life be worth living without it?

Lika You play us one off the other.

Anton It's my deprived childhood. Can never get enough attention from women.

Lika You love talk me and then you do the exact same with every skirt that crosses your path. You want a finger in all the pies.

Anton Is that what I want?

Lika I saw you.

Anton What?

Lika Smooching the astronomer, the big owl eyes of her sucking you in.

17

Anton You know it's you I want, sweetheart. What can I do? I've a big band of lazy siblings to support as well as the old folks.

Lika Are you sleeping with her?

Anton We're not married, are we?

Lika Are you or aren't you?

Anton Don't tell me there's a grumpy little housewife lurking behind those golden curls.

Lika So it's a crime to want to be your wife?

Anton We wouldn't last a month. You're going to be an opera singer. Men will throw roses at your feet. You think I'd allow that? Believe me, you wouldn't like me as a husband. Where I come from a wife is a slave. So Lika, Lika, sweetheart, enchantress, let me take off your dress.

Undoing her buttons.

Lika Here? You must be joking.

Anton We've never done it outside. It's much better. Everything is better outside. I want to take you up, up into the mountains and . . .

Lika No. They'll see.

Anton Do what your doctor tells you.

Unbuttoning her, kissing her, making love to her. She holds the glass of champagne, smokes.

Just look at you.

Lika Men'll say anything in heat.

Anton Yeah we will . . . You know the only proof of God's existence?

Lika Women?

Anton You could ask me for anything now and it's yours, that's what jackasses men are in the presence of beauty.

Lika All right. Marry me.

Anton First I need to sample the goods. I'm a shopkeeper's son, after all.

Lika You won't marry me and you know it.

Anton I'll give you a life of misery if that's what you really want.

Lika You don't have a very high opinion of marriage.

Anton No, I don't. People marry for the stupidest reasons.

Lika And what will you marry for?

Anton For sex of course.

Lika Stop, will you, someone might come.

Anton They're all at the same by the river. Everyone's doing it, Lika, everyone except us.

Lika They're playing cards in the music room. Suppose I get pregnant.

Anton Suppose you do?

Lika I only want to be with you.

Anton Then be with me.

Lika And then you'll cast me aside like an old coat.

Enter Masha.

Masha There you are. I've been all over. Lika, come and sing for us.

Anton (*covering Lika*) Would you ever get lost, Masha!

Masha You're a right pair of tarts. I'll have to write to the bishop.

Exit Masha.

Anton Another reason I don't need a wife. I have Masha.

Lika I'm getting the first train out of here in the morning. No more love letters. No more invitations to this harem you keep here. And don't you promise me anything again.

Anton So serious, Lika.

Lika Three years you've kept me on a string and behind my back riding half of Moscow.

Anton Flattered you've such a high opinion of my 'riding' abilities.

Lika I hope someone breaks your heart soon. That's assuming you have one.

Exiting.

Anton Look at the flounce of that ass. She'll be back!

Lika (*calls from offstage*) Not this time. I'm off now to bed the first man I clap eyes on.

Anton Go ahead, who's stopping you?

Running after her.

Lika, Lika, wait, don't be getting thick over nothing.

Lika (*off*) I'm not listening to you any more, Anton Pavlovich.

And both off by now.

Lights.

SCENE FOUR

Dacha at Lintvariov's estate.
  Enter Kolya in nightshirt, trousers, socks.
  *He is in the middle of a massive haemorrhage, reels
and fights for breath.*
  Alexander runs on.

Alexander (*shouts off*) Anton! Get in here now! Anton!

Anton Ice. Get some ice and my bag. It's in the hall.

  Alexander runs off.

Anton (*holding Kolya*) Breathe. That's it. Let it all
down, don't stop it, just breathe, don't swallow.

  Muffled sounds from Kolya. The blood keeps coming.

Kolya, listen to me. Don't panic. This is nothing. You're
going to be fine.

Alexander (*throws bag beside Anton*) There's no ice.

Anton The fuckin' country's falling down with ice and
snow. Get snow! Jesus!

  Exit Alexander, running.

Anton Kolya, I'm going to give you another shot, okay.
Calm now. This'll help. Let's keep it calm. That's it.
Good man. That's it.

  Injects him. Another avalanche of blood.
    *Alexander runs on with a fistful of snow. Anton
rips Kolya's shirt.*

Pack it on here.

Alexander Is he gone?

Anton Get more. Go get more.

Alexander runs off.

Breathe now. Come on. Come on. It's only a bit of snow.

A terrible breath from Kolya.

That's more like it. Normally. Don't force them. That's it. The worst is over now. You're all right. I'm here, Sasha's here. You're with us and everything's all right.

Kolya You smell like a hoor.

Anton You wish.

Kolya No point washing when there are no women around. What I wouldn't do to a woman right now.

Anton Goes with the territory, Kolya.

Kolya What do you mean?

Anton Oh, when I worked the TB wards as a student the smell of semen'd knock you out, and the women's section, they'd try to pull you into the bed on top of them.

Kolya I should've been a doctor . . . Never knew dying was such hard work.

Alexander (*who has come on, cleaning up*) Can I get you anything, Kolya?

Kolya Vodka.

Anton Yeah, get him a glass.

Kolya's head drops.

Alexander He's gone. He's gone.

Anton He's just passed out . . . Have them disinfect the floors. Now. And his sheets changed.

Alexander Is this the end?

Anton Surprised he's still with us. Look at his hand, like tissue. I'm out of here this evening.

Alexander But he'll want you with him.

Anton Masha's coming.

Alexander And if he dies while you're away?

Anton I've been nursing him ten weeks round the clock. Where were you?

Alexander I was working.

Anton Drinking your head off more like.

And exit Alexander. Anton sits there holding Kolya.

Kolya (*waking*) These are not my socks.

Anton They're mine.

Kolya I'd take the shirt off your back.

Anton You would. You have.

Kolya I'm keeping you from your writing.

Anton I'm a doctor first.

Kolya So you keep saying.

Anton I only write for money. Whereas you, you're the genuine article.

Kolya No. No finishing power. That's the hallmark of the artist. Finishing power. Get it done. Get it done. On to the next. It's only a sprint against time because nothing turns out as you've truly imagined it. Couldn't be bothered finally, sooner fuck and drink red wine.

Anton Wouldn't we all?

Kolya You either live or watch other people live. That's the choice. You can't do both. I chose to live.

Anton To the hilt.

Kolya You think I wasted my life?

Anton I think you could've been a little more faithful to what you were given. You know how many artists in this world? Real artists?

Kolya None.

Anton Almost none. Maybe one in every two million. If even. So when I say you are an artist I'm telling you, you were born like that, with the gift, and no one can take it from you except yourself. The battle with others pales in comparison with the battle we wage against ourselves.

Kolya I've always thought the only thing to do is surrender, surrender with grace. We're shadows, shadows on someone else's path, parasites on the soul, like ticks in a haycock. We know nothing.

Anton A bit esoteric for me.

Kolya You think we're all dust.

Anton I've dissected a few corpses in my time and even the most hardened spiritualist must sooner or later ask himself, where exactly is the soul located?

Kolya Sweet words to sing me to my rest.

Anton Yeah . . . well . . .

Kolya Don't worry, the auld fella'll be in flinging incense and icons at me in a minute. Where's Sasha gone with the vodka?

Anton Come on, we'll get you back to bed . . . Can you walk?

Kolya Let's see.

A painful struggle. Anton half carries him off.

24

And what is it about Masha?

Anton What about her?

Kolya She hangs on your every word.

Anton Does she?

Kolya You ask too much of her.

Anton I ask too much of everyone.

And they're off by now.

Lights.

SCENE FIVE

A restaurant in Petersburg.
Sound of violin. Bustle of people eating, laughing, talking. In Russian.
Enter two Waiters. They set a table.
Enter Suvorin. He takes off his coat, hat, gloves, hands them to waiter, looks around.

Suvorin This the best you can do?

Waiter We're overbooked, sir.

Suvorin (*nods to someone*) This place is gone to the dogs. Next I'll be dining with nurses. Vodka. Blini. Caviar.

Waiter Yes, sir.

Enter Anton in an immaculate suit.

Suvorin Well if it isn't the escaped convict.

Kisses him, hugs him.

I've missed you.

Anton Good to be back in Petersburg. This city is intoxicating if you could get rid of the people.

Suvorin Wait till I take you to Europe.

Anton Are you taking me to Europe?

Suvorin Next month. We're going to see Duse, we're going to La Fenice, we're going to Monte Carlo. We're going to kiss Il Papa. On the lips.

Anton But I just got back. I'm broke.

Suvorin When did that ever stop you?

Anton Beginning to feel like a kept woman.

Waiters arrive with food and drink, lay it out, serve them.

I have to settle down, at least that's what everyone keeps telling me. I have to work, read, I'm a complete ignoramus. Hong Kong was fantastic, fell for a Jap, didn't get out of bed for three days. Have you ever done it with an Oriental?

Suvorin Have you ever done it with two Orientals?

Anton They're very straightforward aren't they, almost manly, none of this coyness and simpering you get from Russian women about how you've ruined them just because you've given them their first decent orgasm. Good to see you, Alexei.

Raises his glass. They drink shots of vodka. Eat and drink throughout.

Suvorin And your cough?

Anton Gone. No blood for eight months. Everyone should go across Siberia in a horse and cart.

Suvorin You're crazy. Crazy.

Anton Yeah, so they're saying in the papers, taking the complete piss out of me. Your hacks are the most vicious. Why do you let them take your friend down like that?

Suvorin Freedom of opinion.

Anton Freedom? We don't know the meaning of the word. It's a fuckin' police state we live in. Spies everywhere, censors butchering everything I write.

Suvorin I protect you from the worst of them.

Anton Why do they hate me so much? People I've never met, spoken to?

Suvorin They hate you because you're brilliant.

Anton Plenty out there good as me. They say the stupidest things. I'm a very simple man, I love lying in a field of new-mown hay, love fishing, being around beautiful women, and they want to kill me over a few little stories and plays.

Suvorin If it's any consolation they hate me too.

Anton And so they should. You run the press. You're a powerful man. Me? What am I? My grandfather was a slave who had to buy his own freedom, his wife's, his son's, he didn't have enough to buy his own daughter back but they threw her in as a bonus – so she could do the washing-up I suppose.

Suvorin Don't you understand that's precisely the reason?

Anton Because my father was born a serf?

Suvorin You're a maverick, a peasant who has risen above his station. The ones who hold the reins in this godforsaken hole of a country are all gentry or what passes for gentry. You're an upstart, Anton Pavlovich.

Why don't you go back to your hovel and chaw on your turnip? They're afraid of you. God knows what you might write next. They have to keep you down. Use it. Turn it on them. Drive them mad. What do they know about anything? Rotten to the core, snub me all the time. I'm one of the richest men here in Pete. Do they invite me in? I have to fight for a table in a decent restaurant. I'm here most nights and look where they put me? While Count Gaga over there dribbling into his kasha, who hasn't paid a bill since the Napoleonic wars and won't ever, has the pick of the room. Let him. He'll never understand what it is to be self-made, to be born without privilege, and he'll never, never, know the thrill of wrestling the world to the ground.

Anton It's disgusting if that's the way it is.

Suvorin They read you, albeit with malice, trying to catch you out, but they do read you. What more do you want?

Anton I want it all. Houses, children, I suppose that means a wife, you can't really have children without one. But please God and his holy mother not a wife yet.

Suvorin What is it with you young men and marriage?

Anton I'd have to poison her. Waking up with this lump beside you, it's not natural.

Suvorin Nothing wrong with a wife about the place as long as you don't get too involved.

Anton Some of us are stupid enough to believe in love.

Suvorin It's not important.

Anton Some die for it. Some kill. It is important.

Suvorin And how is Lika?

Anton Don't talk to me about that one. She ran off with my friend, my ex-friend.

Suvorin Who?

Anton Potapenko.

Suvorin I thought he was married.

Anton Well, of course he is, and now the little trollop is pregnant somewhere between Paris and Berlin, writing me the most heartbreaking letters. He doesn't give a damn about her.

Suvorin Well, he got her on the rebound.

Anton I never finished with her. I just didn't jump when she said jump. And now I'm expected to leap into the breach and rescue her and unborn child from the whole sorry mess.

Suvorin And why don't you?

Anton After what she's done? No way! I'm rid of her now.

Suvorin But it rankles.

Anton She's made her bed as they say, besides she wasn't bright enough, and I've a very low tolerance for those without the spark. Anyway what use would I be to a woman? Grigorovich told me I'll be dead by forty. (*Raises his glas*s.) Well, here's to an early exit.

Suvorin How dare he say that to you? I don't care if he is Grigorovich.

Anton He dared. You know why? Because he's lived his whole life as a dare. That gives him the right. The maestro speaking. He also blessed me. He was the first to tell me I could write, that I wasn't a hack, and at a time when I didn't know who or what I was. You don't forget people like Grigorovich. You pay attention and every silver lining has its cloud. So? Live with it. Besides it wasn't news, only confirms what I already know. (*Drinks.*) Sakhalin was an eye-opener.

Waiter Are you ready to order now, sir?

Suvorin Get us a better table first.

Waiter It'll be a while.

Suvorin We have time. I'm sick watching the rats waltzing across the borscht and your chef scratching his arse with the teapot. Look at him! Look at him! When I was in prison the biggest stick they could threaten you with was Sakhalin.

Anton And well they might. I arrived at night, fires all over the island, smoke like great dragons swirling in the wind as if some God had taken off his hat and tossed his hair. It was straight out of Dante or Bosch. Bodies writhing round the fires, lawless, naked, screams from the shadows, girls of nine and ten working the waterfront in slips and lipstick. I disembarked with the convicts, all in chains. Some of them didn't know what it was they had done. One man had his five-year-old son with him, clinging to his father's chains for fear he'd lose him in the swarm . . . I saw a man get ninety lashes. By thirty I ran from the courtyard.

Suvorin Sights a man should not subject himself to.

Anton Maybe . . . And because there were more men on the island than women, any consignment of women convicts caused huge excitement. They'd line up at the pier to watch them coming off the boats, trying to smarten themselves up a bit so as to appear attractive to the women. And then filing into this barn, the women sitting on their beds, the men looking at them, smiling, trying to catch their eye. And if she smiled back or nodded or just returned the look, they asked the guards to go and speak with her. And the women asked questions like, 'Do you have a bed?' 'Is it flax or straw?' 'Do you have a samovar? Plates? Pots, a table, chairs, how many?' And if the men had all of these things or some of them, then the woman would say, 'Will you hit me?' And to watch them, talking in whispers, trying to build a life out of nothing, out of the lash and ignorance and despair, you wouldn't do it to a dog and these are our people. And the men for the most part were courteous, made no distinction between old and young women, just wanted a woman, though when I asked they said they'd prefer a woman who could have children, you'd walk by the huts in the evening and see them holding their infants, playing with them after another day of back-breaking savagery and insults. I went to Sakhalin expecting a chamber of horrors and I found one. But I also found beauty. Didn't expect that. Men, women, children condemned for life and shining out of them the soul's magnificent determination to wrestle from this world more, far more, than it is prepared to yield.

Suvorin So what are you going to do now?

Anton Going to ask you for more money.

Suvorin Against the next few stories?

Anton Don't feel like a writer these days but yeah, I suppose.

Suvorin Come to Europe with me, recharge the batteries.

Waiter We've a table by the window if it's to your liking, sir.

Suvorin And bloody time too.

Anton I'll need another advance for that but I'm there already.

Suvorin puts his glass on Waiter's tray.

Waiter I'll take that, sir. (*Glass.*)

Anton The clientele here are incredibly rude, aren't they?

Waiter Pigs. Sir. The lot of them.

Anton Yeah. Well, as my old mother says, offer it up. Offer it up. (*Puts his glass on Waiter's tray.*)

And exit. Waiter clears table and exit.

Lights.

SCENE SIX

Melikhovo. Chekhov's estate outside Moscow.
Enter the Black Monk. Takes papers out of Anton's desk. Reads.
Enter Anton in fur coat and fur hat. Doctor's bag.

Black Monk You're writing about me.

Anton Trying to.

Black Monk And building three schools?

Anton A nightmare. Committee lining their pockets, peasants stealing the timber and brick and not a child within fifty miles who can read. And now we're in the middle of a cholera epidemic. They'll all be dead before there's a school finished.

Sits wearily.

Black Monk You're tired, Anton Pavlovich.

Anton I'm very tired.

Black Monk And how is Lika?

Anton Her daughter died, so she's devastated obviously.

Black Monk And you?

Anton She wasn't mine. Have to keep remembering that.

Black Monk Those distinctions mean nothing in the eternal scheme.

Anton Yes, I know, but I can't live in the eternal scheme. I have to live here. I have to do it here . . . And they laughed, booed, hissed my beautiful *Seagull* out of Petersburg.

Black Monk Good. That's good.

Anton How on earth could that be good?

Black Monk It'll make you a better writer.

Anton I disagree. We need encouragement to flourish, like a plant needs the sun. They're a bloodless, loveless, passionless lot. Don't they drink? Don't they have hearts? Don't they yearn at all? Wouldn't know a decent sentence if it bit their nose off.

Black Monk Then don't write for them any more. Write for the one in a million. Write for two thousand years from now.

Anton I'm not that altruistic. Yet.

Enter Pavel. The Black Monk dissolves. Anton sharpens a pencil, then another. Pavel lays tea tray on table. Pours for Anton.

Anton I pay the servants good money to do that.

Pavel Yeah, well, afternoons kill me.

Anton Could you ask them to keep the noise down, just for a few hours?

33

Pavel Crowd of wasters. Apart from you. Where would we be without you?

Anton We'll be out on the side of the road if I don't get some work done, that's where we'll be.

Pavel Then work. Work.

Pulls up a chair. Sits.

I've a bit to do myself. I won't bother you. Farm accounts. The temperature, forgot to record it. (*Notebook.*) Was minus eighteen this morning. Minus ten at midday. (*Writing.*) We had to bring the bull in. Imagine, we're landowners now. I hope my poor father looks down from time to time, hope he sees if I didn't rise, my son did.

Anton Would you ever stop making the peasants call you 'sir', it's ridiculous.

Pavel They like it, they feel safer when they know who's boss. I watched my father being smashed in the face by thugs who thought they were better than him. By God they'll call me 'sir' and watch me have my wine in the evening, champagne in summer, piano music, ladies and moghuls visiting. All thanks to you, God bless you, let me kiss your hand.

Anton Papasha, stop will you.

Pavel No listen, listen, I'm your father, I deserve your ear, I deserve your respect, a little of your precious time. Everything went wrong for me. Everything. I had no luck. You got all the luck in this house. But lucky or unlucky I'm your father.

Anton Have I ever denied it?

Pavel I'm barely tolerated here. Sasha hates me, Misha and Vanya too, only Masha has a kind word. Is it my

34

fault? I worked as hard as the next. And Kolya to be taken so young, my little son, I miss him every day.

Anton You were very hard on Kolya, Papasha.

Pavel What do you mean, hard on him? If I was hard it was because I wanted him to get on. It's not easy out there.

Anton You were brutal to him as a child, to Sasha too.

Pavel And was I brutal to you in your childhood?

Anton What childhood are you talking about, Papasha?

Pavel You're a writer. You make things up. You think too deeply and too long. I won't hold it against you but please don't confuse me with your stories about peasants and slaves, the scum of the earth. I'm a good father, just had no luck because you robbed the quota from this family.

Anton I wish you'd stop lying. For once? I know these things haunt you now. Why not just say, yes, that's the way it was, forgive yourself, try a little tenderness now, a little self-censoring before you speak. It's not too late.

Pavel But admit it, Antosha, you robbed my place as head of this house when my back was turned.

Anton Someone had to take charge, Papasha. You ran, left us with nothing. You really think I love you all hanging round my neck?

Pavel Maybe if you went back to mass, back to your prayers, you might learn a little humanity.

Anton I don't have time for prayers, I'm too busy feeding all the religious maniacs round here.

Pavel It's your duty. The young must look after the old.

Anton And who looks after the young?

Pavel You're spoiled, soft with privilege. What I wouldn't have done had I your opportunities. You don't know what it feels like when you look at your children and know they're ashamed of you.

Anton Look, Papasha, I'm not responsible for your unhappiness, I wish you'd realise that, and really you must learn to keep your temper to yourself. Do not shout at my mother again under my roof.

Pavel So now you're telling me how to treat my own wife?

Anton I won't have you treat her badly. Not here. Not anywhere. Those days are gone. Now please, if I don't get this finished and in the morning post there'll be no mortgage paid.

Pavel Fine, have the last word, you always do, I know where I'm not wanted.

And exit Pavel. Anton sits there, staring out, picks up pencil, begins writing. Enter Masha.

Masha Do you have a minute?

Anton What is it?

Masha You're working, I'll come back later.

Anton No, what is it?

Masha Don't know where to start.

Anton Start in the middle, trust your listener, don't invent psychology and always, always cut your first paragraph, sometimes your last. Cover your tracks and sing.

Puts down pencil.

Masha Smagin has asked me to marry him.

36

Anton And what's that got to do with me?

Masha You don't think it's a good idea?

Anton I didn't say that. If you want to marry him, you marry him, you don't need my approval.

Masha I'd like it.

Anton Are you in love with him?

Masha It's just so sudden, I don't know.

Anton Marriage is a ludicrous institution. Marriage without love is insane. And I don't mean the kind of love you have for your grandmother, we're talking white-hot-poker love if there's any chance of it surviving.

Masha I'm not saying I'm not in love with him. I mean it wasn't love at first sight, nothing wild, but he's grown on me. I could live with him, have children, know I'm not beautiful, but where is it written I can't have my portion like everyone else?

Anton He'd be lucky to get you, you should have a higher opinion of yourself.

Masha But what about the old folks?

Anton What about them? Haven't they a home here?

Masha I'm afraid it's too much for you, you've taken too much on.

Anton We'll be fine, I'll probably shoot them in their beds but we'll be fine.

Masha Just say yes or no. Say no and we'll go on as we always have.

Anton I can't make a decision like that for you. You must make it.

Masha But it'd be easier if I said no?

Anton Well of course it'd be easier, you practically run the place, but that's not the point. Look, I brought you up, sent you to school, college, so when the time comes you make the big decisions yourself.

Masha You're a fantastic help, Antosha. What would I do without your advice?

Enter Yev.

Anton Maybe it's time to grow up, Masha.

Masha (*exiting*) Grow up yourself!

Anton What is it now?

Yev There's an old woman at the back door, something wrong with her neck, she's in agony, poor creature, I know you're not to be disturbed but I couldn't send her away.

Anton Bring her in. I'm coming.

Gets his bag. Stands there a minute.

(*A whisper.*) Lika, Lika, Lika.

Lights down.

Act Two

SCENE ONE

A sanatorium in the Urals. Aksyonovo.
  Enter Olga reading a letter.

Olga Masha doesn't invite me to Autka, I notice.

Anton Since when do you need Masha's invitation?

Olga She's raging. Well, she's every right to be. Why did we have to get married in secret?

Anton You wanted a big posh party with our mugs all over the papers.

Olga And what's wrong with that?

Anton It's vulgar, that's what's wrong with that.

Olga It's like we're not married at all. These rituals are important. You won't announce me to the world, you're ashamed of your wife.

Anton I just couldn't take the speeches.

Olga Or worse. You're afraid of Masha.

Anton This has nothing to do with Masha.

Olga Then why wasn't she told?

Anton No one was told.

Olga That's not true, my mother was, my uncles, your brothers. She's afraid I'm going to take her place, well yes, I am.

Anton You're too hard on Masha.

Olga Always Masha, Masha, Masha, like having a guard dog in my flat, clocking when I come in, when I go out, where I'll be, who I'm having supper with. I work in the theatre, I'm not a nun.

Anton That's for sure.

Olga You Chekhovs live in one another's ears. It's not normal.

Anton If it's so hard having Masha around, tell her to find somewhere else to live.

Olga Jesus Christ, it's Masha I married.

Anton You can throw my mother in while you're at it. Anyway, it was you wanted this marriage. I was fine and dandy the way we were.

Olga I thought you wanted children.

Anton I can't throw them out, they're helpless.

Olga Thought that was the one good thing about marriage, you get to throw them all out.

Anton They don't have the cop on to leave us alone so we must leave them, promise me now.

Olga Be nice to Masha.

Anton Just say nothing and she'll come round.

Olga Men are great at saying nothing.

Anton Maybe because women say too much, like living with a flock of geese.

Olga And your mother? She'll go mad.

Anton She won't, she'll pray for you, you'll just be another cross for her to bear in this valley of darkness.

Wraps himself around her.

Isn't it great we're together though? Aren't you lucky you
got such a good catch?

Olga You're the lucky one! Writers are ten a penny these
days.

Anton Don't I know it.

And they're off by now.

Lights.

SCENE TWO

Garden at Autka.
Enter Masha with glass and bottle of vodka.

Yev (*off*) The trees are parched.

Masha Ah, give over babbling for the sake of it.
What the hell am I supposed to do here all summer?

Drinks.

If he'd only come home.

Yev (*entering with watering can, gardening gloves*) Let
him enjoy his bit of happiness. He works too hard.
Everything we have is thanks to him.

Masha I work too. You think I love teaching those
teenage brats? And then I race back to this wilderness
to see this house runs, scrubbing, polishing, cooking,
weeding, planting, making sure he eats properly. Don't
talk to me about happiness. It's for other people.

Knocking back the vodka.

If he doesn't show up soon I'm going back to Moscow.

Yev Then go.

Masha And leave you on your own?

Yev He'll be back when the weather turns.

Masha Different ball game now he's tied to that one. She's some operator, sneaking off behind my back like that. Suppose she'll give up the stage now and lord it over us all here, probably throw us out.

Yev I don't care for her either, but he does, so let him live a little. We won't have him much longer.

Masha She'll lead him some dance, you wait and see, a tough little madam, that steely German blood, not a drop of Russian in her veins. And she loves the men, a total come-on. Thought he'd have more taste. She doesn't come in till six in the morning reeking of champagne.

Yev You like your drink too.

Masha She sleeps around, she's Danschenko's doll for God's sake.

Yev Mariya, she is Anton's wife now.

Masha Sure she did it here under our very noses. Heard her creeping across the hall.

Yev Well, maybe you should take less interest in your brother's affairs.

Masha What do you mean by that?

Yev If you're not careful you'll turn into one of those hysterical old maids. My family is full of them.

Masha I don't need to listen to this. I'm going into town.

Yev In this heat?

Masha I'm going to send him a telegram. GET BACK HERE RIGHT NOW! He has cut the ground from under me.

Exit Masha. Sound of a bell.

Yev (*looks out*) They're burying someone. Of all the places on earth you could build. What does he go and do? He goes and builds beside a graveyard. A muslim graveyard. Well, God knows one of you had to get married.

And exit Yev.

Lights.

SCENE THREE

Estate near Yalta.
   Enter Tolstoy with newspaper. He stands there reading. Long white beard. Peasant smock. Panama hat. Riding boots.
   Enter Servant.

Servant Your Excellency, Chekhov is here.

Tolstoy Anton Pavlovich. Bring him in. Bring him in.

Servant Right away, Your Excellency.

Tolstoy If I gave you fifty lashes every time you said 'Your Excellency' you wouldn't be long changing your tune.

Servant But Your Excellency, I grew up on Yasnaya Polyana, I've called you Your . . .

Tolstoy Just go, will you, don't keep him waiting.

Servant Yes, Your Excellency.

Tolstoy You try to raise them up a little, take their snouts out of the trough and they refuse, whole bloody game is impossible.

43

Enter Anton.

Tolstoy Anton Pavlovich.

Kisses him, holds his hands.

This is a treat.

Anton Maestro.

Tolstoy Let me look at you.

Examines him.

Anton I'd have come sooner but wanted to let you settle in.

Tolstoy I'm going out of my mind. Why does anyone bother getting out of bed in Yalta?

Anton Now we're both exiles.

Tolstoy You're too thin. You heard I'm sick too? Course you did, front page of the newspapers, all polishing their obituaries, and did you hear I was excommunicated?

Anton I did. Congratulations.

Tolstoy Can't be buried in consecrated ground.

Anton Do you want to be?

Tolstoy Don't want to be buried at all. Come, sit, we'll have some tea. (*Rings bell.*) Are you hungry?

Anton Always, but I can keep nothing down, better if I don't try.

Tolstoy (*mopping forehead*) This bloody malaria, can't shake it. I want to go home, can't stand the stupidity of the locals and the women are ugly as sin, how can you bear it?

Anton I've no choice in the matter.

Servant appears.

Tolstoy Bring tea. You want anything stronger?

Anton Tea is fine.

Tolstoy Saw your *Three Sisters* before I was carted down here.

Anton Haven't seen it myself yet, how was it?

Tolstoy Stick to the stories. You're Pushkin in prose, at times even better than Pushkin, and that's saying something, but your plays Anton Pavlovich, your plays, I'm sorry but they're woeful.

Anton This one is particularly bad, the censor cut it to ribbons.

Tolstoy Censor aside, where's the drama is what I want to know? Nothing happens, where do your characters take you?

Anton I've no idea and I care less.

Tolstoy I'll tell you where, from the sofa to the spare room and back again.

Anton Isn't that a journey of sorts?

Tolstoy It may be an odyssey for a mouse but not for a member of the human race.

Anton Well, God knows I don't care much for anything I've written, love to burn everything, start from scratch.

Tolstoy And I saw the Knipper one. She's no beauty and past her first flowering, but a dangerous something in her eye and not a bad actress.

Anton We eloped to a sanatorium. For our wedding breakfast we had mare's milk and six raw eggs each.

Tolstoy Mr Romance himself.

Anton Never thought I'd marry.

Tolstoy But you're not really married, are you?

Anton What do you mean?

Tolstoy Well, she's in Moscow prancing the boards and you're here in Yalta spitting blood. Aren't you jealous?

Servant arrives with tea, serves them.

Anton But if she left the theatre she'd be unbearable, she's a peacock, needs to be admired all the time.

Tolstoy They're all the same, there's no peace with them.

Anton And my doctors won't let me live in Moscow. I sneak up now and again and she comes here when she can. I know it looks a bit off, but I am very married.

Tolstoy You're not in love, are you?

Anton Wildly, like an Arab. Weren't you in love with your wife?

Tolstoy I was, yeah. For about two weeks. After our wedding we took the carriage to Yasnaya Polyana, fucked the whole way home, ate roast chicken and champagne between bouts. When I can't stand her I think of that. I think of that a lot. Did you hoor around much as a young fella?

Anton Enough. And you?

Tolstoy The biggest tart in Peter and Moscow, I'd have put it in a letterbox. Don't regret it, though I was poxed to the eyeballs at one point, out of action for a couple of years. It's one of the many tenets of our Church Fathers I can't stomach. What are we sparing it for? Look around you, the lord of all creation, the superfluity,

46

the gargantuan excess of the birds and the bees. One
glance out the window on a spring morning and you
realise the man above was the greatest hoor of all.

Anton The vagrancy of tulips, the musk of the rose, the
come-hither of virgin snow. Will I ever see snow again?

Tolstoy I admire you so much, Anton Pavlovich.

Anton As I do you.

Tolstoy There are so many gangsters out there, merchants
of literature, cynical, hard-nosed, out for gain. You're
the only one of the new crop who has a soul. Even when
the sentences are terrible, and they often are, but even
then your soul is there, naked on the page. Wish I was
so brave.

Anton You're braver than any of us.

Tolstoy They're trying to silence me.

Anton I know, and you mustn't let them.

Tolstoy I'm watched all the time. Followed. Even here.

Anton They snoop around my house too.

Tolstoy They leave you with nothing to live for. If you
only knew how I clutch at straws . . . Are you afraid of
dying?

Anton Pointless being afraid, ahead of us all. I try not to
think about it.

Tolstoy And how do you do that?

Anton Keep busy. Work. Work. Work.

Tolstoy But if you can no longer work?

Anton Trust your track record. It'll come back, stop
fretting.

Tolstoy I'm telling you the well is dry.

Anton And I'm telling you it's just refilling, be patient. You've been writing for nearly fifty years, not even Shakespeare put in fifty years.

Tolstoy No, something happened after *Karenina*, don't understand it but I think when I killed her off, killed some vital part of myself. Whatever alchemy went on in the writing of that book. But I can't put down the pen even though the clear true thing is gone. It's like breathing, Anton Pavlovich, you know that.

Anton It's like nothing else, but writers are too hard on themselves, on one another. You think the world cares we can no longer express ourselves as eloquently as we once could? Water off a duck, but listen to me now. (*Takes his hand.*) People are good because you are alive, they're afraid not to be. You have written beautifully and you will again. Trust me on this.

Tolstoy Can I read you something I'm trying to hammer out? I've no idea what it's about. Maybe you can tell me?

Anton Of course, love to hear it, knew you were writing.

Tolstoy The dog wrote it. It's a complete mess. Have you anything with you? A new story?

Anton takes manuscript out of his pocket.

Anton I'd like to hear you on this.

Tolstoy takes it with great interest, weighs it, skims it.

Tolstoy Ten thousand words?

Anton Bang on.

Tolstoy And heard you're writing another play.

Anton Don't believe anything you read in the newspapers.

Tolstoy I don't. Got this from the horse's mouth.

Anton Stanislavski?

Tolstoy What do you make of him?

Anton He likes to set us one against the other.

Tolstoy Yeah, wants a play from me too. On what?
I said to him, on bloody what? Malaria? Senility?

Skimming Anton's story.

I used to write five thousand words a day.

Anton Tell me about it. At one point I'd get two stories
out a night. And then I'd polish them.

Tolstoy (*reading*) A lot of commas.

Anton Yeah, falling in love with the comma lately.

Tolstoy Commas are great when you want to move it
on quickly. The dash is a full stop plus.

Anton Yeah.

Tolstoy (*reading all the time*) Notice a lot of the younger
ones are using the full stop where I'd only use a comma.

Anton Sentences are definitely getting shorter.

Tolstoy They are, aren't they? You rarely see the semi-
colon now, don't think they know what it's for.

Anton Have you come across this recent phenomenon?
They're now beginning sentences with 'and' or 'so'.

Tolstoy That's pure Asia. I haven't come across it. 'And'
is good. I'll use that. Where did you see it?

Anton Forget, one of those dreadful new writing journals
I think, a couple of gems, the odd half-sentence for
plunder.

Tolstoy This is great, no adjectives, clean, clean, clean, that's the ticket, the rest is manna.

Anton Manna and maths. None of our esteemed critics have yet figured out that writing is basically mathematics.

Tolstoy One of us should tell them. How much do you bet they wouldn't believe us?

And they're off by now.

Lights.

SCENE FOUR

Evening. The garden at Autka.
    Masha comes on with glass of wine. Book. Cigarettes. She drinks. Smokes. Reads.
    Enter Olga in nightdress. Dressing gown.

Olga Do you have a cigarette?

Masha hands her cigarette case. Olga lights one. Stands there smoking.

The crickets just like in *Vanya*. All we need is a guitar.

Masha And a gun.

Olga You're making it very difficult for me here, Masha.

Masha Anton asleep?

Olga He's reading Ibsen, keeps slapping his knee and shouting, 'This man couldn't write "the cat is on the mat".' He's in ecstasy over Ibsen's faults.

Masha You've made a right fool of him now.

Olga What?

Masha We're not as stupid as you think.

Olga Spit it out! Stop torturing me with innuendo.

Masha Know damn well what I'm talking about!

Olga I've no idea.

Masha That baby you lost wasn't Anton's.

Olga You're crazy.

Masha Am I?

Olga This is so twisted. How dare you accuse me like that!

Masha Let's talk gynaecology for a minute. I know a couple of things about it. Did a medical course to assist Anton when we had our clinic at Melikhovo. Anton knows a few things about gynaecology too. That was no five-week miscarriage you had. That was an ectopic pregnancy of eight to twelve weeks. It couldn't have been Anton's because you weren't here at the time and he wasn't with you in Moscow.

Olga You're insane.

Masha Just admit it and I'll leave you alone.

Olga You're trying to split us up.
Does Anton think this too?

Masha Very hard to know what Anton thinks, know he received a full report from the surgeons who operated on you in Petersburg.

Olga I've been so sick, nearly died, and now this sneaking around your brother's desk, opening his letters. You're unbelievable, Masha.

Masha Think you can leave me out in the cold while you swan round in your costumes?

Olga I? Leave you out in the cold? I live like an

uninvited guest in my husband's home, don't go near the kitchen, the cook, the servants, don't open my mouth about the filthy ship you run here. He doesn't eat, doesn't wash, freezes in winter, but you'd rather he died of loneliness here than share him with me in Moscow.

Masha Suicide for him to be in Moscow in his condition and you know it.

Olga Lots of consumptives live well in Moscow. The cold hard air is considered better. I've got several opinions on this but you overrule me every time.

Masha And I'll continue to do so where his health is concerned.

Olga Just who do you think you are? I include you in my life in every way, a room in my flat, hanging out of me at every gathering, falling around because you can't hold your drink. The Art Theatre crowd only put up with you because you're my friend, because you're Chekhov's sister, and I'll tell you it's the only reason I put up with you too.

Masha Well, I won't burden you again or your arty clique. I won't interfere with your trysts and liaisons. I'll look after Anton because someone has to.

Olga You know I love him and would never do anything to hurt him. Don't destroy it on us, if not for my sake then for his. Go and find your own man. You're young enough.

Masha Anton doesn't want me to get married, wants me here for himself. Didn't you know that?

Anton (*entering*) That's complete nonsense, Masha.

Masha Then why wouldn't you let me marry when I wanted to?

Anton What're you talking about? I never stopped you marrying.

Masha Well, you never gave it your blessing either. And now you rejig it all to your advantage. Now you have her you haven't a kind word, just orders, orders, do this, do that, hurry, hurry, hurry.

And she exits.

Anton You scrapping with her again?

Olga I'm not welcome here.

Anton Don't be stupid, they wait on you hand and foot.

Olga Why do you never call a spade a spade? Your mother and Masha hate me.

Anton Not this again.

Olga They do. They blame me for losing the baby. My crazy lifestyle. Your mother said it straight to my face. Maybe this marriage is over, never see you anyway, you blame me too.

Anton Have I said one word? Nursed you round the clock and I'm meant to be the invalid here.

Olga Masha said you wrote to Ott and Jakobson.

Anton Masha should mind her own business.

Olga That all you're going to say?

Anton What is there to say? No escaping the surgeon's report. It wasn't mine.

Olga Then whose was it?

Anton You tell me.

Olga You'd trust those surgeons over me. Nearly killed me. Can't believe what you're saying.

Anton Convince me otherwise.

Olga What are your brothers saying?

Anton You don't want to know.

Olga I absolutely want to know.

Anton Danschenko. Nemirovich Danschenko, that's what they're saying.

Olga Do you want us to part?

Anton (*looks at her a long time*) Don't know.

Olga Because I like my glass of wine after a performance I'm accused of lying down with Danschenko?

Anton Look, I'm here a million miles away fighting for every breath. You don't write, you don't phone, I don't care whose baby it was only don't lie to me. Let me know who you are whatever the cost.

Olga It was yours, whatever they say, it was yours. And if you don't believe me I'd rather we split.

Anton Don't threaten me now.

Olga I'm not that devious.

Anton Aren't you? I think I've a fair idea of how it was. You were lonely, I wasn't there, drink on the table, high on your triumphs, the toast of Petersburg and Danschenko hovering as always. And then your surprise trip here to bed me down. Shh, don't say anything. (*Kisses her.*) I don't care. You're here now, with your husband who adores you. We don't have a lot of time left. I wish I could be better to you.

Olga Yes, that's how it was. How do you see so clearly?

Anton Oh, I'm a bit of an expert on human frailty if nothing else, besides I've committed every sin against love myself. Now no more tears. Let's just be good to one another.

Olga We have to get away from them all, they're killing us, we can't live like this.

Anton We can. We are. Let's go to bed.

And exit wrapped around each other.

Lights.

SCENE FIVE

Garden at Autka.

Enter Yev.

Yev Are you gardening in the dark?

Anton (*coming on slowly*) The trees can't stand Yalta either.

A coughing fit.

Yev You should be resting. Is that blood on your hanky?

Anton One hundred per cent Russian.

Yev Come in out of the cold. Isn't it enough your father's gone, and Kolya, my poor Kolya, and now you. The Lord above must surely think I need a hammering.

Anton Leave the Lord out of it, Mamasha, the Lord's world is good, only one bad thing in it. Us. And don't be so quick to bury me, I've put on four pounds since I got back.

Yev What do I need these left-over years for? If I could give them to you.

Anton And if I could take them I would. You sure there was no post today?

55

Yev I told you.

Anton Sometimes you forget and I find them in the hot press, under cushions.

Yev There were no letters, none from Masha, none from Olga.

Anton Well, you needn't sound so pleased with your news. Why don't they write? Too busy getting plastered. I love to drink too. *The Cherry Orchard* is opening tonight and here we are, Mamasha, might as well be on Mars, could float away right now and no one would care or notice.

Yev Spring'll soon be here, you can be on your travels again when the thaw comes. Goodnight.

Kisses him.

Anton Night.

Yev Don't stay out, there's a breeze in from the sea.

And exit Yev.
Hands in pockets, Anton stands there. Looks up. Stars. Breeze. Sound of the sea.
Enter Lika.

Lika Anton.

Anton Lika. Lika. What are you doing here?

Lika Trip with my husband. Thought I'd come by to say hello.

Anton (*kisses her, holds her*) This is fantastic. You're a life-saver. A life-saver. Are you well?

Lika I'm okay. You?

Anton Never better.

Lika Olga isn't here?

Anton You know she isn't.

Lika Yeah. She's never here, they say.

Anton Is that what they say?

Lika They say lots of things. I asked her to drink a toast with me at this party. She refused. A bit of a wagon all said.

Anton You think so?

Lika She has a moustache, Anton.

Anton I'm trying to get her to grow a beard so we'll look like twins.

Lika Well, you got what you wanted in the end.

Anton What was that?

Lika A part-time wife.

Anton I never wanted that.

Lika Didn't you? Can I? (*A drink.*)

Anton (*pours for her*) Of course. I heard you gave up the opera.

Lika You heard the opera gave me up.

Smokes.

I was a disaster. Didn't even make the chorus. You don't know how lucky you are to be gifted. No idea what it's like for the rest of us . . . Why did you shine your light on me so brightly and then just snap it off?

Anton Never snapped it off. You mistook my dithering for banishment.

Lika It still goes through me. You loved me, know you did, don't deny it now.

57

Anton I love you still.

Lika Nothing is right since I lost you. Only went off with Potapenko to make you jealous. Thought to take him from you but I was the one left high and dry. He scurries back to his wife and my daughter dies. Yeah, my baby died at my grandmother's house. Wasn't even there with her. You know why she died?

Anton It was diphtheria, wasn't it?

Lika She died because none of us wanted her to live, not Potapenko, not my mother, not you and terrible though it is to say it, not even me, and so the little creature obliged.

Anton Our infant mortality rate is a disgrace. You shouldn't blame yourself, Lika.

Lika I don't blame myself. I blame you. You should've been big enough to take us both on. Don't talk to me about mortality rates. That baby should've been yours.

Anton Lika, Lika, Lika, don't be like this, it's pointless.

Lika It's not pointless. Lives are ruined or not ruined and you ruined mine, and in ruining mine ruined your own. Those weekends in the country. Everyone laughing, singing, shouting, champagne sloshing like there's no tomorrow, you in your summer clothes as loud as anyone. You were so beautiful, so shockingly beautiful. I couldn't take my eyes off you.

Anton Am I so terrible to look at now?

Lika (*hugs him*) Anton sweetheart, you're dying, aren't you? They're all saying it, I can't bear it and it won't be in my arms.

Anton I'm not taking it too well myself either. But what can I do, apologise?

Lika And you wrote *The Seagull* about me?

Anton Bits of you.

Lika Come on, Anton, Nina is me.

Anton Did you mind?

Lika Got several free dinners on the strength of it. But I sometimes wonder is my life a mess because you wrote *The Seagull* or was it the other way round? Did I follow your plot or you mine? Suppose it doesn't matter now.

Drinks. Anton kisses her.

You'd be unfaithful to your wife?

Anton More I'd be faithful to you for once.

Lika My husband's waiting at the hotel.

Anton All these waiting husbands.

Kissing her over and over.

Lika I'm a respectable girl now.

Anton Not a trait I ever admired much.

Lika I have to go, Anton.

Anton Well don't get too respectable.

Still kissing her, her hair, throat.

Look at you. How did I ever let you out of my clutches?

Lika Think of me sometimes.

Anton I'd walk you to the end of the road if I had the lung power. Be brave, sweetheart. Don't take it lying down. That's all we can do.

She blows him a kiss and is gone. The Black Monk stands there as Anton watches her going.

Black Monk Mark her going and mark it well.

Anton I'm marking it. Was she in the weave?

Black Monk Was she in the weave?

Anton She was the weave . . . Well, goodbye youth, happiness . . . love.

> *And exit Anton. And exit the Black Monk.*
>
> *Lights.*

SCENE SIX

Gypsy music.
> *A restaurant in Moscow.*
> *Enter Maître d', followed by Suvorin. A Waiter pours wine for him. He reads menu.*
> *After a while enter Anton.*
> *They embrace.*

Suvorin So how's it feel having all of Russia at your feet?

Anton Hardly all, with ninety per cent of them illiterate and the other ten don't read except maybe reviews.

Suvorin You're angry with me.

Anton I am.

Suvorin Because I let them have a go at you in my paper?

Anton Look, Alexei, I'm so far from caring what they say about me any more. I write now what I want to write without ambition or hope.

Suvorin And you're pissed with me over that big-mouth Zola.

Anton It would've been so easy to take his side.

Suvorin Are you out of your mind! They'd have shut me down.

Anton Would that be so terrible?

Waiter comes and pours wine for him. Blini, caviar, etc.

Suvorin (*taking out cigar*) So now my paper's a rag?

Anton It usen't be.

Suvorin My paper made you.

Anton It paid when I needed money.

Suvorin Think it did more than that. When I met you, you were scribbling for every trash magazine in the country. Now you no longer need me, now you can get up on your high horse and preach to me about Zola. What has he to do with anything? A year on Devil's Island'll be the making of him. You're using him to break with me. Fine, but remember this. I made you and my paper made you.

Anton (*gets up*) I think this conversation is over.

Suvorin (*going after him*) Anton, don't let's part like this. Don't do this to me. I've loved you more than my own sons.

Anton No one made me, Alexei, no one except myself. I had to draw the slave out drop by painful drop, so don't you ever presume you were remotely involved in my making or unmaking. You flung me a few roubles when I needed them. I gave you back gold every time. It's people like you keeps us all beaten down. You did it to Pushkin. You're doing it to Zola. You're trying to do it to Tolstoy. You won't do it to me.

Exiting.

Suvorin Anton, come on, lighten up for God's sake.

Anton I've never been part of any faction or gang, don't think a writer can, you're playing dangerous games, Alexei.

Suvorin What dangerous games?

Anton Contempt is a dangerous game. Contempt for the truth? The most dangerous I'd say.

And he's gone.

Lights.

SCENE SEVEN

Enter Masha drinking a cup of tea.

Followed by Alexander. Dishevelled.

Alexander (*a groan*) Oh God, God, God, where have you hidden the vodka?

Masha You've drunk us dry, Sasha.

Alexander Where do you keep your stash? My head's exploding.

Masha Have some tea, it's not even twelve yet.

Alexander And ask the genius for a thousand roubles.

Masha Ask him yourself.

Alexander I owe a year's rent, these are the only trousers I have.

Enter Olga.

Masha You can forget all your schemes, he stays here.

And exit Masha.

Olga Good morning to you too.

Anton (*entering*) What's up with her?

Olga She's in a stew because I'm taking you abroad this summer.

Anton Oh, so you felt the need to tell her already?

Olga Damn right I did.

Masha (*coming back*) I'm not in a stew. You think it's all fun and games. He stays here at Autka and that's the end of it. Anton, you promised.

Olga Did you?

Anton The doctors won't let me.

Olga But you said you'd come to Moscow next month.

Masha You what?

Anton And I will. I will.

Masha You're out of your mind.

Alexander (*to Masha*) Just one glass.

    Exit Masha.

Olga No, you won't. She always wins.

    And exit Olga in a huff.

Anton And exit prima donna in a strop. We don't notice these things here in the sticks.

Yev (*sitting, reading her Bible*) Either of you boys realise it's your father's anniversary.

Alexander (*hungover, standing there*) So?

Yev So, he was your father.

Alexander Do my best to forget that fact.

Anton Oh I liked old Pavel at the finish, playing his fiddle in the small hours, polishing his icons, that puzzled look on his face, something about living he never grasped. We're no better, just trumped-up peasants like old Pavel.

63

Alexander He was a nightmare, destroyed Kolya.

Anton Kolya destroyed himself.

Enter Masha with large glass of vodka for Alexander.

Masha That's it, Sasha.

Alexander You're an angel.

Masha Tell that to your brother, he's acting like I'm his jailer and executioner.

Anton Sit down will you, making me dizzy.

Masha And who'll take the roast out of the oven?

Anton Sasha will.

Yev I'll do it.

Exit Yev.

Anton Sasha, will you? She burnt herself the other day.

Sasha This should be interesting. Mother and son fight to the death over who takes the roast out of the oven. There's a plot for you. I'll take my usual ten per cent.

And exit Sasha.

Masha He said last night that there's something wrong with me, that I live too much for you, said I'm sick.

Anton Sasha's a wreck, never sober now. Ignore him.

Masha But he's right. I do live for you.

Anton I want you to know this place is yours when I'm gone.

Masha That all you have to say about it?

Anton Also the papers, manuscripts, pretty much everything.

64

Masha I don't want your house, your papers, those bloody manuscripts.

Anton Then what do you want?

Masha Olga'll go crazy if you leave me this house.

Anton She won't. You're too hard on her. Try and see her through my eyes.

Masha You may be in love with her but Olga's in love with herself.

Anton You think I don't know that? I'm not in love with anyone. That's the problem. Beware writers who fall out of love. And I'm going abroad with her as soon as the weather turns.

Masha You can't walk to the end of the garden.

Anton I've defied the odds this long.

Masha Have you finished that play yet?

Anton Why?

Masha You're a long time at it.

Anton There's no play.

Masha What? I thought . . .

Anton Said everything I want to say. Only subject interests me now is eternity but I never believed enough in it. And now I find eternity doesn't believe in me.

Masha If you go you'll come back in a box, but I suppose that's stating the obvious.

And exit Masha.

Lights.

SCENE EIGHT

Hotel Sommer, Badenweiler.
  Anton stands there. Loud, painful breaths.
  Enter Olga with ice.

Anton Can't we move to a cooler room?

Olga There's a heatwave.

Anton (*through terrible breaths*) A room facing north.

Olga We're in a room facing north. Don't you remember?
We moved a few hours ago. Let me open your shirt.

Anton You don't put ice on an empty stomach.

  Pushes her hand away.
  Enter Dr Schworer with the student Kolya.

Olga Thank God you're here.

Dr Schworer At least the sun's gone down. (*To Kolya.*)
Go quickly and get champagne, the best they have.

  Exit Kolya.

Anton That bad?

Dr Schworer I'm afraid so.

Olga He can't drink.

Dr Schworer It's a doctor thing, we order champagne
for one another when . . .

Anton When it's hopeless.

Dr Schworer That's right. Now let's get you comfortable.

Anton It's easier standing.

Dr Schworer Okay.

Silence as he breathes and breathes. Dr Schworer takes his pulse.

I ordered one of your collected stories today. God knows when I'll have time to read them.

Anton (*a whisper*) This is it, isn't it?

Dr Schworer Yes it is, my good man, and it's all right. Don't fight for the breaths. They'll come, slowly, slowly. That's good. See, they're coming.

Anton I've done this before . . . many times.

Dr Schworer With others? Sure you have, that's it . . . You're doing fine.

Enter Kolya with champagne, glasses.

Pour for us there, good lad.

Olga Don't be afraid. I'm here. Give me your hand, sweetheart.

Anton Another Russian disgraces himself again.

No sound except Anton's breathing. Cork popping.

What are those scars on your face?

Dr Schworer Duelling.

Anton I thought so. Who was she?

Dr Schworer She wasn't worth these and that's for sure.

Anton They're very dashing, don't you think, Olga?

Olga Very romantic.

Anton When I was a boy all I ever wanted was to fight a duel like Pushkin, and then to lie on a couch with my fatal wound, eating cloudberries.

Dr Schworer Cloudberries?

67

Anton Yeah, he died eating cloudberries. What else would a poet be eating on his deathbed?

Kolya hands around the champagne, three glasses. He doesn't drink.

Long time since I had champagne.

Dr Schworer Now what'll we drink to?

Anton I've always hated toasts.

Dr Schworer Then we'll drink to silence.

Anton A man after my own heart.

He drains the glass slowly.
  Looks out.
  Hold.

Blackout.

PHAEDRA BACKWARDS

Phaedra Backwards was first performed at the McCarter Theatre Center for the Performing Arts, Princeton, New Jersey, on 18 October 2011. The cast, in alphabetical order, was as follows:

Nanny Susan Blommaert
Inventor Christopher Coucill
Pasiphae Angel Desai
Minos Sean Haberle
Aricia Julienne Hanzelka Kim
Ariadne Mariann Mayberry
Minotaur Julio Monge
Theseus Randall Newsome
Phaedra Stephanie Roth Haberle
Hippolytus Jake Silberman

Director Emily Mann
Set Designer Rachel Hauck
Costume Designer Anita Yavich
Original Music and Sound Designer Mark Bennett
Lighting Designer Jeff Croiter
Projection Designer Peter Nigrini

Characters

Phaedra

Theseus
her husband

Hippolytus
her stepson

Aricia
girlfriend of Hippolytus

Girl
her daughter by Theseus

Minotaur
her brother

Pasiphae
her mother

Minos
her father

Ariadne
her sister

Inventor

Nanny
the housekeeper

Child Minotaur
six

Child Phaedra

Child Ariadne

Setting

A terrace. A stone terrace. A stone floor.
The bay and the mountains surround this terrace.
The ever-changing light.
The sound of the sea a constant score.

Two other scores inhabit the place.
Phaedra's score and the Minotaur's.

A formerly good dining table, now a battered vestige
of itself.
Destroyed chairs. A lonely chaise longue.

The light is magical, from some dark fairy tale.

Time. Now and then. Then and now. Always.

PROLOGUE

Image which covers expanse of the back wall:
  A field of daffodils.
  The sound of the sea.
  Music under that.

Enter Phaedra.
  *A glass of champagne in her hand. She lies on chaise
longue.*

Image on screen:
  *The Child Minotaur, side profile, stands in a field of
daffodils with the Child Phaedra and Child Ariadne. He
is handing out daffodils to the girls.*
  *In her own world Phaedra raises a hand to take the
daffodil.*
  *The Child Minotaur runs off screen. He is being
chased by Child Phaedra and Ariadne: now we see them,
now we don't, laughing, intoxicating children engrossed
in some elaborate game.*
  Then the Child Minotaur turns.
  *We see the horn, the hooves, the sickle scar on his
brow, the tail.*
  *He stands there talking, we can't hear him, but he
talks animatedly, then he stops, is very still. Then slowly
he begins to eat a daffodil and then another one. The
three lie down in the daffodils, heads touching, eating
daffodils. Music to underscore this.*

SCENE ONE

Enter Theseus. Looking at his phone. Image on screen fades.

Theseus Went over the cliff.

Phaedra The cliff?

Theseus But I could hear it in her voice.

Phaedra What?

Theseus She enjoyed saying it.

Phaedra He went over the cliff.

Theseus She was breathless telling me.

Phaedra Well, it is sort of dramatic.

Theseus But I'm his father.

Phaedra Was it steep?

Theseus I've never heard of a shallow cliff.

Phaedra Some women love giving dramatic news.

Theseus She sounded like she was talking to her lover.

Phaedra Was there a bull in the field?

Theseus You and your bulls.

Phaedra A white bull with a garland of windflowers on his horns?

Theseus Sounds like an accident.

Phaedra Don't be ridiculous.

Theseus He had everything to live for.

Phaedra Unless the bull pucked him off with his horns, but even that wouldn't be an accident. Or maybe, just maybe the sea came up to meet him, the waves caught hold of his hair, but that's the stuff of lyrics. We're past the lyrical, but was he?

Theseus Just can't believe the way she said it . . . He went over the cliff . . . What does that mean?

Phaedra Can I have another glass? . . . Pour for me please.

Theseus You want to mark the occasion?

Phaedra By God I do. I want to mark this evening. This evening melding into all the other gargoyle evenings of my life.

Theseus But my son . . . My beautiful . . . My only.

Phaedra You'll be fine in a year or two. You must learn to trust time. I've buried too many to take grief seriously. It's a formality. Go through it if you must but spare me the lamentations and outward display. I have gorged on grief. It no longer tempts me.

Theseus Stop babbling. My son. Your son, is gone.

Phaedra You spoke about him differently last night.

Theseus Last night he was alive. Last night has nothing to do with tonight.

Phaedra Last night was the cause of tonight as tonight will spawn tomorrow and all your tomorrows until the . . .

Theseus I just wanted to frighten him. In time I would've forgiven him. He knew that. I was angry.

Phaedra You weren't even angry.

Theseus I was standing up for you.

Phaedra You weren't standing up for me. You were ranting about yourself and your battered carcass. How the women don't look any more unless you buy them. You, who once had a cradle rocking in every town land. Last night was about your grey hair and his black. Last night was about that tremor in your hand. When did that tremor appear? Last week your back was straight. Now it's curved like an old seal. Last night was about you in a white rage, looking for any excuse to rip through your son. Well, he went over the cliff. You've won again and now I'll have another glass of champagne. Go and cry in some other room.

Theseus I thought you loved him too.

Phaedra Don't you dare talk to me about love.

Theseus Just why did you tell me?

Phaedra You knew all along.

Theseus Then why state the obvious?

Phaedra Told you on a whim . . . I was bored.

Theseus Bored?

Phaedra Wanted to wring some juice from the evening.

Theseus But is it true?

Phaedra You bring something that beautiful into my house and expect me just to look?

Exit Theseus. Phaedra on chaise longue.

SCENE TWO

The low croon of the white bull. Enter Pasiphae.

Pasiphae I hear you. I hear you.

Enter Nanny.

Where the hell is he?

Nanny He's coming. He's coming.

Enter the Inventor, wheeling a life-size cow covered with a cloth.

Inventor Pasiphae. (*Nods.*)

Pasiphae A month late. How dare you keep me waiting like this?

Inventor I've been working day and night.

Pasiphae Is it finished?

Inventor I believe so.

Pasiphae Well, show it to me then.

Inventor takes off white cloth to reveal a beautiful white cow. Pasiphae walks around it, examining, touching.

Inventor Well?

Pasiphae The eyelashes are good. The legs are good.

Inventor But?

Pasiphae I thought she'd be more beautiful.

Inventor It's a cow. You asked for a cow.

Pasiphae But not just any cow. This cow has to woo the white bull. Out of a herd of five hundred this cow has to be noticed.

Inventor She'll be noticed.

Pasiphae You've driven me mad with the waiting.

Inventor It's not me has you driven mad.

Pasiphae You think this is just a notion? That it'll pass like all the other notions?

81

Inventor It's an unusual request.

Pasiphae You're not paid to have opinions on my requests.

Inventor I'm not paid full stop. If your husband knew what you have asked, what you have ordered me to make.

Pasiphae Minos? You don't need to concern yourself with him. All his fault anyway. How do I get into her?

Inventor Here, under the belly.

Pasiphae Climb in. Show me.

Inventor You climb in. I need to align the rump. Precisely.

Pasiphae I bet you do. (*Taking off her dress.*) How do I breathe?

Inventor There are holes along the stomach. I've also fitted air pipes you can suck on.

They are under the cow now.

Pasiphae I see them . . . like this . . . The smell . . . God!

Inventor That's a real cow hide.

Pasiphae Dung and all.

Inventor Can you climb in?

Pasiphae You find me obscene?

Inventor Completely.

Pasiphae I'm only doing what women imagine.

Inventor So we should act on everything we imagine?

Pasiphae Yes.

Inventor Why?

Pasiphae Because that's the only way we'll become human. All right, I'm in.

Inventor Creep backwards and lean towards me . . . Higher . . . a bit higher . . . Lean . . . okay . . . How's that?

Pasiphae I'll know in a minute.

Inventor If you'll excuse my hand.

Puts his hand into cow's uterus.

Pasiphae I'll excuse it.

A gasp from Pasiphae.

Inventor Well?

Pasiphae I need some more height under my knees.

Inventor How much?

Pasiphae A bit of cloth will do it. Pass me in my dress.

Nanny does. Pasiphae moves around in the cow, settles.

Inventor All right?

Pasiphae Yeah, that's fine.

Inventor There are two leather handles on either side.

Pasiphae I have them . . . for leverage.

Inventor And ballast.

Pasiphae Yeah, they're good.

Inventor That's it then . . . You can come out now.

Nanny You swore you'd never finish this.

Inventor I'm just the servant here.

Nanny There'll be war over this.

Inventor It was you put the idea into her head.

Nanny Me?

Inventor Wringing obsessions and confessions out of her.

Pasiphae (*out of the cow*) You can stop your hissing. This will be ready for tonight?

Inventor Can no one talk sense to you any more?

Pasiphae You'll wheel me into the sea field and get me into position for the white bull?

Inventor You're young. You're grieving for your son. I know what it's like. I lost a son too.

Pasiphae Then you should get another one.

Stroking the cow.

She's beautiful. I love her. Look at the legs on her, more like a deer or a horse. Aren't you proud of your creation?

Inventor Suppose he goes mad? Tramples you?

Pasiphae Suppose he does? Meet me in the lane at dusk. We must be brave. Come on, Nanny, it's time for the children's lunch. Ariadne! Phaedra!

And exit Pasiphae followed by Nanny. The Inventor wheels the cow off.

SCENE THREE

Music. Enter the Minotaur. From a great distance. Ripping through a dimension. Sees Phaedra on the chaise longue. She doesn't see him. Look at those Picasso Minotaur drawings. Goes to her.

84

Minotaur I made it. Here again. Thank you, God. Thank you.

Walks around, sizing the space. Taking it all in.
Phaedra drifts off as Nanny enters with drinks tray. Followed by Hippolytus and Aricia. Nanny pours for them. Minotaur watches them.

Old Nanny.

And exit Nanny. Followed by Minotaur after a good sniff of Hippolytus and Aricia.

SCENE FOUR

Aricia Does she ever shut up?

Hippolytus Who, my mother?

Aricia Yeah.

Hippolytus She's not my mother.

Aricia Well, my head is rocking with her. It's not fair such a wagon gets to live in such a place . . . Look at this beautiful bay.

Hippolytus Sick looking at it.

Aricia As if a great heat is sifting through the mountains . . . The boats rust as the sunset.

Hippolytus What are you, the tourist board?

Aricia Then you tell me what colour those mountains are.

Hippolytus They're just mountains.

Aricia Then describe the water.

Hippolytus Only fools describe water.

85

Aricia Then describe last night.

Hippolytus You're the expert describer.

Aricia I smelt something on your skin.

Hippolytus Skin usually smells of something.

Aricia Tainted . . . an old tang . . . Your mother will be here in a minute eyeballing me.

Hippolytus Eyeball her back.

Aricia She hates women.

Hippolytus Who doesn't?

Aricia I just don't do it for you, do I?

Hippolytus That sounds about right.

Aricia Then why do you keep calling?

> *Enter Phaedra and Theseus in evening clothes, with glasses of brandy, cigars, cigarettes. Phaedra stands there watching Hippolytus and Aricia.*

Phaedra We were just wondering how many lovers you've had.

Aricia Me?

Phaedra None, I said.

Aricia I didn't think people talked like this in houses among the tablecloths and things.

Phaedra You think it's rude to talk about your sex life after dinner?

Aricia My intimate life is not up for grabs.

Phaedra What intimate life? I bet you're wondering how many lovers I've had.

Aricia I'm not.

Theseus She's not.

Aricia I wasn't until now.

Phaedra You see the anthropologists have been looking so long for this missing link, the great silence that happened between the baboon and homo sapiens. There's no missing link. We are the missing link. We lay down with the gorillas or our not so distant ancestors did and – *voilà*! Here we are, half-breeds with the wild undertow of jungle, reptile, Doberman, shark. We got it all. We got the whole swill in spades. Thirteen.

Theseus Thirteen?

Phaedra Not counting you.

Theseus Always good to know where one stands.

Phaedra And you, my navy-eyed boy, Hippolytus, Hippolytus, Hippolytus, made for the women and the dusk. How many have drunk at your well?

Hippolytus I'm not a mathematician.

Theseus And I think the night is over.

Phaedra The night is over when I say it's over. You have decided too many things for me.

Theseus You're moving into prophetic mode.

Phaedra And you? Old bull-slayer, how many?

Theseus Not enough. Nowhere near half enough.

Phaedra You put me to shame with my paltry thirteen.

Theseus Fourteen.

Phaedra And the ones we can't confess without the roof falling in.

Theseus I say good luck to them. They deserve everything they get if they find themselves naked before you.

Enter Girl.

Girl When did you get home?

She kisses him.

Theseus Don't I always come home in the end? Homework done?

Girl Yeah, Nanny checked it.

Phaedra Go to bed, darling.

Girl There's a moth in my room.

Theseus A moth won't harm you.

Girl And I heard hooves.

Phaedra That's only the goats on the cliffs.

Girl No, these hooves sound like they're from some cave.

Theseus Bed. Bed. It's late. I'll come and kill the moth in a minute.

And the Girl kisses Phaedra and goes.

Phaedra A few thousand years ago we could blame Aphrodite.

Theseus For what?

Phaedra For this. For you. I could blame Aphrodite for you or any of those mad medieval saints. The Italians were allowed to whip their statues if they withheld favours. Say you lost your ring and St Martin de Porres refused to find it for you, then you were entirely within your rights to drag him from the altar into the field and

whip the daylights out of him till the paint fell off or he
found you your ring or a decent husband. Now I have
to take the blame for everything myself. That's the thing
I really cannot abide about being modern. Open another
bottle.

Theseus You've had enough.

Phaedra I'm sober, always sober, have to be drunk to
put up with you. When you swim and sway before my
eyes then you're almost bearable, when there's three of
you I can fantasise there's half a man.

Theseus Not in front of the guest, please.

Phaedra She needs to know how we operate here. I
don't hate you, it's just you have innocence without
intelligence. That's the one unforgivable. I can put up
with anything except stupidity.

Aricia I have a degree.

Phaedra It's so obvious you have a degree.

Aricia Something you don't have.

Phaedra You've been nosing around my past. And you
think I'm jealous of your little economics degree?

Aricia Should I go?

Phaedra Yes, go. What right have you to assault me with
your perfect teeth and your undyed hair? But you know
something, little girl with your little degree, I have
something you will never have, not if you live for a
thousand years. You're meant to say, 'And what is that,
pray?' I'll tell you anyway.

Theseus Ignore her.

Phaedra You have no capacity for suffering. The first
wind will blow you away. The only ones who interest me

now, who have ever interested me, are those with the scars and still standing. From here on in I want only the company of witches and wizards.

Theseus So that's my crime? I am not Merlin.

Phaedra I am chock-full of other people's stupidity. Why am I the only one in the room capable of conversation?

Hippolytus You never give us time to respond.

Phaedra There is no time.

Hippolytus We must pretend there is.

Phaedra It's all closing in. Can't you see it's nearly over?

Aricia Are you flirting with him?

Theseus She flirts with everyone.

Aricia But your own mother?

Phaedra I'm not his mother. You didn't tell her? I'm flattered.

Hippolytus I told her.

Theseus He's my son. I had to wrestle his mother to the forest floor to make him.

Phaedra I want to tell you something, Theseus.

Theseus You always want to tell me something.

Phaedra I refuse your verdict on me. I refuse this life, this non-existence by the shore. I am not a mermaid.

Theseus Go to bed. For once go to bed without being carried.

Phaedra I have to be unconscious before he'll carry me. Just what do you do to me when I'm out?

Theseus In the beginning all sorts of unspeakable things.

Phaedra And now?

Theseus When I hurt you now I want you to know.

Aricia Are they always like this?

Phaedra My husband would like me to behave like an auld biddy at a tea party. Next he'll tell you I'm a great gardener.

Theseus She is.

Phaedra Only with aspens.

Aricia Why aspens?

Phaedra There on the willow trees we hung up our harps. Why not aspens? The trembling, racing leaves. I like to sit under them when I'm hungover. It was on an aspen our saviour met his end.

Aricia What saviour?

Phaedra What would you say if I told you it is only the trees that keep me here?

Aricia Maybe you should have been an aspen.

Phaedra (*close to tears*) That's the first interesting thing you've said all evening.

Theseus I met a man once with an oak tree growing out of his palm. There it was, a miniature oak woven into the cartilage, flesh, veins of his palm, so cunningly there they couldn't remove it without taking the whole hand off. So he grew the oak and pruned it, a bonsai oak, and there were leaves, in autumn a bronze scattering. And he was proud of this tree, said he only started to live when the oak appeared.

Phaedra How did he make love? Which palm was the oak on?

Theseus (*looks at his palms*) I don't remember but I'll wager the left. I would say oak trees always grow out of left palms. I saw it in winter. The oak was bare. The women couldn't get enough of it. He said when he'd be buried he wanted his palm raised so the oak could be planted, take root, maybe survive.

Aricia I feel sick, all this bitterness and oaks growing out of hands.

Phaedra And what did you grow out of? A can of beans? Corpses. That's what fertilises us. There isn't one square inch of earth or ocean floor that has not been flowered by corpses. That cedar perfume you're wearing this evening was decanted from your great-grandfather's backside.

Aricia I've always hated trees. Someday I will run a concrete empire and there will not be a tree for a thousand miles. I know we need them for air and all of that but technology is marvellous. Some day we'll have moved beyond air and the only place you'll see an aspen will be in some Eastern European museum, an illegal exhibit in the freak section. And they'll marvel how we could live alongside such monsters without fainting with terror. That's my wish for the future. Steel and stone. Green will be a distant memory. People on the street will be asked to define 'tree'. They'll think it's an obscure term like 'Mycenaean' or 'miserabilism'.

Phaedra That little soliloquy because you hate me.

Aricia You haven't seen my hatred yet. Seems I'm the only one here can hold in what she thinks, the only one with a shred of manners.

Phaedra Unfortunately my husband has impeccable manners, he even wears his underpants to bed.

Theseus Where I grew up underpantses were a luxury.

Phaedra He had a deprived childhood, shot one of his brothers by accident and the mother didn't notice for months, there were dozens of them all sharing the one luxurious underpants.

Theseus And in my time I have found the best lovers are those who conceal, a languorous revealing in sun and shadow. It goes without saying my wife sleeps in her birthday suit. She'd take that off too if she could.

Phaedra (*to Hippolytus*) And how do you sleep, my lazy boy?

Aricia He doesn't.

Phaedra You mean he doesn't in front of you . . . it's the highest definition of love. You like to watch me sleep.

Theseus Yeah, I nearly understand you when you're catatonic, dreaming of bulls and aspens.

Hippolytus Letting someone watch you sleep? More like a preview of how you'll look in the coffin emanating all those odours.

Phaedra I've seen you asleep.

Theseus I have too. Mints and sweating curls is what I remember.

Aricia Everyone talking of sleep and no one goes to bed.

Phaedra Oh, we sleep. We're not vampires, but when we crossbred with the sharks we diluted sleep. Besides it's only what? Three? Four? We should see the dawn in, the brave little sun blazing on as if we're worth it.

Theseus The brave little sun blazes on because it can't do otherwise. Nothing to do with you or me. I'm going to bed. I at least have things to do tomorrow.

Phaedra Like what? Abducting virgins.

Theseus Goodnight, my dear.

Phaedra There's something you should know before you take your beauty sleep.

Theseus There's nothing I need to know.

Phaedra I want to sleep with your son.

Theseus (*laughs*) Any ruse to keep me here. It's me you want and what is he but a carbon copy of my younger self? You always over-speak with wine. Who doesn't have these uncivilised yens from time to time, but must you inflict them on us? You should have a better sense of yourself.

He kisses Aricia's hand.

Despite my darling Phaedra, you are most welcome to the fold. I have a soft spot for those who hanker after stone. If I wasn't scaling down I'd want you at the helm. (*To Hippolytus.*) Be good to her, someday she'll hit upon the antidote to air. Let her watch you sleep. It's easy keeping women happy.

Kisses Phaedra.

Most of them.

And exit Theseus.

Phaedra Suddenly the night is over when he's gone. He knows that too. He never lets you come down. The same in bed. Gone. Always gone.

Aricia We should go to bed too.

Phaedra Goodnight.

Aricia I take it that's a command.

Phaedra Stay if you want, have another bottle with me, you'll regret it till your dying day.

Aricia (*taking Hippolytus' hand*) Goodnight.

Hippolytus I'll be there in a minute.

Exit Aricia.
Hippolytus looks at Phaedra.

Hippolytus You going to sleep tonight?

Phaedra I may.

Hippolytus In my father's bed?

Phaedra What's it to you where I put my head? Think I'll go and sit in the sea field. (*Exiting.*)

Hippolytus Why do you pretend you still love him?

Phaedra I don't pretend . . . But you . . .

Hippolytus You're wrong . . . She's very bright.

Phaedra List her virtues. I heard it before.

Hippolytus Pull your age, your thirteen lovers.

Phaedra My thirteen lovers . . . there was one . . . an Arab pilot, my God, beauty, and before he made love he'd tell me about his wife and the thing was he wasn't married. But each time he got me down, he'd wax lyrical about this wife. Maybe he couldn't get his tenses right, past, present, future conditional, all the same to him, but always before, a love poem to the ideal. The point was, I wasn't it. I didn't seem to mind, my younger pathetic self. I'd listen to how they made love in the tent in the desert under the tamarind trees or the tamarisk trees or whatever the hell they were. And on nights when the heat was unbearable they slept in the garden with their feet in the fountain. Don't resent me my thirteen lovers. I was very young and we were as sad and various as all creatures who think they have the in on ecstasy.

Hippolytus You tell him and he laughs.

Phaedra And so he should. It's ridiculous. You're my son in everything but name.

Hippolytus And blood.

Phaedra It's sordid. It's disgusting. I want none of it.

Aricia (*standing there watching them*) Are you coming or not?

Phaedra Yes, he is, but first let me kiss him, my beautiful son.

A strange thing to watch. Aricia looks on, looks away.

Hippolytus Just who do you love? Come clean, for once come clean.

Phaedra You misunderstand me. You misunderstand everything. This is not about love, this is about guilt and terror, my two trusty knights who'll see me to my lonely grave.

He pushes her away. Exits.

Aricia Can I take a glass with me?

Phaedra Help yourself.

Aricia What are you at?

Phaedra What are you at? Why haven't you run screaming from this house?

Aricia I'm not a screamer.

Phaedra You'd watch anything if it was lit properly?

Aricia Probably.

And exit Aricia.
Film image on screen. The Child Phaedra, the Child Ariadne, the Child Minotaur in a graveyard on a cliff. The little girls hold the Child Minotaur by the hand.

96

They face us. Standing there very still, looking out. Music to accompany this.

Phaedra Dreamt we were on the moon when I lay down earlier this evening. Ariadne and I holding you by the hand and it was green and tropical there. A whole colony swarming, villages, bistros, the inhabitants dining, having coffee, taking their ease. But we wanted to see our one-time home, this bay, these cliffs, so we climbed a hill of stone, searching the horizon as night came on. Then, there it was, the sweetest orb and we longed to return until we realised we were looking at the sun and would never see the earth again. And as we're looking the thought comes, maybe this is not such a terrible thing and the thought comes, what is it we must do to be allowed a brief residency on the sun.

As she is speaking the Minotaur enters. Goes to her.

Minotaur The Druids align. Dinosaurs in St Paul's again. It is time. It is way past time.

Phaedra Who's there?

Looks through him. Doesn't see him.

Who is it?

Minotaur blows on her face. Taps his hoof. She shivers, exits quickly.

SCENE FIVE

Enter Pasiphae. She pours a glass of wine. Wanders the terrace. The sea. All calm. Suddenly noises, cries off. Child Phaedra and Child Ariadne run on in nightdresses. Run to Pasiphae.

Pasiphae What is . . . I sent you to bed an . . .

Enter Nanny running.

Nanny He's home. Minos is home. He's heard. He's heard all the rumours.

Enter Minos with the Child Minotaur in a vice grip. Flings him to the ground.

Minos You're obscene! Let this thing in the house? In a nightshirt?

Pasiphae Don't speak like that in front of him. Come here, darling.

Helps him up. Minos grabs him again.

Let him go. I said let him go.

She puts the Child Minotaur behind her.

Say hello to your daughters. You probably don't even know which is which. This is Phaedra. She's seven now. Ariadne is . . .

Minos That! Is that a tail?

Pasiphae You've seen a tail before?

Minos I've seen them. Where they're meant to be seen.

Pasiphae But look at his hands, his legs, his torso, look, his belly button. This little thing grew in me, grew out of me. Do what you want with me. I won't give him up.

Minos Can it talk?

Pasiphae Of course he can talk.

Minos Let me hear it talk.

Pasiphae In his own time. He's not a performing monkey. You're frightening him.

Minos I'm frightening him?

Pasiphae You'll get used to him. His nature is good, passionate, gentle, infinitely suffering.

Minos And its purpose?

Pasiphae And what is your purpose? What is mine?

Minos Where did you find it in you to do this?

Pasiphae You dare ask that? What did you expect when you bring a force like that into our fields? Just what did you expect? Embroidery? Well, this is what I stitched together while you were away. This strange, beautiful little fellow. Every morning I marvel he's still breathing, that he's still among us.

Minos He belongs in a shed or the open meadow or the last stall in some abattoir.

Pasiphae He belongs with me.

Minos What's that on his forehead?

Pasiphae You've seen that before, the mark of his father reversed, the sickle moon.

Minos The white bull who came from nowhere.

Pasiphae The white bull you stole, penned in. The white bull who trampled down our son because you refused to return him.

Minos How can you return a thing when you don't know from where it came?

Pasiphae There are ways.

Minos What ways?

Pasiphae There are laws unwritten, laws that reside just past language, just past thought. You have no mystery but mystery doesn't care, mystery will have you.

99

Minos And where is my white bull now? He's not among the herd.

Pasiphae We don't see you for years and the first thing you do when you come home is look for your white bull.

Minos Where is he?

Pasiphae And you think he hasn't seduced you? Here is our only proof he ever existed. Hold him. Let him get used to you. In time he may graft himself on you.

Minos Keep away from me with that. I had a son. We had a son. We have no son now. We will never have another . . . I stayed away because . . .

Pasiphae You fled! I had to bury him. Three years old. I had to burn his clothes. You let the white bull in, you let him mow down our son, you let him haul me into the unimaginable and I have returned with him. This is our dead son reborn from the white bull who took him. You're looking at the impossible. He is yours and mine. Hold him. Please. Make him possible.

Minos You're insane. A bull-fancier, a monster-maker.

He grabs the Child Minotaur.

Look at him! This ox-faced mutant is no child of mine. No son reborn. He's some evil growth from some horrific urn.

And exit Minos.

Nanny I'm afraid.

Pasiphae What do you think I am? What do you think I've ever been? What's to become of us, my little man? He won't let us be, if I know him.

Nanny Give him to me here. I'll take him. I'll settle them all.

Pasiphae (*holding Child Minotaur closer*) No, I'm not letting him out of my sight. Everything is against us. Everything. (*To girls.*) Go with Nanny.

And exit Pasiphae with Child Minotaur.

Nanny Come on, girls. It's all right. It'll all look better in the morning.

Image. Of Pasiphae and Child Minotaur hurling through space, blue sky, grey rock, turquoise sea. Suspend them there. Also here a possible place for image of Child Phaedra and Child Ariadne coming out of the sea with the Child Minotaur in great distress. Maybe both images, one after the other.

SCENE SIX

Nanny enters with coffee pot and plate of fruit and rolls. She stops. Looks around.
Adult Minotaur charges on, hooves, horns and tail stamping and flying. He charges for audience, veers at last second and butts the back wall with his horns. He snorts and taps and charges again. And then again. He stops. Sighs. This has given him some relief.

Minotaur Yes, this is how I was sent into the world. All the nobility of the white bull. But unfortunately too in my mix, the shadowy faculties of your race.

Nanny I can't see you but I know you're near.

Minotaur sniffs her, circles her.

Away with you now to the pastures of the unknown.

Minotaur I bet you dream about me.

Nanny All women dream of the bull.

Enter Theseus.

Minotaur Yes, and all men too.

Nanny I said away with you. There is no place for you here.

Minotaur No, and never was.

He stands beside Theseus. Menacing.

Theseus I've yet to walk out here without the sky clouding over. They just sit up there, waiting for me. Only here. Everywhere else the sun goes before me.

He sits. Nanny pours coffee for him, arranges his napkin, puts a roll on his plate. Minotaur on the table. Puts a hoof to Theseus' throat. Music. Some sound. Minotaur withdraws hoof. Theseus clocks this. Something is amiss.

Nanny Some eggs?

Theseus No, thank you, Nanny. This is fine.

He peels an orange, drinks some coffee. And exit Minotaur.

A woman wrote a story about me once. 'Dining with the Enchanter' she called it. And yes I was. I am. I deserve that title. It was a wonderful story, full of food and atmosphere. A French restaurant, that's where she set it. But it was the things she had me say that upstaged the food and wine. And when I read it I decided to take her to a French restaurant like the one in the story, only better. And I surpassed myself with enchantment. I won't attempt to repeat what I said, suffice it to say, after that evening she knew she could never capture me. She stopped writing I believe soon after that. I was long gone by then of course. What's the point of this? Women find me enchanting. That's the point. That's the only point.

Even my wife. I only have to look at her in a certain way and she dissolves. Or my daughter's little school friends, they know too I possess the enchantment. You think this is vanity? It isn't. I was born with it. And owning up to what you have been given is not vanity. It is courage. To date I have slept with three thousand and eleven women. I keep a record of them. Once I've been confused and bedded a woman thinking it was for the first time. Only once. Do I remember them all? Yes, I do. Every last one of them. Don't ask me for names but I could recite to you textures, crevices, alignment of limbs, the way light falls on certain backs on certain evenings in certain seasons, et cetera, et cetera. A friend of mine, his thing is dreams. He can't wait to get to bed every night to dream, has written them down since he could hold a pen, has a whole room full of dream books, bound in calfskin leather, a gift from me. We meet for tea in his dream room every now and then. I talk about women, he tells me his dreams, really they're the same thing. It's good for the soul to have an obsession. So. That's how I spend my time, my real time. Here is by the way, an afterthought, like all duty.

Enter Phaedra in sunglasses, bathrobe, high heels. She eats salad from a packet.

Theseus The sun isn't even shining.

Phaedra That's why I'm eating lettuce. I thought you were gone.

Theseus I'm going.

Phaedra Yesterday I ate daffodils. We used do that when we were children. Sit in the sea field eating daffodils, grazing like cows.

Theseus I want to say something to you.

Phaedra No way, no more conversations between us.

Theseus You said something unsavoury last night.

Phaedra I say something unsavoury every night.

Theseus Something about my son.

Phaedra What do you care about your son? What do you care about any of us?

Theseus It's not a question of caring.

Phaedra Your precious layabout is safe with me. Unlike you, I am no debaucher of the young. Too much pride to inflict this old carcass on them.

Theseus You have some sort of effect on him. He's not advancing. How does he pass his time? Sailing? Sitting around, living off my generosity.

Phaedra And indifference.

Theseus A new woman every season.

Phaedra Where did he learn that, I wonder?

Theseus But without my passion for any of them. It's as if they're all on trial for something. I mean, what are young women for but fucking? Otherwise what are you doing near them? What is he masking?

Phaedra His problem with me, of course.

Theseus His what?

Phaedra It may seem ridiculous to you but people fall for me . . . a lot. Don't pretend you haven't noticed. He's in love with me. We're too isolated here, nothing but mountain and sea, our own little kingdom to fester in. Really I'm very normal considering except for one thing, I don't care any more for prolonging this. All I think of these days is departing. It's no longer a question of when but how? Will it be black or white? Will I go in a sulphur halo or on wings of light? Will I be allowed that brief sojourn on the sun? I want it white, no one's destruction but my own.

Theseus What exactly are you saying?

Phaedra You give me nothing to live for.

Theseus I am not the sort of man to become fixated on. That you've always known.

Phaedra Then why did you marry me?

Theseus Because you asked me.

Phaedra I asked you?

Theseus At your sister's funeral, as they shovelled the clay in.

Phaedra Why didn't you say no?

Theseus I was intrigued at the timing of the proposal, the promise of redemption which I still believed in then. And after all, it's not every woman understands the erotic potential of the tombstone. You were magnificent that day.

Phaedra I am often magnificent with my legs open.

Theseus When you deign to open them.

Phaedra My sister died over you. You! You and your kisses of death.

Theseus We die for ourselves as we live. I refuse to deal with what others put on to me. I am who I am.

Phaedra An aging bull past his prime.

Theseus That's a matter of opinion.

Phaedra Your arrogance is astonishing. My family made you. You throve on my sister's, my brother's graves.

Theseus I throve? I rescued you from that museum of monsters. Your brother? To even call him that? He was a wild animal! Ariadne? Yes she was something different, something else.

Phaedra I don't know why you bother coming home.

Theseus Children, darling, children, that's why I come home. You know this. No love lost between us. We're one big mistake, a sewer for all the ghosts.

Phaedra You come home the way the murderer comes home to the scene of the first crime. And as long as I am here you can fool yourself what you did was right and true and not a desecration of every law, human and divine.

Theseus You and I? From the start, fascinating bad news, a doom-eager pact. Never! I repeat, never speak of my son the way you spoke of him last night.

Phaedra You have long lost the right to tell me anything!

Theseus You touch him and I'll tear you both limb from limb.

Phaedra I'll touch what I need to touch. I have always and I always will. I'm my mother's daughter after all.

Theseus (*ready to kill her*) Someone should throw you off a cliff.

Phaedra It feels as if someone already has.

And exit Theseus and exit Phaedra.

SCENE SEVEN

On the screen. The Minotaur carries Phaedra into the sea. We watch them walking into the sea. Point of view is of them coming towards us. Slowly, step by step, they

*enter the waves. They are calm, unpanicked, resolved,
a pact here, this is right and fitting, enjoyable even, but
the film must portray: this is not a dip. This is it. She's
not coming back. The Child Minotaur gleeful, splashing.
Running alongside Phaedra and Minotaur. Music to
accompany this.*

SCENE EIGHT

Evening on stage.
  *Nanny arranges table for dinner: white tablecloth, a
steaming casserole, opening wine, etc. She mutters the
first lines of a Sappho poem about infantry and oars.
Enter Phaedra in evening clothes.*
  Nanny pours a drink for her.

Phaedra What's with all the food? I hope you don't
expect me to eat it. Where's my daughter? Bring her out.
We'll dine together.

Nanny She has school tomorrow. She doesn't need one
of your onslaughts.

Phaedra You just stop feeding her in the kitchen. She'll
grow up thinking she's nothing.

Nanny She likes the kitchen.

Phaedra I should write a novel, a *roman-á-clef*. The
opening sentence would go like this: 'Once there was a
beautiful woman and a bay and an ugly old housekeeper
who overfed everyone.'

Nanny (*exiting*) And then what happened?

Phaedra I swear to God one of these days something
will. Everyone telling me what's wrong with me. If
someone turned round and said they actually liked me
I think I'd faint.

Music. Enter the Child Minotaur with an extravagant armful of daffodils. Phaedra watches him come towards her.

Phaedra What world blew you in?

Minotaur You've forgotten me?

Phaedra Never . . . never . . . And the daffodils? . . . will we eat them?

Minotaur You must earn these daffodils.

Phaedra How must I earn them?

Minotaur Set me free.

Phaedra How set you free?

Minotaur You know.

Phaedra Theseus?

Minotaur Fair is fair. He killed me.

He makes to exit.

Phaedra Wait . . . Don't go.

Minotaur Ariadne's calling me from the field.

Phaedra Ariadne?

Minotaur Our sister? . . . You've forgotten her too? You've forgotten everyone.

And he's gone. Phaedra stands there, looking after him. Enter Hippolytus. Goes to table. Pours a glass of wine. Lifts casserole lid.

Hippolytus What's this?

Phaedra From the German butcher. Shark, dolphin, you'd want to see him tear a dolphin apart.

Hippolytus I've seen him.

Phaedra He goes purple in the face. When I'm bored I take a jaunt to the pier to watch his frenzies. He has something personal against fish.

Hippolytus And do you have something personal against me?

Phaedra Something personal against everyone.

Hippolytus It's my father you want.

Phaedra It's your father I want.

Hippolytus But he doesn't want you.

Phaedra runs her fingers through his hair.

Phaedra You think not? When I was young, I locked myself away from the young. And now everywhere I turn I see them, the beautiful, slothful young, who know nothing, understand nothing, consider me ridiculous.

Hippolytus The old consider you ridiculous too.

Phaedra I don't care about the old. They're all in the waiting room. They've had their turn. I won't let them take mine.

Hippolytus Everything gets taken.

Phaedra You know this for a fact or you're just chancing your arm?

Hippolytus Isn't that what living is? A whittling to bone till everything you believed is gone, then you're allowed to depart.

Phaedra Is that what you believe?

Hippolytus What I believe is doing the opposite of what I'm told.

Phaedra That is no way to survive.

Hippolytus Who's talking about surviving?

Wraps himself around her, kisses her, the beginnings of a seduction which she almost goes for.

Phaedra But yours is the wrong mouth on mine, the wrong hands. Go away, little boy, little boy blue, you don't interest me beyond five seconds.

Hippolytus You're afraid.

Phaedra As I should be. As should you.

Hippolytus I'm not afraid.

And exit Hippolytus.
  Enter Child Minotaur with Ariadne following him. She carries an assortment of bones, is arrayed in them. She is a bone or near as.

Child Minotaur Here she is.

He bows and departs.

Phaedra Ariadne? Are all the graves open tonight?

Ariadne They're always open. Hello, little sister, husband-stealer.

Phaedra You took him from me first.

Ariadne Let's not argue about the small things. That's not why I'm here.

Phaedra Then why are you here?

Ariadne To play you the bones. I learnt them out on the islands. I make seagulls shiver, hares keel over, snails explode when I take out the bones. When I die again I want to be hung in an open place where the wind can play all the notes through me, all the notes denied me now.

Phaedra How are you still walking the earth?

Ariadne I'm wondering the same about you.

Phaedra I'm barely here.

Ariadne Does he haunt you?

Phaedra Nothing haunts me.

Ariadne You hear his hooves from time to time?

Phaedra I keep thinking of the crescent moon scar on his brow. Who was he? What was he?

Ariadne He was the original nightmare and vision, slipped through eternity's seam.

Phaedra But he bled, he suffered, he loved, all that blood over the stones. I never knew blood smelled, grass and iron, that was his tang as he lay here dying. You and Theseus didn't even have the decency to kill him clean. I can understand cold, clean murder, but that torture, like he was some ancient sacrifice on your depraved altar.

Ariadne It had to be done, no place here for that sort of manifestation.

Phaedra Ever occur to you it's here is all wrong? Not him! No place for the impossible, the unreal, the unbelievable, just take a knife and cut out what lies under the maggoty stones no one dares turn.

Ariadne He asked me to take him out.

Phaedra He asked you?

Ariadne Yes, he appalled himself. He couldn't go on, he was terrified when the man took over the bull or the bull took over the man.

Phaedra I don't believe he asked you.

Ariadne Then ask him yourself.

Music. Enter adult Minotaur. They take a long look at one another.

Phaedra So. You're finally here.

Runs to him, flings herself into his arms, kisses him wildly, madly.

Miracles . . . miracles . . . There must be . . . How did you? . . . Haven't slept in . . . Oh God in your . . . Thank you thank you thank you . . . Oh never thought . . . Miracles . . . It's been . . . Oh my God . . . It's been so hard without you.

Minotaur Yes, hard to leave one's former playground. But you have to find it in you to release me.

Phaedra I thought the dead were free. Free to roam, wander between all the worlds and home.

Minotaur You're thwarting my advance to the next strange shore. Time for me to shed these hooves, this tail, these horns.

Phaedra I planted aspens where we used to play. It's as if you were never here.

Minotaur But I was.

Phaedra They were all so afraid of you.

Minotaur All except you.

Phaedra All except me till I saw those globs of leftovers in your teeth.

Minotaur Some sea creature or worse.

Phaedra That old woman on the hill.

Minotaur Those girls.

Phaedra All those girls. All those disappeared without

a trace.

Minotaur All those. I would swim across the bay. And watch. And wait. To meet me by moonlight in some shadowy lane. Yes. Terrible. Pretending to graze, a clump of furze in my mouth, head down, tail swishing the dung flies. And after I'd done with them, the long swim home, floating on my haunches, sometimes cloudy skies and sometimes clear, and sick, sick with terror, knowing this is no way to live and knowing there can be no other.

Phaedra I'm not equipped for this. I'm sorry. Please leave my terrace.

Minotaur Your terrace?

Phaedra Yes. Mine. Shoo. Go on! Away with you, both of you.

Ariadne Give me back my husband and I'll go.

Phaedra This is not happening.

Minotaur You've seen nothing yet.

Minotaur taps his hooves on the stones of the terrace. The stones open, like graves, tombs, vaults. Out climb Pasiphae and Minos. Pasiphae is the first to emerge.

Pasiphae (*taking a terrifying mouthful of air*) Oh, the beautiful world, the living, breathing stew of it. Who in their mercy has allowed me a brief return visit? (*Looks out.*) That's where I saw him first. The white bull who came in from the sea. (*Looks at Phaedra.*) Phaedra?

Phaedra Mother. The last time I saw you, my father was dragging you across the stones in the dark.

Pasiphae To hurl me off the cliffs, ripped from our beds, half asleep, next thing the wave.

Phaedra What am I supposed to do with you?

Pasiphae Kiss me. Kiss me. You're older than me now.

Goes to her.

Phaedra No, keep away.

Pasiphae Pour me some wine, little daughter. There's a good girl.

Phaedra I don't pour for the dead.

Minos comes out of the stones.

Pasiphae You!

Minos Am I in the right place?

Pasiphae No, and you never were.

Minos Pasiphae, I owe you an apology.

Pasiphae Save it. What grave doesn't teach regret? Is that food? You must serve us. Don't you know we're not permitted to take what isn't offered.

Phaedra Then it isn't offered.

Minotaur Go easy, she's afraid.

Pasiphae Don't talk to me about fear. I could tell you volumes on fear. But you must go and meet it as I went to meet mine. Oh my God, what I gave away for the snow-white bull who came in from the sea. An enchanted thing who swam in to drive me mad. And though his taint would be in the blood of offspring, well, that was the chance I took. And what woman doesn't take chances for the thing she wants? The thing she must have. The thing she cannot not have. Don't look on him, they said, this thing that shouldn't come out of a woman, this throwback, this aberration, no, I said, this creature, this beauty is mine. And they put him with the calves and prayed he'd die. But I stole him back and made a nest

114

for him on my pillow where he slept his fitful sleeps,
gnawing on his hoof, singing of eternity, wept when he
looked in mirrors.

Minotaur Do you want to know what happened after?
After your protection was removed?

Pasiphae I don't want to know.

Minotaur I lived in the caves mostly, the house barred
to me. I trapped hares, dogs, sows, foals, lambs. The
lean times. The times of plenty? I hurled myself on your
kind, women who dream of the bull, women who cry to
be abducted from their lonely beds, Women who thought
they wanted the raw animal steam above them, behind
them. They were the willing ones, until they saw where
their will had led them. Did I care? I like a tussle and
though it wasn't deliberate I left them in tatters. And
then the times of frenzy. Did your white bull show you
his frenzy? The scalding heat, the dripping eyes, the hoof
on the throat, the screams as limbs fly and bones crack,
the thrill of carnage, the banquet, blood of fresh thigh
on this insatiable tongue.

Minos See what you grunted into the world, sullied us
all with.

Minotaur Do you remember how I died?

Phaedra I remember. I found you.

Minotaur Then how can you be with him?

Phaedra I protected you till I no longer could.

Minotaur But to marry him?

Phaedra It was either that or kill him.

Minotaur I want Theseus. I want him. I want everything
he owns. Everything he loves. I want to see his face

when that moment occurs.

Phaedra But I have a child by him, a daughter.

Ariadne We'll take her too.

Phaedra You lay a finger on her!

Minotaur We will. We will. We'll have what we need in the end.

Pasiphae You cannot continue to live with your sister's husband, your brother's killer.

Minos Why should you live when we don't? Why should you eat while we starve?

Phaedra You had your turn. Please let me live out mine.

Minotaur Am I there when he holds you?

Phaedra No one holds me. No one.

Minotaur So it was all in vain? All for nothing?

Phaedra No, he's necessary to keep you at bay. Maybe that's why I love him. He was the one, the only one, could bring a bull to his knees.

Minotaur You'll pay for those flippant words.

Phaedra I pay every day and what I ignore in the sun comes up with the moon. And everything tells me there is no salvation for me, only things that happen to me, things to be endured and then forgotten. Please. Let me pass.

Arranging themselves around her, they surround her, paw and scrape and lunge. Minotaur lifts her up with one arm, suspends her there, whatever way it's done she is hanging in mid-air.

Minotaur Would you like to be a hanging woman?

Ariadne Skin her to a harp and play her with those horns.

Pasiphae takes a bite from Phaedra's leg. Blood and roars.

Pasiphae (*chewing, blood dripping from her chin*) Fresh, fresh, fresh.

Minos No! No! Burrow to the spine first. You must get her there first or she'll escape us.

Pasiphae Look, she's trying to scream and the scream won't come. We have her. We have her. They all do that at the finish.

Minos (*voracious*) Move over! Make room!

Pasiphae I want some neck. Stop shoving, will you?

She pushes Minos violently away to feed.

Ariadne (*playing the bones*) Save some for me. This is breast of hare against rib of sparrow. You have to imagine the wind.

We hear the wind.

And the lone fiddle.

We hear the lone fiddle.

Pasiphae (*a growl to Minos*) You're taking more than your portion.

Minotaur Enough! Enough!

Pulls them away, Phaedra gasps and heaves, stunned, blood pouring. Pasiphae snarls for more, a starved wolf, blood on her mouth.

I said leave her alone!

Ariadne I got nothing! I got nothing!

Minotaur (*fending them off*) Now see what we are capable of. You bring him to us this evening or we'll leave you with nothing. Run! Run! And do our bidding.

They watch as Phaedra runs off, follow her with their eyes.

Pasiphae Never to run like that again, thud of living foot on solid ground. (*A wail.*) I was too young to be taken. Too young. Will I ever get another turn?

And Pasiphae and Minos retreat to their graves. Ariadne wanders off with the bones.

Ariadne This is egret on an infant's knee –

Playing as she exits.
Minotaur looks out. Taps a hoof three times. Stands. Holds. And exits.

SCENE NINE

Enter Nanny, who cleans and tidies, followed shortly by Hippolytus and Girl in waders and sailing jacket.

Girl No, she was young, this woman, and she's there sitting at the end of my bed.

Hippolytus When was this?

Girl This is every night, she comes and sits on my bed and she has a little boy with her.

Hippolytus Is this a dream?

Girl If it is I'm always awake and she holds this little boy and there's something wrong with this boy.

Nanny What boy? What's wrong with the boy?

Girl Something on his face and the other night the three of us were waltzing on the bed and I held the little boy's hand only it wasn't a hand, it was, I don't know, velvet and something else at the same time, and then last night the little boy spoke to me.

Hippolytus What did he say?

Girl He went like this – (*A beckoning gesture.*) He kept going like this. Standing on the windowsill and I flew off after him.

Nanny You're sleeping in with me tonight.

Enter Phaedra, bloodstained, scratched, bitten, a weeping leg, a torn neck.

Hippolytus What, what happened?

Phaedra (*shaking*) Don't ask me anything. Don't talk.

Girl (*giving her a drink*) Here, Mom, have this.

Phaedra (*looking around in terror*) Are they gone? Nanny, they're here. They're all back.

Nanny They never really left.

Phaedra My beautiful girl . . . I need to . . . I can't . . . You see, sweetheart, I always believed we get one gallop here. One lawless gallop and then oblivion. But I didn't reckon on them. Where can I go? There is no place for me. I am forever cast out, forever watching others live while my lips rot with my song. I've seen them, dressing up, holding hands, like some secret society. What is it? Why is it not allowed me? I can dance. I love to dance. My sister loved to dance. And where did it get her? A wind chime hanging from a tree, crows in her hair. That's where dancing with the wrong man on a Friday night gets you.

Enter Aricia.

Aricia (*to Hippolytus*) You said you'd wake me.

Phaedra She sleeps! She sleeps!

Aricia Maybe I'm sleeping for all of you.

Phaedra Don't be so smug about it. I've seen them after thirty-year sleeps. They don't look any better.

Aricia Let's go.

Phaedra Go with her. Don't be a fool.

Hippolytus (*to Aricia*) I look at you and all I see are weddings, christenings, funerals, one endless ritual in white. I'll pass.

Aricia Don't you contact me again.

And exit Aricia.

Phaedra Don't blame me for your sickness.

Hippolytus It's what you want, isn't it?

Enter Theseus. He stands there looking at Phaedra, Hippolytus, Girl. Eventually:

Theseus Go to bed, little girl.

Girl It's still early.

Theseus Go on away with you, Nanny.

And exit Girl with Nanny.

Phaedra And what do we owe this unexpected pleasure to? Let me see. You've had your first refusal. Was she young?

Theseus With a big Greek nose and she didn't refuse. No one refuses me. No one.

Phaedra Except me. I'm the expert in that department. I was born with the gift for saying no.

*Theseus takes her by the chin, examines her, fingers
her wounds, her arm, her neck, her leg.*

Theseus It's nothing to be proud of, this genius for no.
What are these gashes? These bruises?

Phaedra I'll give you three guesses.

Theseus I'm not in guessing vein.

Phaedra Ask your son.

Goes for him.

You did this! You! They're going to take us all out.

*And exit Phaedra.
Theseus stands there. Hold.*

Hippolytus What?

Theseus I'm wondering what you think you're at?

Hippolytus This and that.

Theseus This and that.

Hippolytus What were you at, at twenty?

Theseus At twenty I had you. At twenty I'd made my
first million. At twenty I wrestled a bull to the ground.
Don't attempt to lie to me. I made my fortune from
interrogations, reading faces.

Hippolytus And what does my face tell you?

Theseus You want. You want. You want.

Hippolytus What I want is none of your concern.

Theseus What is mine is my concern. If I wanted like
that I'd pursue it to some grizzly end. You're a runt, a
nothing, a lout, a dreamer of crimes who is seedily
immaculate, obscene in your pristine torpor.

Hippolytus Because I don't plunder and rampage I'm not fit for your presence?

Theseus If you had fucked her and repented I would've forgiven it, but this girly dithering. I need to see some shadow of the young bull in you, some shade of the bull-slayer that came down from me.

Hippolytus You would forgive that?

Theseus That kind of power never asks forgiveness. People back off astonished. Get out of my sight. You are forbidden this house until further notice.

Hippolytus I have nowhere else to go.

Theseus Then go there.

Hippolytus All right . . . I will.

And exit Hippolytus.
   Theseus stands looking after him, pours himself a drink.
   Image on screen. Minotaur tied to a stone slab. Theseus standing over him with a knife. Close up on both their faces. Strangely still. Then blood dripping from the stones. A terrible sound.

SCENE TEN

Enter Phaedra, changed, patched up, made-up, pours herself a drink, looks out on the bay.

Phaedra The waves Cleopatra-black and me so wanting to be wise. Not this time round it seems . . . (*Listens.*) Did you hear something?

Theseus What are you listening for?

Phaedra I wonder how he'll do it.

Theseus Awash in your fizzy flights of doom.

Phaedra I saw him heading for the cliffs, a lithe shape behind him. You've had this long on the earth and you've learned nothing. Tonight you'll learn.

Theseus What are you planning?

Phaedra If I had the courage to plan, my children would be safe and you in your grave. I don't have the wherewithal to sink the blade but I can do the next best thing.

Theseus Which is?

Phaedra Just let it happen. My son who is not my son will fly off the cliff tonight. My daughter? Please God let them spare my daughter. Long past time I went to join my people.

Theseus Go then. You've been threatening for years. Go. I never knew what happened in caves till I chanced on you.

Phaedra Yes, I am what happens in caves. Me. My sister. My brother.

Theseus Your brother! He was an animal, a furious bull who scorched the air here. He's scorching it still.

Phaedra And you're not an animal? And I'm not? And are we not surrounded by animals? You call the way you live human? This country human? The passions of the upright two-feeters human? We're animals. We suffer, we die, we're forgotten. But the price must be paid here for the transgressions of here. You think to exit freely after what you've done? Do I think I can slip away under the aspens after what I have allowed? No, it'll be bloody and violent and then it's over. Yes, he was terrifying, my brother, the voracious marauding fact of him, the smell of him, the appalling eyes that struggled for the light and

123

failed, failed each time, sinking back to what was his nature. But that nature, that force in him was the same as what's in you and me and every other specimen I've come across that is called the human race. That was life. Life with nothing to cloak it. And you took it.

Theseus Someone had to.

Phaedra But it was you.

Enter the Minotaur carrying Hippolytus, both dripping from the sea. He is followed procession-like by Pasiphae and Minos.
Minotaur lays Hippolytus at Theseus' feet. He arranges him with great care. Theseus stares in shock.

Minotaur The wounds on his face are from the rocks but the hoof mark on his back is mine. The rest I believe are yours. And when you recover your equilibrium, which won't be today or tomorrow. But when you think you have, wander down and absent-mindedly find yourself in the caves. And sit and ponder how you got from there to here and here to there. And forget about the tricky tides that swell and turn and fill that place of booming stone. And panic and climb to the highest ledge, my one-time monkish lair. And strain because you hear a different rhythm that is not the mounting waves or the slap of shell on sand or your own racing heart. And listen to me breathing, and when I offer you this cloven hand against the rising surf, refuse it, let the sea have you. It will be easier by far.

Bows to Phaedra.

Thank you.

Phaedra Where's my daughter?

Ariadne enters carrying the Girl. Lays her at Phaedra and Theseus' feet.

Silence.

Ariadne All in harmony again. All fair and square. Thank you.

Pasiphae walks up to Phaedra and bows.

Pasiphae Thank you.

Minotaur Come, I owe you a daffodil feast.

Phaedra The time for eating daffodils is past. The distance travelled from myself too great. I'll go on my own steam. I won't be long.

Minotaur We understand.

They turn and exit in procession. Minotaur stops to look back at her, nods, exits.
  Image of Phaedra on screen, staring out, huge, all face. Looking. Or reprise of the Minotaur carrying Phaedra into the sea.
  Blackout.

End.

SOME EXTRA IMAGES
TO PLAY AROUND WITH

Child Minotaur with Child Phaedra and Child Ariadne in a field of daffodils. Playing. A two-minute sequence, chasing, tumbling, making garlands.

Child Minotaur running along the shore with Pasiphae.

Minos watching them with a face of murder.

Minotaur being dragged, tied to a cart in crucifix position by Theseus and Minos. Ariadne and Phaedra watching.

Ariadne hanging from a tree.

Close up of Minotaur. Very still.

Pasiphae and Child Minotaur falling through the air.

Girl and Ariadne talking in a bedroom. Child Minotaur looks on.

Theseus and Phaedra in bed making love. Minotaur watches.

Theseus with a hoof at his throat.

THE MAP OF ARGENTINA

Characters

Deb
late forties

Sam
late forties

Darby
late forties

Father
nineties

Mother
eighties

Argentinian
forties

Mark
sixteen

Natalia
fifteen

Ted
ten

Holly
eight

Jess
five

Waiters

SCENE ONE

*Evening. Deb paints her toenails. Drinks from a glass of
red wine. Sam watches her.*

Sam You going out?

*Deb looks at him. Drinks. Resumes painting her
toenails.*

What's the colour?

Deb You don't recognise red when you see it?

Sam There's red and there's red.

Deb Certainly is.

Sam You see red when you see me.

Deb Sam please, not tonight, I'm exhausted.

Sam This is our house. Our home.

Deb looks at him.

I'm your husband.

Deb Lucky you.

Sam It's time you had another baby.

Deb To calm me down?

Sam Pregnant women don't usually go running around.

Deb Last year I'd have had another baby.

Sam Why didn't you tell me?

Deb I'm too old.

Sam Yeah, you're a middle-aged woman. Maybe you should start acting like one.

Deb And how does one act middle-aged? Like you, is it?

Sam Yeah, like me, accepting one's portion, knowing the best is gone, over, never to be retrieved and still to wring the dregs. That's the proper way, the dignified way.

Deb I used to believe that too.

Sam What time did you get in last night?

Deb You know what time I got in.

Sam Must've been good.

Deb What do you want me to say? It was great?

Sam We partied till five in the once-upon-a-time.

Deb Yes, we did.

Sam Dancing naked on the table to Johnny Cash.

Deb All over now.

Sam I don't believe that.

Deb Gone with the swallows.

Sam It'll come back. Always does.

Deb It's gone, Sam . . . Whatever that was – calf love – this is the real thing.

Sam You're so in love with him.

Deb Don't make me say things that'll hurt you more than I already have.

Sam You were in love with me once.

Deb No not like this, Sam.

Sam He's a thug.

Deb You're the thug.

Sam Me?

Deb If you'd any pride you'd leave.

Sam It's because I've so much pride I'm staying.

Deb You think you're in competition with him?

Sam I know I am.

Deb It's not a competition.

Sam If you can turn that quickly, you can turn back again. I'll be here. In the marital bed.

Deb To take your revenge?

Sam I'll be humble in victory.

Takes hold of her. Looks at her. Feels her up and down. This should be lovely. He's trying to woo her. Soften her.

Kiss me . . . Go on . . . surprise yourself.

Deb No.

Sam Show me what I've been missing.

Deb I don't know how to kiss you any more.

Sam You can pretend I'm him.

Deb Sam, please.

Sam kisses her. Long. Passionate. Should go on too long.

Sam I want you and it'd be nice if you could make it mean something for a change.

Deb I can't.

Sam You think you only want him?

Deb Stop second-guessing me. I know I only want him.

Sam You're mistaken. You'll see. He doesn't love you. He's a wrecker. It's me he wants.

Deb You?

Sam You don't know very much about men.

Deb Look, I'm trying to end it.

Sam But you can't help yourself? I can end it.

Deb No doubt you can.

Sam I'm going to have you declared an unfit mother.

Deb You dare!

Sam You're a drunken whore.

Deb I'm the drunken whore you married.

Sam I like whores.

Deb I've been the perfect wife, mother, for twenty years. Doesn't that count for anything?

Sam Not a damm thing.

Deb If you even think about coming between me and the kids!

Sam Just stop this madness! I know about desire! I know how addictive it is. How thrilling. I know all about a man, a woman, a shining bed. I am that man. You are that woman. Upstairs is our shining bed.

Deb Suddenly you're in love with me.

Sam You're my wife. You won't let me near you.

Deb I can't.

Sam Saving yourself for him. What is this born-again virgin act?

Deb I don't want it sullied.

Sam It's already sullied, Deb.

Deb If I get pregnant –

Sam What?

Deb I have to know whose it is.

Sam What are you saying to me?

Deb So I can make decisions accordingly, be clear, know what the options are.

Sam Are you pregnant?

Deb Don't know.

Sam Are you trying to get pregnant?

Deb I don't know.

Sam You want to risk everything?

Deb Is that what it's called? Risk?

Sam Why?

Deb So we'll find out.

Sam Find out what?

Deb Just leave me alone.

Sam You're not seeing him tonight, are you? It's a bit late now, not your pattern. So are those red toenails for me?

Deb Stop looking at me. Stop clocking everything I do.

Sam He might show up . . . You need to be ready, painted, perfumed. Is he going to show up here tonight? Am I supposed to wave the two of you off from the front door like the maiden aunt? Is he going to bring me chocolates?

Deb He's not coming. He wouldn't do that.

Sam To me?

Deb No. To me.

Sam To you. Good. Thought you were trying to make him out to be a gentleman there for a minute. If I'm not mistaken you're trying to woo me tonight. Keep me on side.

Deb You were always an egomaniac.

Sam So how about it? Pretend I just met you in your new perfume, what is it? Let's say the Victorian era, fog, mist, Jack the Ripper on the loose, I just picked you up, can do anything I like with you.

Deb It won't work.

Sam Why not?

Deb You'll start telling me you love me.

Sam Well, I do. Even still. What's so terrible about that?

Deb I can't do this any more, Sam. There's not enough of me.

Sam Admit it, Deb. You've turned away from me. Six months ago you shifted your gaze to the middle distance and he walked into it.

Deb You shifted your gaze too, many times.

Sam Never. Never like this. For me it's very simple. I've loved you since the first minute I clapped eyes on you.

Deb It's only because of him. It's not for me.

Sam I know I wandered from time to time, but in my heart . . .

Deb Please no talk of your heart.

Sam In my heart! It's always you. And that's the truth, isn't it? You have to come back to me.

Deb If you leave me alone I might.

Sam I'm not leaving you alone.

Deb Then I'll walk, Sam, I swear I'll walk. I'll leave you here with the whole lot of them.

Sam Who's doing the school run?

Deb I always do the school run. That's not changing, is it?

Sam And Natalia's concert is tomorrow evening.

Deb I can't make it.

Sam At eight.

Deb I said I can't make it.

Sam You have plans?

Deb I have plans.

Sam Cancel them. We're going together.

Deb I've been to hundreds of their concerts. On my own! You go for a change.

Sam What's his number?

He lifts her phone.

Deb No, give me that!

Sam scrolls, fends her off.

That's my phone. Am I allowed anything? That is my phone!

Sam Paid for by me. Here we are.

Rings, we hear ring tone. Enter Darby in dressing gown.

137

Darby Darling.

Sam Sweetheart.

Darby Sam?

Sam Darby.

Darby Hello, Sam.

Sam Hello, Darby, and how are you getting on?

Darby I'm getting on mighty thank you, Sam, and how are you?

Sam Oh, I'm in great form except for the weather. It was a mucky day, wasn't it?

Darby It was.

Sam Mind you, it cleared up.

Darby It did.

Sam Apart from the rain.

Pause. Let them hold it standing there with their phones.

Look I won't keep you, I just wanted to let you know, Deborah is really sorry but she can't meet you tomorrow evening so you can cancel the dinner, the flowers and whatever else you'd planned with my wife. My wife. Because you see Natalia has a concert. At her school. She's playing her cello and she wants us both there.

Darby I see. Is Deb okay?

Sam Deborah to you. And she's fine.

Darby Can I speak to her?

Sam That's not necessary and in fact I'd prefer if you never spoke to her again.

138

Darby I'd like to see if she's okay.

Sam Are you afraid I'll do something to her? You're the one doing things to her. I'm the one who's afraid here.

Darby I'm told you have a temper.

Sam We all have tempers.

Darby We certainly do, Sam. Now I'd like to speak to her.

Sam I'm just delivering a message. Thought I'd save her the bother. She's exhausted with our five children. Five.

Darby I've got your message, Sam. I've got all your messages and now I'd like to speak to Deborah.

Sam (*hands her the phone*) He wants to speak to you.

Darby Hello? . . . Sam?

Deb No it's me . . . Sorry about . . .

Darby What the hell is . . .

Deb Sorry, sorry, he just grabbed my . . .

Darby Are you all right?

Deb Yes yes, I'm . . . I'm . . .

Darby You have me worried – do we need the police?

Sam The police!

Grabs phone.

You want to call the police on me?

Deb Give me that!

Darby Look, Sam, leave her . . .

Sam I can't believe I ever let you sit at my table!

Deb (*shouts into phone, which Sam won't give her*) We're fine! We're fine! I'm fine!

Sam She's nearly fifty!

Darby If you lay a finger on her –!

Deb (*shouting into phone as Sam fends her off*) Just hang up on him. I'll call you later.

Sam (*at the same time*) I'm not the one laying fingers!

Darby I'm coming over!

Deb (*phone*) Give me that! Darby. Darby.

Darby Are you okay?

Deb Yeah! Stop! Christ, I'm perfect! I've been married to him for twenty-two years, he doesn't own a chainsaw, what are . . .

Darby I don't like the tone of his voice.

Deb Text me later.

Hangs up. Silence. Hold.

Sam I mean . . .

Deb I can't take this any more!

Sam Have I ever laid a finger on you?

Deb You have to leave me be, Sam.

Sam Did you tell him I have a temper?

Deb Well you do, don't you?

Sam Never with you!

Deb I don't think I ever said that except maybe to keep him in his place.

Sam What place?

Deb He wants to marry me.

Sam But you're already married!

Deb God, that never occurred to me!

Sam Does he have a temper?

Deb Yes he does.

Sam Has he used it on you?

Deb Have I made him angry? Yes, I have.

Sam Has he done anything?

Deb Like what?

Sam Is he rough?

Deb How do you mean?

Sam You know damm well how I mean!

Deb I'm different with him. Grow up, Sam.

Sam I can't allow this. He'll put an axe in your head.

Deb He'll do nothing of the sort.

Sam I'm afraid for you.

Deb So am I, but not the way you think.

Sam He wants to call the police on me.

Deb We should all be locked up.

Lights.

SCENE TWO

Enter Darby. Suit. Sunglasses. Sits.
  Enter Deb. Dressed to kill. Darby jumps up. Wraps himself around her. Kisses her. Extends her. Admires her. These people adore each other. The attraction and pull

should be electric. They find it difficult to restrain themselves in public. Take this as far as possible.

Darby What the hell was that about last night?

Deb I love the tie.

Darby My girlfriend got it for me.

Deb Which one?

Darby The big fat married one with the twelve children.

Waiter has arrived.

Black Bush . . . please. Neat.

Deb Two Black Bushes.

Waiter Sure.

Darby Three Black Bushes. Four. You sort your marriage out okay? Stop trying to implicate me.

Deb (*kissing him*) But you are implicated.

Darby I don't want to have to speak to him again like that.

Deb What did you have to say that for anyway?

Darby Say what?

Deb The cops. What were you at?

Darby He was losing it.

Deb He wasn't. He's always like that. Tell me how much you love me? Tell me how glad you are to see me?

Darby I'm not. You should be at Natalia's concert.

Deb I don't need this from you. I can get that at home, okay?

Darby I want out. This is going nowhere.

Deb But where can it go?

Darby You're spewing it all over me. You want me to step in, carry you off like some medieval knight.

Deb Yes, please carry me off like some medieval knight.

Darby How?

Deb I'm too old for you.

Darby You're too messy. Old? I don't mind old. Love old like good strong wine or one of those oak trees you see standing alone in the middle of a beautiful field. I've been after you for years.

Deb And a whole slew of other women. Sam said you're a wrecker, that it's him you want.

Darby (*laughs his head off*) He said that? He wishes.

Deb And I heard you plucked the bride from under the groom's very nose. Last summer. My cousin was at the wedding. She said you ran for the car with the bride.

Darby She wanted rid of him. She thanked me, stopped her ruining her life. You can't ignore a woman in distress.

Deb Well, I'm in distress.

Drinks arrive. Darby gives the Waiter money.

Darby I think we'll have two more.

They clink. Drink.

Deb You're so . . . What am I supposed to do with you?

Darby (*kisses her*) What do you want, Deborah? Love that name. Deborah. Deboorah. Deb.

Deb I want to wake up and all of this is sorted. I want to wake with you. My kids. I want to be able to talk to Sam reasonably, like an adult, whatever that is, whoever they are.

Darby I hate adults, can't stand them, wherever you see an adult you can be sure everyone is miserable.

Deb Natalia's not playing till the second half. I have to be there.

Darby I thought you made a decision.

Deb I did. I have. Okay, no concert. She'll have a fit.

Darby You said you'd spend the evening. The night.

Deb I'll come back after.

Darby No, you won't. You'll go for pizza with your husband and your children.

Deb Look, Natalia was in tears. She's fifteen. She wants me there. She eats junk non-stop, she's going to be a heifer if she doesn't watch it.

Darby Poor Natalia, depending on you.

Drinks arrive.

I wish I'd met you twenty years ago.

Deb You'd have ignored me.

Darby You think?

Deb Wouldn't even have registered me.

Darby What're we going to do? The whole thing's a disaster.

Deb We have to. If it kills us then it kills us.

Darby But Sam? All those kids?

Deb The kids are fine. They're doing really well. Honestly they are. None of their bloody business what I do in private.

Darby I've said this to you before but I'll say it again. I'll take you on, mess that you are. I'll take your kids on though they'll despise me. I'll take it all on. But I can't sort you and Sam. You have to do that.

Deb But there's no sorting Sam and me. Yeah, I love him. He's my husband, but it's not the way I love you. Want you. Every time I see you I want to die. I want to die because I'm so afraid you'll slip through my fingers. I can't sleep. I can't eat.

Darby You can drink.

Deb I can drink. Am I crazy?

Darby I'm crazy about you.

Deb I mean, is it my age? Is it I'm looking at the coffin? Is it every third thought I won't be here much longer? Is it I've had too much prose? I want the lyrics now, the epics, the ballads. I want to be a sonnet they'll recite a thousand years hence, not some cautionary tale to keep everyone in line.

Darby I better cancel.

Deb What have you planned?

Darby Doesn't matter.

Deb It does matter. I'm not going to Natalia's concert. She can hardly play the damn thing anyway.

Darby All the more reason you should be there.

Deb I give her oodles of time. What, are you the parents' association all of a sudden? The Catholic marriage advisory board? I don't need advice from you on the state of my marriage. You're the reason for the state of my marriage.

Darby She's a kid. She wants her mother there, looking at her.

Deb I'm always there.

Darby Your decision.

Deb I really hate you! No matter what I do it's wrong.

Darby Kind of the definition of woman, isn't it?

Deb You had more respect when you couldn't have me.

Darby Sure I had.

Deb I'm going to break my children's hearts over you, drive Sam to drink or an early grave. But what Sam will never acknowledge is he played around too.

Darby Is that what this is?

Deb No, I didn't mean that.

Darby I'm not playing around.

Deb I'm not either. But Sam, when I was pregnant with Ted, he had an affair.

Darby I'm not an affair.

Deb I'm talking about Sam.

Darby I'm not an affair. I'm not revenge for Sam's affair.

Deb Affairs.

Darby Lucky Sam.

Deb Maybe Sam's right. You'll tire of me very soon. You're tired of me already.

Darby I don't get enough of you to be tired of you. I was looking forward to spending the evening with you. You promised me a whole night and now I've to drive you to your daughter's school, park around the corner like a thief. Come on, you'll be late.

Deb Hang on, I haven't decided.

Darby I have.

Lights.

SCENE THREE

*Drawing room. Sam's mother in twin-set, skirt,
emeralds, heels, a beautiful white-haired woman in her
eighties. She pours sherries. Sam sits there.*

Sam Have the others been around?

Mother I think so, yes. David was here yesterday or was
it the day before? And Stella made me count backwards
from a hundred. She was really annoyed I managed it.
And now you. How's everybody?

Sam All good. All fine.

Mother Deborah?

Sam Deb is Deb, busy running after the kids.

Mother No doubt she is. Give her my love.

Sam You missing Pincy?

Mother Pincy was a cat.

Sam But you miss her?

Mother I miss people. People, darling. Life too short to
be crying over a cat. Sure I miss her. Since your father it's
just been me and Pincy against the world. You and Deb
okay?

Deb We're okay, why?

Mother Just wondering.

Sam A mother's sixth sense?

Mother Only Stella said that Deb was spotted dancing
in some club, a bottle of champagne in her hand. You
were there?

Sam You know I wasn't.

Mother She's at that age.

Sam What age?

Mother The age of unravelling.

Sam And at what age does that happen?

Mother For men? Well, you're constantly unravelling, aren't you?

Sam Are we?

Mother For women, it's the forties. It was for me.

Sam Can't imagine you ever unravelling.

Mother Can't you?

Sam You've always been here.

Mother You're mistaken, darling.

Sam Always thought you and Dad were really happy. Old lovebirds.

Mother I left him once.

Sam You did not?

Mother Think your mother was just a boring old psychiatrist all her life?

Sam You left Dad? When?

Mother Before you were born. David and Stella were ten and nine. I left him for a year, fifteen months actually. Stella still gives me a hard time about it. Stella remembers.

Sam Why did no one bother to tell me?

Mother When I came back, your father said, let's just pretend that whole nightmare never happened. And we put it behind us. And then we had you.

Sam And was it a nightmare for you?

Mother The only nightmare was coming back.

Looks around.

We should not be creatures of habit.

Sam Who was he?

Mother Argentinian. A heart doctor. Still dream about him. He was referred to me with stress and addiction problems and somehow we ended up on the floor of my office and he had a dog that he used to bring into the operating theatre with him and he'd throw the fat that he cut away, the guts, innards, he'd fling them to the dog. He died young.

Sam And why did you come back?

Mother I've no idea . . . Children? And your father, suppose I was very attached to him.

Sam In a calf-like way?

Mother Probably.

Sam That's what Deb said about me.

Mother Worse things than calf love. No. Maybe there isn't.

Sam But I don't feel like that about Deb. I want her the way a man wants a woman, being married, having kids gets in the way of everything. You and the Argentinian?

Mother I'm a crone now. I wasn't always.

Sam Poor Dad. And I was always so proud of you when you collected me from school. What am I going to do?

Mother Who is he?

Sam Never mind. You'll take Deb's side anyway, always sticking up for the women.

Mother Someone has to. How long has it been going on?

Sam Not sure. She lies all the time now. I think he makes more than me.

Mother They usually do. Sex and money. Money and sex.

Sam Will you stop talking about sex? You're eighty-eight! And what really pisses me off is that he's good at what he does. Respected. The shark.

Mother I may be eighty-nine, darling, and I may not have the carapace, the upholstery, any more, but inside there is a fourteen-year-old dreaming of one last great love.

Sam Oh for God's sake, Mum, I don't want the details. How did Dad get you back?

Mother He didn't. Not really. Not ever. Another drop?

Sam No, I'm going.

Mother Be good to Deb.

Sam I am.

Mother Take care of her.

Sam She won't let me.

Mother She hasn't left. That's something, Sam. I know what I'm talking about here. Listen, she's very fragile right now.

Sam Fragile? She's driving through me like a tank.

Lights.

SCENE FOUR

Enter the Argentinian in scrubs. Covered in blood. He holds his dog. Smokes a cheroot.

Argentinian (*kisses the dog*) I lost him, Maria Bernadetta. Be sad for me. Sad. No smiling. Stop wagging your silly tail. It's not good to lose them, not good for me. You liked all the fat? Four pounds of fat. No dinner for you this evening, Maria Bernadetta. He was too young. Three small children. Who will teach them how to ride a bicycle now? Who will kiss them better? Who will pay for them? You? Will you explain to his wife that you just ate four pounds of fat from her dead husband's heart? Will you tell her that his heart was delicious?

Throws down cheroot.

Come, Maria Bernadetta. Come, we talk to the wife.

And exit with his dog.

SCENE FIVE

Two girls, Holly and Jess, eight and six, colouring like mad, in their pyjamas. Deb reads a book, pours a glass of wine.

Jess (*colouring*) But even when Mom's dead, I mean stone dead like that rabbit we saw in the ditch, even if Mom gets that dead I'll never ever forget her.

Holly I'll never forget Mom even when she's a ghost.

Jess Even when she's two ghosts I'll never ever forget her.

Ted, a boy of ten, sticks his head in the door.

Ted Can I watch a movie?

Jess Mom, can we have a little chat?

Deb School night.

Ted Please, Mom.

Deb Where's Natalia?

Ted In the bathroom putting on your new make-up. Can I?

Deb (*yells*) Natalia! Tell her to get out of the bathroom. (*Yells louder.*) Natalia! (*Louder again, a growl.*) NATALIA!

Holly Give it back!

Ted Can I, Mom?

Deb (*roaring*) Natalia, if you dare!

Jess I got it first!

Holly It's mine! Mom! Jess stole the top of my marker!

Ted Just for half an hour?

Deb Do you understand the word no? (*Yells.*) Natalia, leave my make-up alone!

Jess But I got it!

Ted But I put out the rubbish!

Deb I don't want a big dramatic scene when I turn it off!

Ted Thanks so much, Mom. (*Dashes out.*)

Holly (*roars*) I said give it back! That's the top of my Twistable! Mom!

Deb Give it to her, Jess.

Holly Mom bought that for me in the shop. As a surprise.

   A struggle between Holly and Jess. Deb tries to read.

Jess You're the meanest sister I ever had!

Holly (*a dramatic scream*) Mom! Jess pushed me really hard!

Jess Ow! My elbow and my daddy toe! Mom! Mom!

Holly It's mine! Mine! Mom! Mom!

Deb I'm not here! I'm not listening! Go to bed, for Christ's sake. (*Pours, covers her ears.*) Holly let her have it, for me, please.

Holly But it's my pink top from my pink Twistable.

Deb Where's hers? Where's yours, Jess?

Jess Doesn't matter, I got this one now.

Holly Pig!

Deb Girls.

Jess Pig's bum!

Deb Girls.

Holly Pig's bum with pooh on it!

Deb Girls! Girls! Please.

Holly No! I want the top of my Twistable.

Deb I'll buy you more tomorrow.

Jess Then you have to buy me more!

Deb I'm not buying you anything.

Jess I hate you!

Deb That makes me really sad, Jess, because I love you.

Jess No, I'm the sad one! I'm the saddest person in this house. And the smallest! The saddest and the smallest ever!

Head under the cushions, bum in the air, a fit of weeping.

Holly Just ignore her. I love you, Mom. You should never say you hate your mom, Jess! Mom's lovely.

Kissing her like a lover.

Deb No tongues, Holly.

Jess Just look at her! She robs all the hugs. You love her better than me! She gets all the attention in this family. (*Punching the cushion.*) This is the horriblest horriblest day of my life.

Deb Come here, darling, and I'll give you a hug.

Jess No, you have to come to me.

Holly (*on Deb's lap*) Sometimes I pretend you're a witch. Do you mind that, Mom?

Deb Come on, Jess.

Jess Only if you buy me new Twistables and only if Holly disappears.

Holly It's when I'm playing in my private tree at the end of the garden I pretend you're a witch who locks me in a cage and the swing is the cage. Do you mind, Mom?

Deb I am a witch, it's fine, sweetheart, if you want me to be a witch that's not a problem.

Holly But you'd never lock me in a cage?

Deb Of course not. (*Hugs her.*)

Jess Just get Holly out of here, Mom, and we can have some time to ourselves for once. Go and play, Holly, in your bedroom!

Holly But you're not really a witch are you, Mom?

Deb How about if I buy you both Twistables, new Twistables, tomorrow after school?

Holly First Jess has to give me back the pink top of my pink Twistable.

Jess But first Holly has to get off your lap. Pick me up for a change.

Enter Natalia.

Natalia Would you two stop being such little farts! Did you call me?

Deb Is that my make-up?

Natalia Can I run over to Maggie's?

Deb Just go to bed.

Natalia To give her back her iPad, she's going mad!

Deb It's far too late.

Natalia It's three doors down.

Jess You heard what Mom said. No! Natalia! No, Jesus, No!

Natalia (*running out of the door*) Shut up you, you little runt, I'll be two minutes. You can time me!

Deb Natalia! Natalia!

Enter Sam with Mark, a boy of sixteen in soccer gear.

Sam Where's she off to?

Holly Dad.

She runs to him. Jess dives for Deb's lap.

Mark Mom, I'm starving!

Sam What're you doing, still up?

Mark Can you run me down to the chipper?

Deb There's loads of food in the fridge.

Mark I want grease.

Sam I'll run him down.

Deb He had a huge dinner. Will you put this pair to bed? They just won't go.

Holly Not bed, please!

Jess (*holding on to the arm of the chair*) Not bed not bed not bed.

Sam (*trying to prise her off*) Bed right now or you're sleeping in the shed with the spiders.

Deb Did you do your homework?

Jess (*clinging on*) Think I'm afraid of a silly old spider!

Holly (*grabs top of Twistable from Jess*) Got it! Hah!

Jess (*a shriek*) Give it back! Mom! Dad! She just grabbed it out of my tiny little hand!

Sam Girls! Girls!

Mark Let's shake it, Dad, or it'll be closed.

Deb Homework? I asked you a question.

Jess (*tears*) But she just grabbed it off me.

　Enter Natalia running.

Natalia One minute forty-two seconds. You should trust me more. No one raped me unfortunately.

Ted (*head in the door*) Did I hear chips?

Deb No way, and turn off that movie now!

Ted I just turned it on! It's the ads!

Holly Yeah, chips! Can I have chips and ketchup?

Jess Yay, we're getting chips and ketchup! Can I put my finger in your wine, Mom?

Deb Everyone's had dinner. It's eleven o'clock.

Mark Come on, Dad!

Deb Bed! Now! Everyone! Teeth! Wees! Bed! And I don't want to set eyes on any of you till the morning!

Pours another glass.

Jess But you promised!

Deb No, it's too late for a story, Jess.

Holly You said, Mom! You said! You said!

Jess You crossed your heart!

Holly About Draphonopholus!

Jess Please please please! Did you know that, Dad, about Draphonopholus? She went and robbed one of Holly's teeth and left no money. Mom saw her flying down the hall last night, not one cent did she leave and Sophie got five euro for a totsy tooth. I'm going to kill Draphonopholus. I'm going to kill her with a knife. I'm going to get hold of her by the wing and stab her to bits till she gives back Holly's tooth. She's the meanest tooth fairy in the whole wide of fairyland. I'm going to get her like this! (*Does it.*) And this! (*Does it.*)

Sam Okay, chips for everyone!

Natalia Was Ryan playing?

Mark Laoise was there with no bra on.

Deb No chips, Sam, they'll be up all night.

Ted But Mark's getting chips.

Natalia I'll have chips and a quarter-pounder, Dad, no cheese, nothing on it, I mean nothing, loads of vinegar.

Jess I want vinegar, Dad, I want vinegar.

Holly May I please have eight chicken nuggets?

Jess Because you're eight. I want triangle chips.

Ted Because you're a triangle.

Jess Am I? Mom, am I a triangle?

Mark You want anything, Mom?

Deb This is ridiculous.

Jess But am I? Am I?

Deb Yes.

Jess No! (*A roar.*)

Deb What?

Jess (*a fit*) I don't want to be a triangle! I never wanted to be a triangle!

Deb Look, if you want to be a triangle then you're a triangle, okay! And if you don't want to be a triangle then you're not a triangle. Jesus!

Sam (*going to her purse*) Do you have any cash?

Deb Bed! Everyone bed!

Ted Can I go with you, Dad?

Sam You're in your pyjamas.

Holly Can I go?

Jess Can I go, Dad?

Deb Everyone's going! Everyone into the car! Dad's taking everyone to the chipper!

Jess But does Draphonopholus really hammer out your teeth when you're asleep with her golden hammer, tell me the truth now, Mom?

Natalia Don't forget, nothing on my quarter-pounder.

Jess Does she? Does she? Does she?

Deb Does she what?

Holly I have my shoes on. Mom, will you tie my laces?

Jess But I really don't want her to hammer out my teeth when I'm asleep.

Natalia But what does he see in her? She's a Russian prostitute.

Deb You'll have to sleep with your hand over your mouth. (*To Holly.*) Go 'way, you don't need your laces. (*To Natalia.*) Who's a Russian prostitute? (*To Jess.*) Or we can use Sellotape.

Holly But Jess, Dracobum is even worse.

Mark I'm going to faint with the hunger. Does anyone here realise I just played ninety minutes and penalties and you didn't wash my hoodie, Mom!

Holly Jess, Jess, Dracobum flies in by your eye and down your nostrils. Dad! Dad! Wait, don't forget about me!

Jess Carry me, Dad. Just carry me, I don't know where my shoes are.

Sam lifts her up, Holly holds his hand.

Natalia Okay, I'm coming. Bags the front.

Mark I'm in the front!

Ted Dad, can I sit in the front for once?

Deb's phone rings.

Mark You all know the front is mine. We're not going there!

Ted You just hog it!

Natalia I'm the lady round here, Dad?

Sam Answer it.

Deb looks at him. Phone continues ringing.

Mark Mom, your phone.

Ted I'll get it.

Deb holds it away. Continues ringing.

Natalia Who is it?

Holly Can I say hello?

Jess No, no, no, me, me first! Me first!

Silence, all look at the ringing phone. Hold. Deb turns it off.

Deb It's no one.

Sam Mr Nobody . . . Okay, let's go.

Exit all. Deb looks after them.

Lights.

SCENE SIX

Deb and Sam sit having coffee, sunglasses. Sunshine. A café terrace.

Sam You going to kiss his tombstone?

Deb You can't any more, they've blocked it off.

Sam Pity. Always wanted to kiss a tombstone.

Deb What did you make of all those lunatics?

Sam What lunatics?

Deb The pictures we just saw?

Sam Oh them. I'd like to have seen a few normal photos of them.

Deb What's normal?

Sam I mean when the camera was switched off.

Deb I love the way the doctors wrote their names on their backs.

Sam Those doctors were the real hysterics. He's here, isn't he?

Deb Yeah.

Sam He followed us?

Deb He's here on business.

Sam Business. You didn't say, 'Don't come'?

Deb Sam.

Sam You didn't say, 'I'm going to Paris with my husband?'

Deb I didn't want to come.

Sam Then why are you here?

Deb Look, we're here now.

Sam Are you going to see him?

Deb How can I? You won't let me out of your sight.

Sam You said last night you were going shopping this afternoon.

Deb Okay. I'm not going shopping this afternoon. Shopping this afternoon is cancelled as of now.

Sam Where's he staying?

Deb I don't know.

Sam You know.

Deb All right, I know.

Sam Where?

Deb None of your business, Sam.

Sam I thought we were having a nice time.

Deb We are.

Sam You even let me . . . Was it very hard for you?

Deb You have no idea.

Sam Felt you're being unfaithful to Darby?

Deb You really want to know how I feel? I feel completely and irretrievably unfaithful to myself. Not to you. Not to Darby. To myself.

Sam I'm going to leave you.

Deb You can't.

Sam I can't? Grow up, Deb. Who do you think I am?

Deb I just need . . . I just . . . Look . . . Give me six months, a year, and it'll be over. Just a year, Sam? What's a year after all the years we've been through together? Then I'm yours again. I swear. Please. All the windows are closing on me.

Sam I look at you now, you're nearly an old woman.

Deb You only have to look. I'm the one changing. I'm the hag in the making. I'm going to die soon.

Sam No, you're not.

Deb I am. I feel it.

Sam We're all going to die soon.

Deb And there's a couple of things I need to do.

Sam Do them with me.

Deb I am. Don't you see I am? I'm trying.

Sam No I don't see. And I'm getting very tired of all this understanding, this patience. You made vows.

Deb What vows?

Sam They didn't register?

Deb I must have skipped that bit.

Sam I could skip that bit too.

Deb I'm beginning to hate you.

Sam Beginning?

Deb You want control.

Sam You need control.

Deb How can you know what I need when I don't know myself. I'll have a gin and tonic, no spoon.

Sam It's too early.

Deb (*hand waving*) Waiter. Waiter.

Waiter comes.

Waiter *Madame.*

Deb A gin and tonic *s'il vous plaît, pas de* spoon.

Waiter *D'accord, et pour monsieur?*

Sam No, *merci.*

Deb No, Sam, listen, listen.

Sam What?

Deb It's like this . . . I love you.

Sam I know you do and that's what makes it so terrible.

Deb You're my man.

Sam Always thought I was.

Deb kisses him.

Deb I want us to have a nice time. We're in Paris.

Sam I made you come.

Deb No kids bawling the house down.

Sam I miss them. They should be with us always.

Deb I know, but they can't.

Waiter brings gin and tonic. Sam pours tonic and stirs it with spoon.

Merci. They're on their way, Sam. I can't believe we had them. I look at them. Are they mine? What do they have to do with me apart from the fact that I'd kill for them?

Sam If you don't come back to me soon I think the best thing all round would be for me to fly to Brazil and top myself.

Deb Why Brazil?

Sam You were in a nightclub drinking champagne by the neck.

Deb What?

Sam You were seen.

Deb I'm not hiding anything. You're the one pretending everything's fine.

Sam Stella saw you.

Deb Stella?

Sam A bunch of eighteen-year-olds pawing you. You kissed them all.

Deb I most certainly did not, Sam.

Sam My mother knows.

Deb Knows what?

Sam You're having an affair.

Deb I'm not having an affair.

Sam Then what're you having?

Deb I don't know, I don't understand it any more than you do. What did you have to tell your mother for?

Sam Stella told her.

Deb Stella's a bitch.

Sam Stella's my sister.

Deb Don't give me that family crap. I don't do guilt. Do you hear? I don't do guilt.

Sam Guilt is necessary.

Deb I've done enough guilt for the two of us. When I was pregnant with Ted you had an affair, hadn't you?

Sam I had a fling.

Deb A fling? Well, I'm having a fling now. And when I asked you at the time you denied it.

Sam It was nothing.

Deb I even know who she was.

Sam You don't know who she was. I kept all of that separate.

Deb I know exactly who she was. You know how I know? She was the one laughed as I breastfed Ted at that party. Had a good look at my boob, my fat belly hanging out and she laughed. No competition, I could see her thinking.

Sam I never fell in love with her. She was no one.

Deb Darby's no one. You carried on with her for a year, this no one.

Sam You were breastfeeding.

Deb Okay, you're breastfeeding now.

Sam (*knocking back her gin and tonic*) What are you, a man?

Deb Haven't the remotest interest in being a man.

Sam Well, you're losing your charm.

Deb That's a matter of opinion.

Sam So this is revenge?

Deb I wish that's all it was, Sam.

Sam What is it then?

Deb I don't want revenge. Can't you understand? I love you. I accept you for what you are. I've let you do what you needed to do. I don't want you doing what I say, what I want – let me do the same.

Sam gets up, walks off.

Wait, where are you going?

Sam The airport.

Deb No, wait, Sam.

Sam Call Darby, he'll rescue you.

Deb I told him not to come.

Sam No, you didn't. I've had it, Deb. Don't bother coming home.

As he exits:

Deb You ordered me here! I'm here! Don't you dare leave me in the middle of Paris. I knew you'd do this. You have the passports! Sam! Sam!

Running after him.

Waiter *L'addition, madame, l'addition, madame! Madame!*

Deb Sam, please!

Waiter (*running after her*) *Vingt euros. Madame! Vingt euros! L'addition.*

Lights.

SCENE SEVEN

A hospital bed. Deb's Father, in his nineties, all wrapped and swaddled in white, like a baby, white sheets, white nappy, white hospital gown. Tubes. Drips. Monitors. He sleeps.
   Enter Deb. She goes to him. Watches him sleep. Kisses him. She stands there. He opens his eyes. Registers her slowly.

Father Darling girl.

Deb Dad. How are you?

Father Oh . . . I'm having Roman thoughts.

Deb What kind of roamin' thoughts?

Father Antony had them when he was with Cleopatra in Alexandria. 'He was disposed to mirth but on the sudden a Roman thought hath struck him.' (*Takes her hand.*) Was I good enough to you?

Deb You were.

Father I was always working.

Deb A man has to work.

Father But was I kind?

Deb Dad, of course you were.

Father But was I there?

Deb What do you mean, were you there?

Father Was I there where I should've been?

Deb Dad, I was mad about you. I am mad about you.

Father You were my second chance. Your mother was my second chance.

Deb I know.

Father You know about my first marriage? You know about Rachel?

Deb Of course I know, Dad. Mum told me all about Rachel.

Father Rachel . . . seventeen . . . found hanging at the back of a flower shop . . . But do you know why?

Deb Is there ever a reason for things like that?

Father It was because of a dress.

Deb A dress?

Father Yeah, a dress . . . a stupid dress . . . imagine that? . . . It was her graduation ball and Anne had bought her this dress. Rachel took one look at it and said she wouldn't be caught dead wearing that thing. Anne was so hurt. She had chosen the dress with such care, attention, love. And Rachel just spat on it. Seventeen. No one is going to tell me what to wear. But for once Anne stood up to her, insisted Rachel would wear this dress and no other to her graduation ball. The row went on and I was dragged in. I took Anne's side. Rachel, this is a lovely, a very expensive dress. Your mother chose it for you and it would make her very happy if you wore it. No way. We could stuff our fucking dress. She wasn't going to her fucking graduation looking like a fucking banshee. This was my Rachel, my little Rachel, cursing like a fishwife. I told her she was out of line, speaking to us like this. That's all I said . . . I swear.

Deb I believe you.

Father Do you?

Deb Of course, Dad. It wasn't your fault.

Father No. What I should've said was, sweetheart, you can have any dress you want. You can have all the dresses in the world. Anne just lost her mind. Standing in the hall wringing her hands. I watched her disappear before my eyes.

Deb Don't dwell on it, Dad.

Father I'm going to meet my maker.

Deb I know, and Rachel should be here too.

Father Yes, she should. Yes, she should. I'm not getting out of here, am I?

Deb No.

Father They're buried together, Anne and Rachel.

Deb Do you want to be buried with them?

Father Would you mind?

Deb You don't want to be buried with Mum?

Father It isn't that. Your mother made me very happy . . . I just have this . . . I should be with Anne and Rachel. Unfinished business there. Unfinished business.

Deb I'll do what you want, Dad.

Father It won't upset you?

Deb Losing you is what'll upset me. I'll be an orphan.

Father You have Sam.

Deb I'm not sure about that any more. I have my kids.

She bursts into tears.

Father Deb. Here. Here, here, what's wrong? What's wrong, child? Deb . . . Deb.

Struggles out of bed, sheet, nappy, tubes dangling.

Deb No, don't get up, I'm sorry, I'm sorry.

Father (*can barely stand, holds her*) Here, here, it's all right, Deb. It's all right.

Deb It's not all right. I've fallen in love.

Father What?

Deb I'm crazy about him. I'm killing Sam. I'm ruining my children's lives.

Father Oh, Deb. Sam. How could you?

Deb I just saw him there. I don't know. This is not me. I think I've gone mad and now you dying on top of it – couldn't you just put it off till next year?

Father Darling, I'm old, I'm sick, I don't want to die, to leave you, I'm sorry, it's out of my control.

Deb What am I saying?

Father But Deb, what're you going to do?

Deb I shouldn't have told you.

Father No no, but what do you want me to do?

Deb Would you meet Darby?

Father Darby? That his name? That's a terrible name.

Deb It's not.

Father It is, Deb, it is. Jesus. Darby?

Deb It's a beautiful name. I'm head over heels.

Father Darling, you can't.

Deb If I can't have him I'll kill myself.

Father Don't say that, Deb. Christ Almighty, don't say that to me.

Deb But will you meet him? I want you to meet him. Can I bring him in to see you?

Father I won't like him.

Deb I promise you, you will. He loves me. He adores me. All my life I've been waiting for him and now he's here.

Father Darling, this is dreadful. Sam. The kids. My grandchildren should not come from a broken home. Sam. Oh my God, Deb, this is bad. This is so bad.

171

Deb I'm sorry, Dad, I'm sorry.

Father I thought you were happy. You were the child who made it.

Deb But I am happy, Dad. This is the thing. I've never been happier. You have to see him.

Father But Sam –

Deb Sam doesn't need to know.

Father It's wrong, Deb. It's just wrong.

Deb Then why does it feel so right?

Father It's a phase. You have to stop.

Deb No way.

Father You have to, Deb.

Deb I'm not. I can't. That's impossible. All the laws are changing, Dad, or maybe they're going back to what they were before in Eden.

Father This is no Eden, Deb, and if you want to talk Eden the tree of knowledge bore fruit of evil as well as good. People always forget that when they talk about their private paradise. No, listen to me.

Deb Just don't tell me to finish it.

Father Deb, the kids –

Deb I know.

Father Sam.

Deb Oh Sam, my beautiful Sam.

Father I can't go to my grave with you in this state. I want a good death, Deb, as good as I can hope for after Rachel and Anne.

Deb I knew I shouldn't have told you, but please, please just see him.

Father No, that is never happening.

Deb For me? I want him to have met you.

Father I can't, Deb. It's not honourable.

Deb Okay. Okay. I have to go. I'm late.

Kisses him, settles him in bed.

I'm sorry. I'm sorry. I'm sorry.

Deb runs out. Father lies there.

Lights.

SCENE EIGHT

A gleaming bed lowers from above and stops vertically about five feet from the ground. In it Deb and Darby. Music to accompany.

Darby I've got something for you.

Deb Have you?

Darby presents her with a large velvet box.

Darby, you didn't.

Darby I know how you love pearls.

Deb Oh Darby, you're going to make me cry. I don't deserve these.

Darby (*kisses her*) Sure you do. For you, my love, anything for you.

Deb takes out a string of pearls. Kisses the pearls. Kisses him.

Deb Put them on me.

He does.

How do I look?

Darby Pearls for a pearl.

Deb They're beautiful, Darby. Where did you get them?

Darby I dived for them.

Deb You didn't?

Darby I did.

Deb No? Really?

Darby Remember I was in Bahrain a while back? See this one here – (*Necklace.*) See it's smaller than the others, rougher. I found that one on the ocean floor.

Deb You did not?

Darby The things I do for you. Has Sam dived for you?

Deb I don't want to talk about Sam tonight.

Darby But has he?

Deb Many ways to dive, sweetheart.

Darby You're wrong. There's only one way. You put on a wet suit, fill your tank with air, throw yourself overboard, pretend you're dead so you sink like a stone, tear at oysters till your nails fall off and your fingers bleed.

Deb Such a romantic.

Darby The opposite, in fact. I just happen to know what I want. I want you.

Deb You have me.

Darby No, I don't.

Deb You have me where it matters.

Darby No, I don't. Not yet. But I will. (*Kisses her.*) Used to be these pearl divers were little boys with wax in their noses, their ears, dived to unbelievable depths, come up bleeding from every orifice, sometimes coming up dead, lungs exploded but clenched in their fists or in pouches round their waist, perfect pearls, or in Japan it was the women were considered better divers because of your extra layer of fat, they'd dive the icy depths, come up half a stone lighter.

Deb With the pearls.

Darby With the pearls. (*Kisses her.*) What are you so afraid of, sweetheart?

Deb Am I afraid?

Darby Petrified. I'm worried about you. If this is too much for you, Deb, I'll let you go. It'll kill me but I'll let you go.

Deb Don't say that. Please don't say that.

Darby That's how much I love you. I want you alive even if it's not with me.

Deb Don't be maudlin.

Darby You think I'm maudlin? You think keeping you alive is maudlin?

Deb Sometimes. Be braver just to go, wouldn't it? Hang myself with these pearls.

Darby Now who's maudlin?

Deb What time is it?

Darby Three. Are you tired?

Deb Exhausted. Let's not sleep tonight. Let's get up and cook and have some more wine. Let's dance.

Darby (*rolls on top of her*) You want to dance?

And music, and bed ascends.

Lights.

SCENE NINE

Mother. Twin-set and emeralds, listening to some Argentinian love song. She sways, sips, sings along, the sherry falls from her hand, she clutches her heart, reels, falls to the ground in the middle of a heart attack.

Lights change, smoke, suddenly the Argentinian is there. In his scrubs. With his dog. Doctor's bag. Smoking a cheroot.

Mother At last . . . you came back.

Argentinian I'm here.

Mother I thought you were dead.

Argentinian I am. What do you think you are?

Mother No? Me?

Argentinian As good as. Say hello to Maria Bernadetta.

Mother Hello, Maria Bernadetta. (*Pats the dog.*)

Argentinian You remember her? Hah, Maria Bernadetta? She remembers you. Now let's have a look at your heart.

Mother Surely you're not going to operate on me?

Argentinian (*straddles her, opens bag*) Most certainly I'm going to operate on you.

Removing her cardigan, cutting open top, bra, with his scalpel.

176

I've waited forty years to have a good look at your heart. You still wearing my emeralds? We can leave them on, I'll just disinfect them.

Sprays them, sprays her torso, wipes her down.

Now? (*Scalpel poised.*)

Mother Don't I need an anaesthetic?

Argentinian Your whole life has been an anaesthetic.

Cutting into her.

You know something, Laura?

Mother What?

Argentinian (*cutting away*) We weren't brave. We should've grabbed life by the cojones. Instead we scurry home. I drank myself to death after you.

Mother I know. I was at your funeral.

Argentinian In a black veil?

Mother No veil.

Argentinian Did you weep?

Mother Buckets.

Argentinian What is it about good-looking women and funerals?

Mother I saw your wife, your children.

Argentinian You saw my dry-eyed wife? She was married within the year.

Mother Good for her.

Argentinian You think? What about me? Hah? (*Brandishing scalpel.*) What about me? You've put on a few pounds. You're too fat. I'm glad you left me! Here, Maria Bernadetta! Eat! Eat!

Flings the fat to Maria Bernadetta.

Nice eh, Maria Bernadetta? That's the fat of the heart from the one woman I ever loved. Eat it up! Eat it all up!

A bark of appreciation from Maria Bernadetta.

Mother Don't feed bits of me to the dog.

Argentinian Don't you tell me what to do! And I followed you soon after you ran out on me.

Mother You followed me?

Argentinian That Saturday, oh yes I followed you. I watched you walk your children to their music lesson. I wanted to knock you to the ground, you looked so smug, carrying their violins, holding their hands, virginal, butter wouldn't melt in your Irish cunt. I wanted to scream to the passers-by, her legs were on my shoulders last Thursday, and her tongue? You wouldn't believe where that woman's tongue has been. You sat at the coffee shop across the street, your legs crossed, you ordered coffee and a cake which you didn't eat. You smoked five cigarettes. You were talking to yourself. You looked mad.

Mother I was mad. I dialled your number every day for almost a year.

Argentinian Then you dropped the children home, came out again straight away, went to the hair salon, had them cut all your hair off.

Mother You saw me do that?

Argentinian Your beautiful hair! How dare you cut off what I love! To do that to me! Savage, Laura. Savage! I knew what it meant. This is it. She's not coming back this time.

Mother I've often regretted that decision.

Argentinian Your regrets don't interest me. And the son you had was mine?

Mother Yes, he was.

Argentinian He knows?

Mother I never knew how to tell him.

Argentinian Your husband knew?

Mother Of course he knew.

Argentinian (*operating throughout*) A little awkward, I would imagine.

Mother We weathered through.

Argentinian He looks like me?

Mother The image.

Argentinian He's happy?

Mother He's alive and I suppose being alive is to be happy and unhappy by turns.

Argentinian More nonsense, Laura! Only people who don't live talk like that. We were put here to be happy. From here I look on, we were made for happiness, to love! To love! And then to die. The rest is fucking lies.

Takes her heart out of her chest.

Here we are. Now let's see. Look at this.

Holds her heart aloft. Lights on it.

Mother How is it?

Argentinian As I expected. Stone. Calcified. Covered in stone. Where's my hammer?

Takes out his hammer, smashes her heart.

179

Mother AAAAH!

Argentinian (*smashing, smashing, smashing*) Stone.
Stone. Stone. The whole way through. See what happens
when you leave me? Look at this marl! You call this a
heart? I'm ashamed for you. Arteries? Stone. Veins?
Stone. Blood? Grey slime. Right aorta? Poison. Left
aorta? A sewer. Left ventricle? Limestone. Right? Sand.
Sand, sand that'd fill the Sahara, the Gobi, the Kalahari.
Oh, but look here, look, a sliver.

Mother What is it?

Argentinian (*waves it at her*) The map of Argentina of
course. Me! Me! Who else? Folded, packed, hidden
under your pyramids of stone. Me. The thing about the
heart, Laura, the heart always, always yields up the
truth. This bit's for me, Maria Bernadetta.

He eats the map of Argentina.

Mother We'd have killed each other.

Argentinian And what of it? You have to die of
something.

Lies on top of her, takes her face, kisses her.

I was the one. Say it. For once, say it.

Mother You were the one.

Argentinian It is given to us once, this beautiful
playground. Admit it. You didn't play.

Mother I played.

Argentinian You didn't play to win and you didn't play
fair. Admit it.

Mother Did I not?

Argentinian You didn't play fair with me. With yourself.
You did not, Laura. (*Kisses her madly.*)

He gets up, packs his instruments, scalpel, clips,
hammer, saw. He puts the stone heart in her hand.

Now hold it. Carry it down with you, down to your
grave. Show this to your Creator. All he has given you,
and this, this is all you have to show him in return. Let's
go, Maria Bernadetta.

And exit Argentinian with his dog and bag.
Mother lies there holding her stone heart. Dies.

Lights.

SCENE TEN

Enter Sam in black carrying Jess in black, followed by
Holly in black, Mark in black, Natalia in black.

Jess Poor Nanny. Poor poor Nanny.

Sam Poor Nanny.

Jess And it was awful mucky when they wedged her into
the ground.

Sam It was, Jess.

Jess Will she drown?

Natalia She's already dead, thicko.

Jess I'm going to be the last to die in this family.

Natalia Would you ever shut up talking about dying.

Sam No, you shut up telling her to shut up. Honestly,
Natalia, when did you get so rude? What is going on
with you?

Natalia I'm sorry, Dad. I'm sorry. Are you okay?

Sam No, I'm not okay, darling, I'm very far from okay.

Jess You're going to die first, Dad, 'cause you're the oldest, then Mom's going to die, then Mark, then Natalia.

Natalia I'm never dying. Never.

Jess Yes, you are, Natalia. Straight after Mark you'll die because you're the next biggest, then Ted, then Holly and last of all me. I'm always last. I'll be here all by my own.

Sam You won't, darling.

Jess I will. I'm the youngest. How am I going to be by my own?

Starts to cry.

This is the meanest family to put me at the youngest. I'll have to get a job.

Sam But that won't happen for ages, Jess. You'll be big. You'll have your own family.

Jess (*wails*) I won't have my first family.

Holly You can get a dog, Jess.

Jess (*wailing*) It's no good, even if I do have a German shepherd it's no good, because I won't have Mom and I won't have Dad and oh my God you'll be dead too, Holly!

Holly But I'll come and visit you, Jess, I promise.

Jess No no no! (*Wails.*)

Enter Deb in black with Ted in black.

Deb What's wrong with her now? Jess?

Sam Calm down, calm down.

Deb Jess? Jess?

Takes her from Sam.

Jess (*still wailing, high drama*) The meanest, horriblest, I'll have to draw pictures for you all where you fall down dead. It's too many there's too many of you, you'll waste all my colours, and how will I get my dinner, you won't let me even touch the cooker, I don't know how to turn it on.

Deb It's all right, Dad's here, I'm here.

Jess But you're not really. None of us are really here.

Deb We're all upset, darling.

Mark Can I get you old folks a drink?

Sam Yeah, I'll have a brandy.

Mark Mom? Red wine?

Deb That'd be lovely, sweetheart.

Holly Can we have 7 Up?

Deb Go on.

Holly Jess, we can have 7 Up?

Jess And a bar?

Deb Yeah, yeah, a bar.

A mad rush to pour the 7 Up.

Ted Can I, Mom?

Deb Yes, Ted. You pour for the girls. I don't want a big mess.

Ted Mom said I'm pouring.

Holly No. I'm pouring. I'm pouring.

Deb No 7 Up then.

Natalia There's only four caramel bars.

Deb I bought five.

Natalia Who's the thief? Ted!

Ted I didn't!

Deb Ted?

Ted I always get blamed!

Natalia Because you always rob!

Ted I swear I didn't! Mom!

Natalia (*forcing his mouth open*) Look at your tongue! Black! You liar! Big liar!

Ted It's not black! Mom!

Natalia Liar! Liar!

Ted Mom! MOM!

Sam Stop it!

Ted Mom, is my . . .

Natalia Black! Black as Satan!

Sam Natalia!

Natalia Black! Black! Black! Liar! And you robbed my chewing gum yesterday! You should be in jail! Liar! He's the biggest liar, Mom!

Ted Mom! Mom! I didn't! Get off me! MOM!

Deb Ah, would ye shut up for fuck's sake.

Ted Ow! Ow!

Natalia Where's my chewing gum? Where is it? Where is it?

Mark I don't want a caramel bar!

Natalia So mature.

Mark I'll have a beer. That okay, Dad?

Sam Yeah, sure, ask your mother.

Deb Did you have wine at lunch?

Mark No, I hate wine – how many times have I told you that?

Deb Okay, just one though. You've school tomorrow and I'm not overly impressed with your maths test while we're on the subject. You promised me an A.

Mark Well, a couple of things happened this week like Nanny died, for example. (*Close to tears.*)

Deb Okay, okay, I'm sorry.

Mark Forget it.

Sam Mark, Mark, it's okay.

Jess Mom, Holly spilled her 7 Up!

Holly Shush, you big tell-tale!

Deb Don't wipe it with your dress for God's sake. Can't you drink a glass of 7 Up without wrecking the joint?

Jess I didn't spill my 7 Up.

Spills it.

Oh no! Oh no!

Holly You big messer!

Jess It just spilled! Oh no! It wasn't me it was Dracobum! (*Wails.*)

Deb Stop wailing! Jesus, I'll go mad. It's only a glass of 7 Up. Look, everyone calm down. Natalia, clean that up please.

Natalia Why should I?

Deb I give up.

Sam Natalia, please.

Natalia Okay! Clean up after the little slobs again! The little fat uncles!

Holly You're the fat uncle!

Jess You take size a hundred.

Ted Mom, I swear I didn't take that caramel bar.

Deb I believe you, Ted, thousands wouldn't, but can I just ask you one question?

Ted Yeah.

Deb Will I find the wrapper under your pillow tonight?

Ted looks at her. Everyone looks at Ted. Ted runs out to dispose of wrapper. Everyone laughs.

Sam Ted. Ted! Ted!

Ted comes back in.

Come here, Ted. Come here. I want to tell you all something.

Deb Sam, not now. Please. Not now. We're all upset.

Sam Then let's get all the upset out in the open.

Deb No, please, wait a few days.

Sam It's all right, I'm not going to say what you think I'm going to say.

Deb What? That sounds worse.

Sam Now listen to me all of you. You know how much your mother and I love you all.

Jess I love you, Dad, so, so much, straight from my heart.

Kisses him, hugs him.

Holly And I do too, Dad. I love you much much more than Jess ever could.

Hugging him. Kissing him.

Jess (*pushes her away*) I was kissing Dad first!

Holly And Mom, I love you so so much. (*Hugs and kisses.*)

Jess No, let me, I wanted to say it first to Mom! Mom, I love you so so so much. I'm not in love with you 'cause you're a girl. I am a bit in love with Dad but he's only a boy so don't be sad 'cause you're the nicest mom I ever had. (*Hugs and kisses.*)

Natalia She's the only mom you ever had, you little clot.

Deb Don't call her a clot. Natalia, would you give her a break? For once? For me? For five minutes?

Mark (*exiting*) If this is what I think it is I don't want to hear it.

Sam Mark?

Mark No! You're not splitting up. I've to do my leaving cert. Don't do this to me! Do not do this to me! Nanny's dead. Just who do you think you are? You think you can do what you want with us. You both stay here and that's the end of it. I've had it with you two. And I know all about that Darby prick!

Deb What?

Sam Mark!

Deb Sam?

Sam He didn't hear it from me!

Mark You think it's a big secret? My friends know. My friends' mothers. The whole city knows you're running round like a tramp.

Sam Don't speak to your mother like that!

Mark I can't believe you allow this, Dad.

Deb Mark, I'm sorry, I'm sorry, darling, but it's a little more complicated than that.

Mark No, it isn't, Mom. It is not. And you can keep your love. Love? If that's your love I'd hate to see your hate.

Sam Mark, Mark, Mark.

Natalia Mom, is this true? You have a boyfriend? I'm the one who's supposed to have the boyfriend.

Jess Who has a boyfriend? Dad's Mom's boyfriend, aren't you, Dad?

Holly No. Dad's her husband, Jess, that's why you and me can't marry Dad because he's already married to Mom.

Jess But when Mom dies then we can marry Dad, can't we, Dad?

Ted Mom?

Deb Yes, Ted?

Ted What're you talking about?

Deb Nothing, sweetheart, nothing. Everything's fine. Everything is absolutely fine.

Mark Get me out of here.

Exiting.

Deb No, Mark, wait, don't go.

Mark I'm going over to Johnny's.

Sam Don't. Not now.

Mark Dad, I'm going to Johnny's house to watch the game. I'll be home by half-ten.

Deb (*hugs Mark*) I'm so sorry. I'm so sorry. Mark. Sweetheart. It's killing me too.

Mark Just let me go, Mom.

Deb lets him go. Exit Mark.

Sam Ted, will you put on a movie for the girls, get them into their pyjamas.

Ted Okay, but I'm not looking at them when they take their clothes off.

Jess Can we have hot chocolate?

Deb No way, you just had 7 Up and a bar.

Holly Please. Please. Please.

Jess (*at the same time*) Please, Mom, I'll never, ever, ever, ever in my whole life ask you for anything again if you let us have hot chocolate.

Ted I'll make it.

Deb I don't have the energy to argue, go on and clean up after. I don't want to find chocolate and mallows mashed into the floor.

Jess I bags the Dora cup.

Holly No, I'm having the Dora cup, you had it last night.

Jess Tough, I bagsed it.

Holly (*grabs Jess by the hair*) I'm having it, missy!

Jess grabs Holly by the hair, both cling on fiercely roaring.

Jess Ow! Mom! Holly's pulling my hair out!

Holly AAAH! Mom!

Jess Let go!

Holly You let go!

Jess AAAH! Let go! I'm begging you Please! I'm begging you, Holly! OW!

Holly AAH! You let go, you pig!

Sam lifts the two of them by the scruff.

Sam That's it! Bed!

Holly No! No! We're sorry!

Jess We're so sorry!

Sam (*dragging them squealing and struggling*) Too late!

Holly No, Mom said we could have hot chocolate!

Sam Not with this behaviour!

Jess Mom! Mom! Dad's capturing us!

Sam You want to sleep in the shed tonight?

Jess You always say that.

Sam With the spiders?

Holly No! We'll be good! Mom, tell Dad we'll be good.

Jess We are so so so sorry.

Sam Say sorry to your sister.

Jess She has to say sorry first! She pulled my hair first!

Sam Say it together. Okay? Holly? Okay? Jess? On the count of three. One. Two. Three.

Holly Sorry.

Sam Jess!

Holly She didn't say sorry!

Jess I said it in my mind.

Holly Dad! Make her! Make her!

Sam Jess, you're on your last warning.

Jess But I can't say sorry.

Sam What do you mean, you can't say sorry?

Jess It's a rude word.

Sam It's not a rude word, Jess, it's a useless word. Bed for you, my lady. Holly, you can have hot chocolate and a movie, maybe even two movies.

Jess No, sorry, sorry, sorry!

Sam Ted, good boy, just get them out of here. Here give me a hug. (*Kisses the girls.*)

Deb (*kissing the girls, to Ted*) You're a sweetheart.

Ted Can I have your laptop when I get the girls sorted?

Deb Yes you can, darling boy, and no one gets the Dora cup.

Jess Holly can have it, I don't mind, Holly you can have the Dora cup.

Holly It's okay, Jess, I'll have the Barbie cup.

Jess No, I'm having the Barbie cup!

Deb *and* **Sam** Out! Out! Get out!

And exit Holly, Jess and Ted.

Natalia Can I go ice skating?

Sam Not this evening.

Natalia They're all going.

Sam Who's all?

Natalia Petra's dad is driving us. It's only for an hour. I'll be out of your hair. You guys need to talk.

Deb How much?

Natalia Twenty'll be fine.

Sam Ten'll be fine.

Natalia It's eight-fifty to get in.

Sam (*gives her ten euros*) So you'll have change.

Natalia exiting.

You're forgetting something.

Natalia Thanks, Dad. Thanks, Mom.

Sam You're welcome.

Exit Natalia. Silence. Hold. Hold. Hold. Sam pours another brandy. Turns. Looks at Deb standing there looking at him. She offers her empty glass for him to refill. He doesn't. She refills her glass.

Deb So I must pour my own drink now.

Sam Been quite some time since you've wanted me to do anything for you.

Deb What were you going to say?

Sam What?

Deb Before Mark started crying.

Sam I wanted to say goodbye to the kids.

Deb No?

Sam Yes.

Deb Where are you going?

Sam Doesn't matter. I asked for a transfer. They've approved it. I leave next week.

Deb But where?

Sam Far, far away.

Deb You can't.

Sam I can't?

Deb The kids'll be devastated.

Sam Are you going to give me the kids?

Deb No.

Sam No. So the kids'll be devastated. For a while. Then they'll forget about me.

Deb You can't, Sam, you can't let them suffer because of us.

Sam Because of you.

Deb Okay, because of me, because of me. Sam, I fell in love.

Sam I know.

Deb I didn't mean to.

Sam I know that too. I didn't think I'd stopped wooing you. I must have. I've just been working, Deb. It was always for you. For the kids. Always.

Deb Don't go.

Sam You've made it impossible for me. What am I supposed to do, sit here and watch you madly in love with someone who isn't me?

Deb I'll give him up.

Sam You won't. You think you will but you won't.

Deb I will. I will. I'll end it.

Sam And resent me to the end of your days?

Deb No, I won't. I swear. I won't. Don't go.

Goes to him, puts her arms around him. He kisses her passionately.

Sam It's too late, Deb. The damage is done and can't be undone. I adored you. I was very lucky. I had your love for twenty-two years. You gave me five beautiful children and now that's all gone like a dream when you've woken. You need to be with him. You need me out of the way, be honest now, you've got the kids, the house, the lover, the car, whatever money we have, you've got it. I'm letting you go, Deb. I wish you all good things. I'm leaving my children in your care, they should be together, they should be with you. I'm letting you all go.

Deb Sam, please, there must be another way.

Sam There isn't.

Deb Mark'll go crazy.

Sam He won't. Mark is his mother's son first and despite all this new-age nonsense they feed us about the role of the father, children belong to their mothers first like back in the caves, Deb. Sure I love them but more out of curiosity and mainly because they're ours. But there's no us any more, is there? I've lost you so I lose them. Maybe they'll find me when they're grown. And now I'm going to check my mother's grave. See they've filled it in properly and then the brave new world, life without Deb.

Deb Please, Sam, not like this.

Sam (*puts his finger to her lips.*) Shh.

And exit Sam. Deb watches him walk away.

Lights.

SCENE ELEVEN

Father lies propped in hospital bed. Trussed up in white. sheets. Tubes. Oxygen mask on.
  Leave him there a while. He's singing through his oxygen mask. Something operatic. Orchestra to accompany.
  Enter Darby. He stands there watching. Listening. Eventually Father clocks him.

Darby You've a good voice.

Father Used to, singing lessons, all of that, took up the piano when I was fifty . . . Mr Darby?

Darby Deb's been at me to come and see you.

Father I don't approve.

Darby I don't either.

Father But you do what the woman says?

Darby As much as possible.

Father Wise.

Darby Deb sent this.

He produces a bottle of red wine and two glasses.

Father I'm not allowed.

Darby That's what I said to her.

Father Go on, pour, might as well go with the grape on my lips.

Darby (*opening wine*) What're they saying's wrong with you?

Father At this point everything. Right now I'm drowning in my own fluid, imagine that, you can drown yourself from the inside. I'm filling up like a bucket at the pump. When the lungs are full, that's it.

Darby And what level are they at now?

Father Very full. (*Takes glass.*) This should do it.

Struggling to take off oxygen mask.

Darby You need some help with that?

Father I have it. Cheers.

Drinks shakily.

Darby Cheers.

Drinks.

You want to put the mask back on?

Father I needed that. I suppose a cigar is out of the question?

Darby I can go out and get you a cigar if you want to set the alarms off.

Father No, I'd upset the little nurses. I'm their pet. They lean over me to to fix my tubes, insert catheters, and I'm thinking if I was only thirty years younger. They smell beautiful. No, I couldn't upset them, their star patient. Your father alive?

Darby No. He died when I was ten.

Father Young to be without a father.

Darby A horse-riding accident. A hunt, a boulder, his head split open.

Father Terrible. You got on? You loved him?

Darby Very much.

Father That's good. I never had sons. I was given daughters. Two daughters. Deb told you?

Darby She told me.

Father But Deb only knows the end of it. She doesn't know a thing about the how or why of Rachel's . . . Can I tell you a story about consequence, Mr Darby?

Darby Darby's my first name and yes, you can.

Father Consequence is an immense thing, a wild animal all said that falls on you from the sky. We're all experts with hindsight – what if? What if? What if? But none of us knows a damm thing before the fact. So I was married to Anne, some sixteen years, happily married even, Rachel was fifteen, a lovely girl, growing lovelier and lovelier and then there's this conference, Berlin, and I fall like the fool I am for this Italian woman, Carla. I didn't think, didn't have to think, couldn't think, went straight to her, got stuck in like a bee in a pot of jam, missed papers, banquet dinners, round tables, the keynote address which I was meant to give, even missed my own book launch, we literally did not get out of bed for five days, room-service trays piling up, champagne bottles so you couldn't move, phone off the hook and Carla lying there, the honeyed skin, the tumbling hair, the nose on her like an Egyptian pharaoh. All fine and dandy you might think. Yes, innocent enough if I could've left it at that. But no, I had to have more, letters, phone calls, flights to impossible destinations, subterfuge, lies, lies, lies, all for a few hours in Carla's arms. She was married too. Children, three was it? Carla. Where is she now? Where have we gone to, that passionate man and woman? I see a sunlit street in Turino, Carla sitting in the shade, sunglasses on, drinking lemonade. Waiting for me. She doesn't see me yet. I stand at the corner and watch, one of those moments no one can describe or understand but everyone feels, this battered heart in this guilty breast hammering, hammering for her, so connected, from the beginning, and so it will be to the end of all feeling. Then she sees me, jumps up, laughs in that crazy Mediterranean way. They do everything with their bodies, hands, torso, feet, lips, all dancing, we do nothing here in these cold northern isles, not since the flight of the earls, and two years rush by, blinding euphoric years, years I knew what it means to be here, actually here. That knowledge cost me Rachel.

Darby I don't see . . .

Father Listen and you'll see. I'd lost my grip. I was a liar, a cheat, not who I appeared to be, I wanted to die when Anne smiled at me, no way for a man who calls himself a man to behave. I deserved none of them, not Carla, not Anne and certainly not Rachel. I was sullying them all and out of this crippling guilt I became more attentive to Anne, presents, dinners, trips, the small courtesies we pay our wives when we're not obsessed with other men's. And then the graduation ball, the graduation dress, Rachel's tantrum and because I had just spent four glorious days and nights with Carla the week before I felt I should take Anne's side in the matter of dresses and so my daughter dies. That's consequence.

Darby And Carla?

Father I never saw her again.

Darby You deprived yourself of that? Of what was right and true? You deprived her?

Father How could I not?

Darby Very Old Testament.

Father Does that make it untrue?

Darby But what's the point of living if . . .

Father The point is to get it right.

Darby Then better not live at all. Living means messing up, making huge mistakes, it's by our mistakes we grow, feel, think. It's almost a duty.

Father Is Deb a mistake?

Darby Never.

Father You walked into a family and took the woman out of it. You've sent a good man packing. There are five children now without a father. Sam was here, devastated. I'm too sick to deal with this. You're the mistake that will haunt Deb for the rest of her life.

Darby I hope what you're saying is not true.

Father But Rachel . . . Rachel, Rachel . . . she should be here.

Darby If someone is going to hang themselves over a dress then they're not fit for this world.

Father But it was I who made her unfit for this world. I took my gaze away, not for long, but I took it away, never thinking all of this costs, all of this must be paid for, and by whom? I'm so worried about Deb.

Darby Deb's a big girl now.

Father But the children. I'm afraid they're the ones the axe will fall on. It only takes a detail, one small detail overlooked.

Darby Job did everything right, didn't he? Good father, good husband, tended his goats and cattle, faithful to his God, and misfortune followed him down the wind to the end of his days. There's no right and no wrong. That's what Job's God is telling us. He's as capricious as us. Stop torturing yourself over Rachel. Things happen and things'll always happen that we can't make sense of. Not here anyway. Maybe not ever. I'll leave you now. You're tired.

Father (*oxygen mask*) I just need to get this thing on.

Darby Let me.

Fixes oxygen mask on him.

Okay?

Father I'll drop off in a minute . . . Would it be too much of an imposition to ask you to . . .

Darby You want me to sit here for a while? Sure. (*Sits back down.*)

Father Always surprised these days when I wake up . . . I'm still here.

Darby You're still here.

Father settles. They stare at one another. Father drops off. Darby sits on.

Lights.

SCENE TWELVE

*Deb stands there looking out of the window. Enter
Darby. He comes up behind her. Kisses her.*

Darby You've been looking out that window all day?
What're you looking at?

Deb Waiting for some monster coming towards me in
the dark.

   Kisses him.

No, you can't see it now but there's a rose out there, one
yellow rose out there in the dark, it's been swaying all
day in the wind, huge, accusing me. Sam planted it for
me when I was expecting Ted.

Darby You want him back?

Deb I want everything, everyone back. I want every
second of it.

Darby It's all in there. (*Touches her heart.*)

Deb And I want you.

Darby You have me.

Deb For now.

Darby What's wrong with now?

Deb It's never enough is it? In a year or two you'll be
gone.

Darby Don't start this.

Deb No, listen, you need children. I know you do. I
can't give them to you. You should have children, you're
so good with mine. In a year or two you'll want to be
heading along.

Darby Stop this.

Deb No, it's okay. I just want to tell you it's okay. Despite the heartbreak, the mess, the madness, I wouldn't have it any different.

Darby You can't tell the future, Deb.

Deb Not all of it, but some things I can.

Darby I might surprise you.

Deb This intoxication can't last.

Darby Why can't it?

Deb It turns on a dime. I'm too full. I've eaten too much, think I'll be a lonely old lady sitting in the darkest corner of hotel bars.

Darby I'll send you over a drink.

Deb I just know I've to pay for this . . . this . . . somehow . . . I mean this kind of happiness is obscene . . . I'm not programmed for it . . . and the kids . . . terrified something'll happen to them.

Darby Lots of things'll happen to them, hopefully good, mostly. Deb, things have a habit of happening but not because of this. If you're so frightened you should woo Sam back, I'll bow out.

Deb No. Don't talk like that. (*Kisses him.*)

Darby What God could curse you for glorying in your life? You live truly. You do. People don't like that and I know you've suffered their judgement, their slights, their high-handed disdain because of me.

Deb They just think I've lost it.

Darby We all lose it, sweetheart, sooner or later, but no God is cursing us, you wait and see.

Deb I'll wait. I'll see.

Darby It's not happening.

Deb Tonight I believe you. Tonight we're all safe. Thank you.

Kisses him.

Lights.

End.

HECUBA

Hecuba was first produced by the Royal Shakespeare Company at the Swan Theatre, Stratford-upon-Avon, on 17 September 2015. The cast was as follows:

Nepotolemus David Ajao
Cassandra Nadia Albina
Hecuba Derbhle Crotty
Agamemnon Ray Fearon
Polymestor Edmund Kingsley
Polyxena Amy Mcallister
Odysseus Chu Omambala
Xenia, Hecuba's Woman Lara Stubbs
Polydorus Marcus Acquari / Nilay Sah / Luca Saraceni
Son of Polymestor Sebastian Luc Gibb /
  Christopher Kingdom / Daniel Vicente Thomas /
  Yiannis Vogiaridis

Director Erica Whyman
Designer Soutra Gilmour
Lighting Charles Balfour
Composer Isobel Waller-Bridge
Sound Andrew Franks
Movement Ayse Tashkiran
Company Text and Voice Work Michaela Kennon
Assistant Director Robyn Winfield-Smith
Music Director Candida Caldicot
Casting by Hannah Miller CDG

Characters

Hecuba
Queen of Troy, wife of Priam

Agamemnon
King of the Achaeans

Cassandra
daughter of Hecuba

Polyxena
daughter of Hecuba

Polymestor
King of Thrace

Odysseus
King of Ithaca

Polydorus
youngest son of Hecuba

Neoptolemus
son of Achilles

Servant
one of Hecuba's household

Soldiers
thousands, Achaean

Hecuba's Women
five of them

Two Small Boys
sons of Polymestor

SCENE ONE

The throne room. Hecuba surrounded by her Women.

Hecuba So I'm in the throne room. Surrounded by the limbs, torsos, heads, corpses of my sons. My women trying to dress me, blood between my toes, my sons' blood, six of them, seven of them, eight? I've lost count, not that you can count anyway, they're not complete, more an assortment of legs, arms, chests, some with the armour still on, some stripped, hands in a pile, whose hands are they? Ears missing, eyes hanging out of sockets, and then Andromache comes in screaming, holding this bloody bundle. My grandson, intact except for his head, smashed off a wall, like an eggshell. They're through the south gate, she says, they've breached the citadel, they're here. I say put him with the rest, put him beside Hector, his father's mangled body. She won't stop screaming, shut up I say, you'll draw them on us. I tell the women to cover her mouth, we have no soldiers to protect us, all dead, or still fighting, trying to save their own women, children. And I don't know where Priam is. He went out a while ago, when was it? Last night? Yesterday? My women are putting perfume on me. Perfume! I swat them away. The smell of blood, wading in it, the tang of rotting bodies everywhere. Bodies that came out of this body and I want to vomit but there's nothing in my stomach, they've cut off our food supplies. And Cassandra standing at the throne, that smirk on her face, I told you so, did I not tell you so? And I could kill her right now. And Polyxena looking at me. Petulant. Willing me to turn this around, make it all right, make

211

sense of it. And I'm glad at least my little Polydorus is
safe. We've sent him to Thrace away from all of this.
And then a soldier comes reeling in the door, Priam's
head in his hands. My husband's head. They've beheaded
him in the Great Sky God's Temple. I say where's the rest
of him? What good is a head? We can't bury his head
without the rest of him. And the soldier says, I don't
know, they've burned the temple. Burned the temple?
The whole city's in flames he says, and he puts Priam's
head into my hands. I sit on the throne holding it like
a baby. His tongue's hanging out, his eyes are terrifying,
a ferocious death. I try to close his eyes. They're caked
with blood, crust, dust. I can't close them. And the
soldier is weeping on his knees, holding my ankles, all
the men castrated he says, not enough to kill them, must
desecrate them too. And I say, the women? What about
the women? The children? The women too, they're
killing the women he says, all the old ones, the ugly
ones, the ones past childbearing, past work. And the
children? I say. Priam's head is oozing on to my dress.
The children he says, all the boys and all girls under ten.
Why? I say, though I know it's a stupid question. Not
enough room on the ships, he says. They're rounding
them up, have them in the cattle pens. And I think this
is not war. In war there are rules, laws, codes. This is
genocide. They're wiping us out. And then there's
shouting, clashing of swords, more screams and
Agamemnon is in the throne room.

Agamemnon Fabled Queen, I say. She hears the mockery
in my voice though it's not complete mockery. I've been
wanting to get a good look at her for a while. And there
she is, perched on her husband's throne, holding what?
His head? The blood flowing down her arms. And what
arms they are, long and powerful. What's that, I say? She
doesn't answer, just looks at me as if I'm a goatherd, the

snout cocked, the straight back, three thousand years of breeding in that pose.

Hecuba They told me many things about him, this terror of the Aegean, this monster from Mycenae, but they forgot to tell me about the eyes. Sapphires. Transcendental eyes, fringed by lashes any girl would kill for. I pretend I don't know who he is. And you are? I say. You know damm well who I am he laughs, and you may stand.

Agamemnon And she says she'll stand when she feels like it. So I lift her off the throne. Now that wasn't too difficult, was it? I say. I can't resist twirling her though I know I should show more respect. Used but good. Still good. I was expecting an auld hag with her belly hanging down to her knees. But she's all right, there's bedding in her yet. I wonder if she still bleeds, will I ask her? No. Not now. Leave her, she's lost everything. She's a Queen, was a Queen. Behave yourself.

Hecuba God bless you, he says as he twirls me, God bless you, but war is hard on the women. He smiles at Cassandra. Cassandra smiles back, the little trollop. So you're the man slit his daughter's throat to change the wind, I say.

Agamemnon And the wind changed, I tell her. The wind changed.

Hecuba And I wonder what sort of wife he must have, this barbarian who calls himself King.

Agamemnon And she's looking me up and down. She has an eye on her. Eighteen children I'm told. I wonder if they're all Priam's. I wouldn't mind making a son with her. Only way to sort a woman like that out is in bed. Take the haughty sheen off her, the arrogance even while she's skidding in blood, stepping over corpses, the lip curling. This is my husband's head she says, brandishing it at me. You didn't even have the decency to give me back his body.

Hecuba These are the remains of my sons I say, pointing to the dung heap of limbs, heads, hearts, necks, necks I loved and kissed. I have to bury them I say.

Agamemnon My men'll take care of it. I see the corpse of an infant. Who's that? I say.

Hecuba Scamandrius. Hector's babe.

Agamemnon I thought his name was Astyanax.

Hecuba No. Scamandrius. Why do you want to know?

Agamemnon I wonder did Hector have two sons then. These Trojans, so sly. Can't have any of them alive. Where's the boy? I say. What boy? She says. You know what boy I say. Polydorus. Your boy. Your lastborn.

Hecuba I don't know.

Agamemnon You know.

Hecuba He's nine. He's a child.

Agamemnon Children grow up fast. Last thing I want is Trojan sails on the wide Aegean, your boy at the helm.

Hecuba He's no threat to you. Where is he? he says. Can see the anger rising in him, a man of sudden rages, can't be thwarted. I must be careful. Priam sent him away for safe keeping six months ago I say. I don't know where. A stab goes through me. Polydorus. They're going to take you too.

Agamemnon You know well where he is and the longer this business goes on the worse it'll be for you. And she starts crying, please, she whispers, please, the face crumpling. I've seen that look before. On my wife's face when they made me drag Iphigenia from her arms. But I

can't let the boy live. This is war. These things have to
be done. Don't you have children she says. I have lots of
children. The daughters are stunners, can see the mother
in them, what she must've been in her prime, not that I
mind the old hens, have a weakness for them, all said.
I'm bored to the nostrils with girls these long years. They
know nothing, understand nothing. But the look in this
one's eye when you're on top of her. I'd give plenty to
see that look, hostile, weighted, challenging, and then
transported once I'd get to the animal in her. The young
ones won't reveal that, think it's all flowers and moonlight
and concealing. Think they've all of time to declare
themselves. But this one in starlight, might take a while
to get her down and willing but by God when you did.
Magnificent in the sack I'll wager and I'm rarely wrong
in these matters. And I say we'll find him whether you
tell us or not. And she's muttering now, the children,
why're you killing the children? Sell them as slaves on
Lesbos, Lemnos, or we can ransom them, they're children,
they've done nothing. My husband's body she says
walking round in circles, this is too much, she has to
bury them all, with her own hands if need be.

Hecuba My husband's body. Where is it?

Agamemnon I tell her there's no time, she has to get on
the ships, but she's not listening, she's losing it. We're
evacuating Troy, burning it to the ground, this city of
liars and rapists. She's listening now, turns on me, blood
rising, hands shaking with rage, goes into a reel, spittle
on her lips as she gives vent. You came as guests she
hisses.

Hecuba You came as guests, rolling in here stinking of
goat shit and mackerel and you came with malice in
your hearts. You saw our beautiful city, our valleys, our
fields, green and giving. You had never seen such

abundance. You wanted it. You must have it. You came
to plunder and destroy.

Agamemnon She rattles on about their paved streets,
their temples, their marbled libraries, their Holy Joe
priests, their palaces of turquoise and pink gold. I say,
where's Helen? We can't find her.

Hecuba Helen? Helen? Helen was never here and well
you know it!

Agamemnon You have to admire her, the brazen stance.
I say you stand here, everything lost and still you lie.
Who is this Helen she says, and if she could get her
hands on her she'd tear her asunder. To enter a man's
house, I say, to bed his wife, to kidnap her, to kill her,
to do away with the evidence. We want Helen back.
We have our dead to bury too.

Hecuba Helen does not exist. You made her up. You
needed a reason to take it all. There is no Helen. There
never was a Helen. Yeah, yeah, yeah, he says, that's your
version. Cassandra snorts, plays with her bangles, stares
at him. We need a treaty I say. I must calm down, save
what I can. We need to hammer out a treaty.

Agamemnon Now you want a treaty? The little
prophetess is wearing the bracelet I sent her. Young, far
too young. The other girl glares though I know she's no
innocent, gave many happy hours with the bold Achilles.
Way past time for treaties my good lady. I tell the soldiers
to round them up, get them on the ships. I'm going
nowhere she says till I've buried these. She waves her
hands helplessly. The place is an abattoir.

Hecuba His men will do it, he says. I know they won't.
And then he sits on Priam's throne. I ignore the outrage,
I say these are my women, they've served me faithfully,
they mustn't be harmed. Okay he says, keep them near,

it's wild out there. He's making himself comfortable on my husband's throne, clicks his fingers, his men produce what? A goblet in the shape of a lion, pour for him. He sits there legs apart, looking at me, drunk on his success, never thought he'd see this day. We never thought so either. He's got what he wanted, Priam, your throne, your head at his feet. I say I have to have my things packed, I'll inform him when we're ready to depart. He says I like your cheek.

Agamemnon You'll inform me of nothing. Different rules now. Everything is in my gift. Show me your gratitude.

Hecuba And he offers me his hand to kiss. Now he's being ridiculous. Come girls, I say, Andromache? She's holding her dead baby. My darling little grandson. Leave the baby I say. She won't. Leave him! And she comes and takes my hand.

Agamemnon I'll excuse your bad temper on account of the day is in it I say. Bury them together she says, find my husband's body, as if I'm her slave. If you don't do this your own death will be terrible.

Hecuba You putting a curse on me now he says. If I had the gift of curses. Take them to my ships, he says. You mean my ships, I say.

Agamemnon She refrains from spitting. Just about. No, mine, I say, my black ships. Where are you taking us, she says.

Hecuba Home, he says, home. And the soldiers lead us out. And there's crushing, swelling, shouting, someone pulls at me, the soldiers push him back, they whoop and leer and spit. His men put up their shields to protect us. Polyxena clings to me, Cassandra walks through them like she's walking through a field in May.

217

Agamemnon You heard what she said, I say to my men, bury them together, find Priam's body. Put it with this head. I'm not afraid of her curses, just something about her should be honoured, her lack of fear though I know she's terrified, when I pulled her off the throne, shaking like a lamb newly shorn.

Odysseus So I find him in the throne room. Of course he's on it, a crown on his head, a jewelled goblet in his hand. He laughs his mad laugh, not bad for a Spartan boy, he says. Not bad I say, was that herself I passed in the courtyard? That was herself he says and smiles. Well, we know whose house she'll be going to. And the daughters? I say. You'd run away with them, he says.

Agamemnon We are, he says, we are. And did you see Hector's widow with her? The one she was holding by the hand? That's Hector's son there.

Odysseus I see a crushed skull, a tiny hand, a knee. Poor little fellah I say, who did that? Doesn't matter he says, had to be done, the temples cleared, he says.

Agamemnon Yeah he says, pouring wine. The libraries? Yeah he says, the granaries? The pleasure houses, the farms, the orchards, the cellars. The flocks? The herds? We found fifty rooms piled to the eaves with forgotten gold he says, just lying there in the dust.

Odysseus These people lived, he says. We won, Odysseus, he says. We won. Barely I say and at huge cost.

Agamemnon You're not still mourning that little prick?

Odysseus He won us the war.

Agamemnon He nearly lost us the war with his fucking tantrums. I won us this bloody war.

Odysseus Not what they're saying on the ground. When they sing this song, Achilles will be the one, I say. Only because he died young he says.

Agamemnon Committed suicide more like, chasing skirt. Trojan skirt. They won't sing that, No, they'll say he fell in the field beating off thousands single handed. Let them, sooner be alive, wine in my belly, a woman in my bed, and then Polymestor arrives, that Thracian horse thief, with his sons.

Odysseus The boys doe-eyed, lithe. I miss Telemachus, not much older than these when last I saw him, waving me off from the harbour at Ithaca.

Polymestor He offers me his hand. He's on Priam's throne. I don't know what to do so I kneel, kiss the offered hand. A great day for you, Agamemnon.

Agamemnon A great day for Mycenae. A great day for Sparta, I say. These your sons?

Polymestor The boys kneel, kiss his hand. Only two? He says. What I was given, I say.

Agamemnon You should get yourself another wife. I'm happy with the one I have, he says, as if I've insulted him. What brings you here?

Polymestor To assure you of our loyalty.

Agamemnon To assure yourself I don't leave Thrace in ashes. I have been loyal, he says, where's the boy? I say. What boy? He says. Don't play girly games with me, Polymestor. You mean Priam's boy, he says. I do I say, where is he?

Polymestor He was given to me for safe keeping by his father. He's my cousin, he's nine, he's playmate to my sons.

Agamemnon He's Priam's son.

Polymestor He's a child.

Agamemnon No children in war, only those on your side and those against you. Bring him to me. I swore to Priam I'd guard him with my life, he says. Priam's dead, I say.

Polymestor Priam's dead? I don't believe it. On Apollo's altar, he says, beheaded, I wouldn't have done it that way, he says, but my men have gone a little mad.

Agamemnon Is nothing sacred to you, he says. He's fighting tears. No, I say, nothing. Priam, he says, we were brought up together. He goes on his knees again. I ask you, he says, a catch in his voice, let his little son live. Would you rather I took one of yours, I say.

Polymestor No.

Agamemnon Then don't thwart me. You think I want to kill a boy of nine? These things have to be done. I'll keep your sons with me till you return with Priam's.

Polymestor Then I beg, useless with a man like this, but my sons, please, I'll bring him, I say, but let me take my sons with me.

Agamemnon When you bring the boy, but no, he's panicking now.

Polymestor I swear to you, I'll hand Polydorus over, only give me my sons now.

Agamemnon You swore to me before and broke your word, I say. Whose infant is that, he says, going white. I think he's going to puke. Hector's, I say. Shouldn't he have a decent burial, he says, his hands are shaking, he holds his sons by their frail necks. He will, he will, I say, the soldiers must've forgotten him. And now he breaks down, his lament. I'm used to men breaking.

Polymestor It has not been easy sandwiched between Ilion and the Achaean these long years. Whatever word I broke was to protect my people. The Thracians. No one thinks of the Thracians in all this carnage. What we have endured, the plunder, the rape, the livestock, the fields ruined, all the young men dead, the women taken and used like mules. You have stolen the bread from our children's mouths. Give me my sons. I'll bring you Polydorus. No you won't, he says, you'll run for the hills with him unless I keep your boys.

Agamemnon Go now. He wrings his hands, kisses his sons, whispers about them being good, staying together, saying nothing, He tells the older one to look out for the younger. The boys hold hands, terrified. It seems I terrify people. I say to them, I have sons too, your age. I say, what colour is Polydorus' hair?

Boy 1 Brown.

Agamemnon And his eyes?

Boy 1 Green.

Agamemnon How many sons does Hector have?

Boy 1 One.

Agamemnon His name?

Boy 1 Prince Scamandrius.

Agamemnon Is that him there?

Boy 1 I don't know. I never met him.

Odysseus Okay let's go, he says. Have them take that throne to my ships, he says.

Agamemnon And then torch the place.

Exit all. Light on dead infant. Music, lights.

SCENE TWO

The beach. Sound of the sea. A blue, blue sky.
Hecuba and her Women.

Hecuba And then they order us off the ships, soldiers everywhere, the scorching sand under our feet, the heat. It's hard to breathe.

Polyxena Why have we stopped here at Thrace?

Hecuba Haven't you noticed? There's no wind, they can't sail, where's my jewel box, I say. The soldiers took it, Cassandra says. Can't you do one thing I say, my bracelets, my rings, my diamonds, my pearls, my wedding crown.

Cassandra All gone. Don't you just love war?

Hecuba No, Cassandra, I do not love war.

Cassandra Sexy or something.

Hecuba Sexy! Your father beheaded, your brothers butchered, their bodies defiled, left for the crow and the rat. All the children slaughtered, pulled screaming from their mothers? Troy a smoking ruin? Our beautiful city of light? Gone? Sexy? Shame on you! Shame!

Cassandra I don't know, all those half-naked soldiers, besides I told you this would happen. You make things up she says, her usual refrain, you guess.

Polyxena They dashed little Scamandrius' head against a wall, he was just starting to walk. I saw it before he was born, she says in her best prophecy croak.

Cassandra I told Hector, I say, he slapped my face. Who's crying now, Hector?

Hecuba And I'll slap your face now unless you shut it. My women are fussing with my things, I tell them to stop and get us something to eat. Get me water, wine, some olives, cheese I say, I haven't had a morsel in days.

Servant There's no food.

Hecuba What do you mean, there's no food? I'm starving. There's none, she says, not a loaf of bread, not a fig, not a comb of honey, not cheese, not wine, not water. Did no one think to bring provisions? Must I think of everything? There was no time she says. Just get us something to eat I say, the girls are hungry.

Servant We all are. They put a sword through my son's heart as we got on the ship. He's seven. Then they flung him into the sea.

Hecuba Don't you talk to me about swords! Don't you talk to me about sons! I've lost more than any of you. What's one son compared with all of mine? Don't you talk to me about sons! He's better off.

Servant He was all I had. His father died for Troy. He fell early on. He was all I had.

Hecuba Did you honestly think you would escape what none of us can escape? Leave her mother, Polyxena says, she's suffering, I saw it, it was horrific, he was still dying when they threw him between the ships. The whole evacuation was horrific, black smoke swirling, walking over the dead, tripping on them. The children with ropes around their necks, the lucky ones, the ones being sold, the pyre of dead babies, were some of them still alive? Flung living on the flames? I take the woman in my arms, hush I say, hush, I'm sorry about your little son, Hector wasn't it? Wasn't that his name? He was called after your Hector, she says. They all were.

Servant Your Hector blessed him, held him up to the sun the day he was born, asked Helios to give him long life and happiness.

Hecuba You have to put him out of your mind, you have to, we have to live through this. Go with the other women, I tell her, go together, go to their kitchens, get us food and water, a bit of bread, anything. And I'm scalding in my robes, want to tear them off, run into the sea, swim till I drown. Priam. Priam. If you could see me now, your wife of over thirty years, your Queen. And the girls are scrapping, Cassandra in full prophecy mode, none of this matters she says, none of it.

Polyxena None of this breaks your heart?

Cassandra It's my own death breaks my heart.

Polyxena Your own death?

Cassandra And yours.

Polyxena I'm not dying . . . am I? I'm far too young.

Cassandra Scamandrius was one. Polydorus was nine.

Hecuba Polydorus is alive, I say carefully. Is he? she says. What? I say.

Cassandra You won't believe me if I tell you. There'll be none of us left, none of us.

Hecuba You sound happy, Polyxena says.

Cassandra I sound right.

Hecuba Anyway, she says, doesn't matter I'm going to have a mad passionate affair with the barbarian king. You're going to have no such thing I say.

Polyxena He sent her gifts.

Hecuba What gifts?

Cassandra These I say, holding up my arm.

Hecuba And this dress she says. Take it off I say. And put on what she says?

Cassandra I'm just telling you what's happening here. I'm not saying I want it. One of them raped me on the ship.

Hecuba What? Who did?

Cassandra Doesn't matter. Knew it was coming. Just glad to have it over with. Another fear down. Ajax. His name is Ajax. Very unattractive but I knew that too. And then just to annoy her I say I heard the servants saying that Agamemnon has a statue of you in his tent, you know, the bronze one from the north temple? That one, and he feels it up and down when he's on the wine. Have you lost the run of yourself, she says, repeating gossip like that to me. But she's interested, my mother is a vain woman, used to adulation, my father adored her, could never see why. He wants you, Mother, I say just to see her confusion. Agamemnon wants you. And it's true. He does. Not my turn yet.

Hecuba He wants us as slaves, he wants us brought low, he wants to parade us in chains through his savage kingdom, all the war widows spitting, screaming, throwing stones, clawing at your eyes, pulling our hair out. Is that what you want?

Cassandra Better than rotting in Troy.

Hecuba Don't you love any of us? No, she says I don't. You get in my way, you're too soft, soft with privilege and arrogant on top of it. You thought Troy was untouchable. You thought your gilded life would go on for ever.

Cassandra Nothing goes on for ever. All of this privilege must be paid for. We need to lie down with the Achaeans now, we need some of that barbarian abandon in our weak perfect blood. Look at them dancing, singing. No Trojan man moves like that. The lightness, they don't care about anything, they're all dead by twenty. He wants you, Mother, he wants the Queen, the legend, the mythic horsewoman all the stories are about. And she tosses her head like a mare. She wants to hit me.

Hecuba Stop this foolish talk I say. I only report what I see, she shoots back. You don't see I say, you see a thing and then you see its opposite. You don't know what's going to happen.

Cassandra She's desperate. She's willing me to give her good news. I wish I could. She's still my mother. We're all going to die I say.

Hecuba Surprise surprise, everyone dies! Soon, she says, and some sooner and she looks at Polyxena.

Cassandra I see you across the altar of some tomb I say to Polyxena, it should've happened already, your throat slit like a calf.

Hecuba And how will you die, I say.

Cassandra An axe, a threshold far away, all my prophecies fulfilled.

Hecuba And she runs off and I let her go. Why can't I love that child? The bane of my life from the day she was born. And the heat. I'm on fire, take them off, Polyxena says. I can't. I have to look the part even though there's nothing back of it now. Will they never come with some water?

Polyxena Sit, Mother, sit here.

Hecuba My darling, always running round trying to help me. Come here, sweetheart. I take her on my knee. My little girl.

Polyxena I'm fourteen. You were married at fourteen.

Hecuba I had Hector at fourteen. Thought he was a doll, put him on a shelf once the way you'd tidy away your toys, only luck he didn't fall off and crack his skull. Polydorus, I hope he's safe. God above, keep him safe.

Polyxena I miss him too. What's going to happen to us?

Hecuba We're going to be all right I say though I know we are far from all right or ever being again, her little face, so frightened. You're going to stay with me I say, though I know they'll separate us, divide us out among their generals, war booty. You're staying with me, there's nothing to worry about, I say. I swear you'll come to no harm.

Polyxena They won't kill us?

Hecuba That would be too merciful I say. And then I tell her they'll bed her down and does she know what that means and she laughs and says she's not a child. And I say it's not what I wished for you. You should've been cherished by your husband, a prince should've come for your hand like out of all the old stories. Not this. You should've known the love of a beautiful man.

Polyxena The way my father loved you.

Hecuba Don't let me think of him. Don't let me remember. They wouldn't even let me bury him, his poor broken body. They wouldn't let me have that. His severed head. Savages.

Polyxena They say it was Achilles' son, Neoptolemus, who beheaded him.

Hecuba Who told you that?

Polyxena The servants of course. They say he's looking for me.

Hecuba You? Why you? Because his father liked me, she says. What? I say. Achilles sent me gifts she says. You never told me.

Polyxena You were running a city, I barely saw you. He came to my rooms, I went to his tent. Don't be angry I say, I'm only telling you because I want you to know I've had my prince. I know what that is, whatever they do to me now. He sang for me, I danced for him. He was entirely beautiful. He even asked me to marry him. I even said yes.

Hecuba He even killed Hector.

Polyxena I know.

Hecuba Put a rope through his heels, dragged him over the stones, round and round our pink walls, unrecognisable when we finally got him back. Your father had to beg, on his knees, for Hector's body from this Achilles. I know, Mother, she says. I know all that. I don't approve, I say. There are tears in her eyes. But these are different times I say, are they? she says and I realise this girl has only ever know war, never saw Ilion in its heyday. People from all over the known world and the unknown came to our city, the learning, the music, the medicine, the crafts, the gold, the banquets. Your father was a great king, just, fair, a lawmaker. He welcomed strangers, even these Achaeans. You never saw him in his prime, on his horse, head of his army, tearing across the plain, barebacked, the sweat, the dazzling eyes, goodness shining out of him. How am I supposed to live without his love and protection? Then the soldiers come and tell us our tent is ready. They give me dark stares, ogle my daughter, how they hate us and I know it's only their fear of Agamemnon that keeps their hands off her.

Polyxena One of the soldiers pulls me aside. Young, his armour too big for him. My mother says no but they push her forward. I'll take her to you in a minute he says, his hand is on my arm. My mother says no again and then she's gone. Polyxena, he says. Yes, I say.

Soldier I'm Neoptolemus, Achilles' son.

Polyxena And now that I look at him I see that he is, the eyes, the shoulders, the shape of the head. Achilles I say and then I don't know what to say. The boy looks at me. I don't know what he wants.

Neoptolemus They told me my father was sweet on you. She says nothing only looks at me with that closed face. She's lovely. I smell cinnamon, eucalyptus off her, under the dirt of the ships. I say I got here a few days ago to fight alongside him and he's dead.

Polyxena They're all dead.

Neoptolemus They also say you lured him, it was a trap.

Polyxena It wasn't. I didn't.

Neoptolemus You had Paris behind the pillar with his knives.

Polyxena No. Never.

Neoptolemus My father was unarmed. He came to you for love and your brother stabs him in the back. I didn't know Paris was there, she says.

Polyxena I swear I didn't. Someone must've seen, told. I suspect it was one of your own who betrayed him. He died in my arms. We returned his body. I washed it myself which is more than you did for my father.

Neoptolemus I haven't seen him since I was three, no memory of it. I get here and he's gone.

Polyxena And then he leans towards me, a thumb on my lips. He had good taste he says, excellent. And he kisses me, a strange kiss, the ghost of Achilles there, and I think it's his father's embrace he wants. God knows I want it too. He asks me do I want to stay with him or go to my mother's tent. I should stay with my mother, I say.

Neoptolemus You'd be safer with me, my men, my father's men would protect you. He was going to be the next king. I am now. We'd protect you, really we would. Agamemnon's word means nothing. The coalition is falling apart. He won't last much longer.

Polyxena No, I want to be with my mother.

Neoptolemus She doesn't understand and I'm frightening her. Okay, I say, then let me take you to her.

Polyxena And he stretches out his arm for me to walk before him.

Music. Lights.

SCENE THREE

The throne in the sand outside Agamemnon's tent on the beach.
   Agamemnon and Odysseus eating. Drinking.

Agamemnon Now Odysseus, I don't like this calm, I say. Not a puff of wind he says. Does it remind you of anything I say?

Odysseus It does. He's sitting on Priam's throne, had them drag it from the ships all the way up here. He mops his face with the tablecloth, knocks back the rough Spartan wine. In this heat. Yes, this blistering calm reminds me of something all right, reminds me of a

morning long ago at Aulis, another lifetime, a time when
we Achaeans could hold our heads up and look one
another in the eye, an innocent time before these terrible
times. The men are already muttering about a sacrifice,
I say.

Agamemnon He's blathering on about, I don't know,
God the man goes on. The men, he says, the men, not
looking at me, Achilles' ghost seen wandering the camp,
in torment, in torment to be left as ashes on Trojan
shores, wandering angrily among the tents, his breath on
your shoulder as you sleep, his voice in your ear at the
fire, floating somewhere between the stars and here.
Don't believe in ghosts I say. All the ghouls are here
I say, meaning him. Achilles is dead and gone I say, and
good riddance.

Odysseus His funeral wasn't big enough, the tributes not
grand enough.

Agamemnon Nothing ever big enough or grand enough
for that little peacock. So hot, so still, the heat like a
wall leaning on us.

Odysseus They're saying there's a lack of symmetry to
the whole thing.

Agamemnon And what would they know about
symmetry? Spit it out! What do you mean? I know damn
well what he means. Well, he says, we sacrificed a girl
before the war. We certainly did, I say. We sacrificed my
girl. Fucking cannibals had me slit my own daughter's
throat for the fucking wind to change. Iphigenia, twelve,
I held her hand, but that wasn't enough for them, you
call yourself king they said, the king performs the ritual
killing. Not where I come from. We don't slit the throats
of children in Mycenae. No. You do it or we storm the
palace and take your whole family out. Her eyes.

Iphigenia's eyes as they laid her on the stony strand, the
obsidian knife in my hand, her throat, a girl's sparrow
throat, the delicate gold necklace they stopped the
proceedings to remove. She was so afraid. I'm sorry, I
whispered as I lowered the blade, I'm sorry I have no
choice. But I had, of course I had, could've fled with her
to our high green kingdom. Could've barred ourselves in,
beaten them off, kept her alive. But I chose the other.
And when you worship at that altar, well, what's there
left to say? She knew. Iphigenia knew. My own eyes
looking back at me. Always the first of them racing
down the palace steps to greet me. Iphigenia with her
sun hat on, blonde hair to her knees, the dimple on her
left cheek, the smile.

Odysseus Seems they want another girl on another altar
now. Glad I've no daughters near is all I can say, he says.
He'll never forgive us that. The men are jumpy, anxious,
want to get home, they're spooked.

Agamemnon Always the way after a bloodbath, the
rape, the plunder, the excess. Now the remorse. Let them
keep it to themselves bunch of auld grannies whingeing
over their knitting. You'd be wise to pay heed to them,
he says. What're they threatening? The usual he says.

Odysseus That you're not the rightful king.

Agamemnon The rightful king is the one who wears the
crown. They've always hated me.

Odysseus One of the Trojan princesses would probably
do it. Calm them down.

Agamemnon Would that shut them up, I say. Long as
the right wind comes and we can get out of here he says.
The right wind'll come when it comes I say. Don't tell me
a girl's throat has the remotest influence on whether the
wind comes or the wind goes.

Odysseus Everything has influence, Agamemnon.
Everything matters.

Agamemnon Only three things matter, Odysseus. Food.
Sex. Winning wars. Give them a girl I say, if that's what
they want, not the little prophetess, the other one.
What's her name again?

Odysseus Polyxena.

Agamemnon Well, Achilles wanted her for a bride and
now he'll have her. And who'll perform the sacrifice I
say, knowing of course it'll be me.

Odysseus You, I say, they'll respect that. They can keep
their fucking respect says our gracious Mycenaean.

Agamemnon How many more kids do I have to slaughter
to keep these perverts off my back? How're we going to
explain this one to her mother? That's one conversation
I'm not having. You do it. You take some of the heat for
a change. I'll do it, he says. I'll do that much. Why not
the little prophetess? he says. Because when things were
really desperate, she predicted we'd win this war. And
we did. And he slinks off, sly islander that he is, bandy-
legged mountain man, invisible, indispensable, the men
love him.

Enter Polymestor with Polydorus.

Polydorus My cousin takes me into the heart of the
Achaean camp. Thousands, thousands of them spread
along the beach, dicing, drinking, gaming, fighting,
eating, the smell of lamb, pig, dog, bird, I see a shark
turning on a spit, the five rows of teeth intact. Some
swim in the sea, naked, the water warm as soup. They
splash, dive, jump one another, cling on amorously, some
race horses, flinging sand in our faces, they're having sex
out in the open for everyone to see, the sun splitting the

sky in half. All the black ships glutting the harbour. Who
are these people? Polymestor shaking by my side. He fears
for his sons, my little kinsmen. His hand on his sword,
ready to draw. This is his land and they've destroyed it.
As we came down from his hill fortress on the horses he
wept. Poor boy, he says, his hand on my neck. They're
going to kill me. Come here child, he says. He's sitting
on my father's throne, mine now. Agamemnon.

Agamemnon That's my father's throne, he says, a
handsome little fellow, a prince to the marrow. That's the
sacred seat of kings he says, it's sacrilege for you to sit
on it. Your father's dead I say.

Polydorus I know and I know you mean to do away
with me too. Where are my sons, Polymestor says, but
Agamemnon silences him with a wave of his hand.

Agamemnon I don't mind for myself he says, but my
mother, I'm her last son, last born, last living. If you kill
me she is unprotected in the world, my sisters too.

Polydorus I ask you to spare my life so I can be with
them, help my mother through this catastrophe. I can't,
Polydorus, he says in a voice of such weariness, sadness
even. I can tell he's exhausted, emptied out, hasn't slept
in years, afraid to.

Agamemnon I can't. I wish it were otherwise but I can't.
That's what I thought, he says, calm as you like, this
green-eyed, brown-haired boy. The Spartans would love
this child, the resolve in him, so young, what is he?
Nine? Ten?

Polydorus May I see her? Say goodbye to her?

Agamemnon No. That would be harder for both of you.
With respect, he says, you shouldn't presume what is
harder for us.

Polydorus I know she would want to see me even under circumstances like these.

Agamemnon His feet are tanned, scabbed boys' feet, he has scars already, swording, they train them up young, these war-torn times. Orestes was about this size when last I saw him. Let me go to her, he says, she needs me now. When my father was king he was merciful and my request is not huge.

Polydorus Priam would've allowed it, I say. This gets to him. I knew it would. His face tightens, the eyes harden. My father often said that Agamemnon wanted to be him. Don't you have your own throne I say?

Agamemnon I certainly have. Arrogant little pup!

Polydorus Then why do you need mine?

Agamemnon Yours? Yes, mine, he says. They're all dead, my father, my brothers. I'm the rightful king of Troy.

Polydorus The great sea god himself made this throne, A god's hand made this throne, dragged it up from the sea floor on his shoulders. Placed it on the founding stone and Troy began. Troy is gone he says.

Agamemnon I don't need you to tell me that he says. By God have they brought him up well. Can I ask you one thing he says. Ask, I say. Why? He says, why? Why do away with us like this? There are laws around the conduct of war. Why torture a vanquished people, why burn their city to the ground, throw salt on the fields, decimate the livestock, poison the rivers, the lakes, the very sea. Why slaughter the old, the weak, the young?

Polydorus My little nephew, Hector's son, it's shameful what you've done. In war, yes, the losers suffer but never before like this. What you and your army have done is beyond understanding, it's personal, it's evil, we have never come across anything like it and my father fought many wars. There are animals, not many but some, who kill for the sheer pleasure of it when they get the scent of blood. But this is not the conduct of humans or anyone who calls himself a member of the human family and it is certainly not the conduct of someone who calls himself king. You may sit on my father's throne, desecrate it, but you will never be Priam. He nods to his soldiers.

Agamemnon Take him away I say and make it clean. He's just a kid.

Polydorus Polymestor throws himself on the ground, kisses my feet.

Agamemnon He raises him up, a gesture of such tenderness, he has studied his father well, the poise, the economy of movement. It's not your fault, he says to Polymestor. In your place I would've done the same though you sense he wouldn't. Polymestor kisses his hand, bows, yeah, he's their little king. God, can he play the part. Bless my little nephews he says, bless my sister, your good wife, thank you for your care these long months. And just before he goes he turns to me. I'm asking you not to tell my mother, he says, let her think I'm still alive, safe with Polymestor, do this for her, don't break her completely. And he turns and walks calmly to his death. My men could take a leaf from his book. I'm . . . don't know what I am. Humbled. Reduced. For a second I want to go after him, revoke the terrible sentence, but the iron in him, wouldn't care to meet him on the battlefield, head of his army, sixteen.

Music. Lights.

SCENE FOUR

Hecuba's tent.

Hecuba Finally there's food. Not much of it, some
bread, a paltry piece of tuna, rough unseasoned wine,
cheese, barley and beans, the diet of footsoldiers, no fruit
but jugs of cold Thracian mountain water. No table
linen, wooden cups and not enough of them, no plates,
we eat with our fingers, sand everywhere. The wine goes
to our heads. We're grateful in spite of ourselves. I try
not to think of the heaped platters I dined from in our
banquet hall now a heap of rubble. The delicacies I
sniffed at and passed over. My bevelled cup overflowing
with the choicest wines of the Troad and beyond,
musicians in the corner as we danced and gossiped and
laughed our heads off. A vanished world, who would
have thought so quickly? Outside the tent the din of men
with nothing to do, only a bit of cloth between us. I'm
terrified for my girls, my women, myself. And there he is,
gawking, no greeting, no deference, just stalks in with
his boar-tusk helmet, a bow-legged gargoyle, the soldiers
stand straighter, he says something to them, they smile,
nod, stand back a bit.

Odysseus I'll come straight to the point. There's no easy
way to say this. I'm here to take Polyxena.

Hecuba You're what? I say. Agamemnon's orders he
says. And who are you?

Odysseus I'm Odysseus, King of Ithaca.

Hecuba Another king and not one of them looks like
one. Priam told me there's forty kings among them, one
more vicious than the next. And where is Ithaca? I say to
annoy him.

Odysseus A kingdom in the Aegean.

Hecuba Never heard of it. How dare you barge in here while we try to put a bite in our mouths. Tell your king this food is disgusting. I'm embarrassed to give it to my servants. And the wine? You have emptied our cellars. Bring me some of my own wine. We need bed linen, blankets, my bath, or do we have to wash ourselves in the sea like horses. I'll see what I can do he says, but your status has changed.

Odysseus I'm well aware of my status, she snaps back.

Hecuba No fear of forgetting my changed status among you pack of dogs. Just hand over the girl he says and I'll be on my way and not inflict my presence on you longer than necessary. Polyxena stands beside me holding on to my dress. Why do you want her? I say.

Odysseus Never mind, I say, just hand her over.

Hecuba Tell me what you want her for. He looks away. No one speaks. I look at the soldiers. They look away too. What, I say, what do you want her for?

Odysseus She's to be sacrificed.

Hecuba No. No. Never. Sacrificed?

Odysseus The gods have asked it.

Hecuba The gods? What gods? Sacrificed? How? For what? I can't believe this. This is not what he's saying. This can't be. On the ashes of Achilles he says, to appease his ghost, to give thanks for our great victory.

Odysseus Your great victory, she says. I think she's going to fall, she holds on to the table, and you mean to kill her, she says, her voice cracks.

Hecuba My daughter a sacrifice? The gods demand it, he says. The men are worried about the wind. The wind!

Odysseus She has beautiful hands, the hair, she's not old, not really, not yet. I wonder would Agamemnon give her to me. I'm owed a high-born woman. You're joking, she says, knowing damn well I'm not. We don't joke about these matters I say.

Hecuba I've never heard . . . This is obscene! I won't allow it.

Odysseus I'm afraid you no longer have the power to allow or disallow anything. You're subject to our laws now. Laws, she hisses, growls, she looks old now, the face clamped with rage.

Hecuba You dare call this a law? It's an atrocity on top of all the other atrocities! You want to sacrifice my daughter to appease your savage gods. No proper god would ever ask such a thing.

Odysseus Oh they would. They do. They asked it of Agamemnon. Ten years ago, his daughter, he submitted. And if they can ask it of a king then how much more may they ask of you, a slave.

Hecuba And if I refuse to hand her over?

Odysseus She looks around helplessly. We'll take her.

Hecuba Take me instead.

Odysseus I knew this was coming. And there are tears now, the endless tears of mothers. We're sick of them. Let her live, she says, she has her whole life ahead of her.

Hecuba And what does it matter if I go now or in a few years?

Cassandra And my proud mother who has never knelt for anyone, kneels now, pulls at his sleeve.

Polyxena I can't bear to see her like this. I'll go with them. I'll go with them.

Cassandra Get up, Mother, don't beg, it'll make no difference.

Hecuba No, please, don't take her, don't harm her, take me.

Odysseus It's the girl they want.

Hecuba But if it's a human sacrifice you want isn't one as good as another? And I can't believe I'm having this argument, that there are words for this. The women have started to wail. No, he says, it's Polyxena they want. Agamemnon's command. I don't know his thinking, I just obey. Get up, Mother, Cassandra says and drags me to my feet. So you were right after all I say.

Cassandra And why is there no joy in it?

Polyxena Cassandra takes me in her arms, not since we were children. Be brave little sister, she whispers, remember who you are, don't be afraid, don't cry out, don't give them the satisfaction. My mother is looking at me with her mouth open. I think she's going to die of grief in front of me. What are they going to do to me? What are they going to do to me? Kiss your mother, he says.

Odysseus Best not to delay. They're all becoming hysterical, the men anxious, I don't want to have to use force. We're too long away from women and the way they go on. Say goodbye to your mother, I say, more gruffly than I mean to. Hecuba stands there like a statue of herself. This is hard. I'm not made of stone. I want to go home, never to have set eyes on Troy. Sweetheart, she whispers to the girl, sweetheart.

Hecuba I'm sorry you were ever born. I'm holding her wrists, my grey-eyed girl, I'm coming with you, I saw you into the world. The least I can do is see you out. Let

your eyes close looking at mine as they opened looking
at mine. No, she says, no, Mother, spare yourself that.

Polyxena She's gripping my hands so tight it hurts, no
I'm coming, she says. And you won't panic, you won't
be afraid, she's babbling now, something about a long
sleep, exhaustion, my father waiting the other side, open
arms, I don't know what she's saying.

Odysseus You can't deny me this she says. Then come,
I say, bring her, she turns to Cassandra, a question in her
eyes. The little prophetess shakes her head. No she says,
I've already seen it. Chilling. Then she looks away.

Music. Lights.

SCENE FIVE

Agamemnon. Priests. The altar.

Agamemnon The priests robe me. Dusk, the stars
coming out. Why do they always pick dusk for these
sacrifices? Get away from me with that fucking mask, I
tell him, trying to smother me. One of Achilles' generals
presents me with the urn. The ashes of Achilles, he says,
grandly, importantly. We're all ashes I say. The men
snake quietly across the sand under their banners. The
word has gone out, Agamemnon is going to conjure the
wind again. Do they actually believe this shit? How they
hate me. They stand there talking softly, the stink of ten
thousand men waiting to see a girl's neck torn. Some
look at the sky for signs. There are none. We are here
alone. What is so difficult about that to learn? Smoke
curling up from the fires, the smell of roasting meat, the
sea with all its bounty surrounds them but no they'd
rather eat a wild dog. They'll go mad tonight, feel it in
the air, once they see her blood on his urn they'll feast

and drink till dawn. What do I care? We've been too
long here. Too long. And there's Odysseus with his men,
coming along the shore, behind him the Trojan queen,
the girl by the hand, her women. They could be picking
sea shells. As one the men turn to look, enchanted. Then
the voice, soaring, dirge-like. Is Hecuba singing? They're
walking into the sea, the women taking up the song,
washing the girl, passing her from arms to arms like a
newborn. Calm, slow and calm, they hold her, kiss her,
pass her along. That's what's called grace. So rare here it
hurts the eyes. An assault on the soul if you still had one.
The men transfixed, not a sound save the women singing,
the waves. Some ritual, their ways are strange. Now
they're lifting her up, up to the stars. Are they giving
thanks for her brief, too brief life or are they begging for a
reprieve? The men can't stop looking and then the drums
start, the charlatan priests banging away, we have our
own ways. I hold out the ritual dagger. Anyone wish to
perform this sacrifice to our high great gods who in their
wisdom have delivered us this far and will deliver us to
the end? This is the script, it's what I'm meant to say. No
one will take this dagger from me, they look at me, lower
their eyes, so be it, more blood on these blood-soaked
hands. She stands before me, Hecuba, the girl, the women,
all dripping from the sea. What were you doing? I say.

Hecuba The drums. He's standing on the altar, robed in
purple. They didn't know what purple was before we
showed them. A hideous mask in his hand. In the other,
the dagger, huge, sickle-shaped, lethal, my daughter
shaking by my side. I hold her tighter. What were you
doing he says, what were you singing?

Agamemnon An old Phrygian parting song, she says,
that I learned on my mother's knee many lifetimes ago.
The girl is so young, she stares at the knife, chin
trembling, don't let her scream.

Hecuba Is there no way to avoid this? I know there isn't, the men leaning forward to see, to hear, breath on our necks, we're surrounded, we haven't a chance, the seething mass of them, they want blood, Trojan blood. More and then more again. Won't be satisfied till the last of us falls and not even then. It's shocking to be hated like this. There's no way, he says. His eyes move over his army, he's afraid too, he holds his power, his crown, his throne by a thread. Are you ready? he says to Polyxena.

Agamemnon The girl nods. You must bare her to the waist I say to the mother, priests hovering, can't wait to get their talons on her. No, she says, why? Her voice rising in disbelief. She's going to scream and then the men'll go crazy.

Hecuba No look, she's here, she's calm, she's prepared, leave her covered please. I'm sorry, he says, it's how it's done, it's expected, I have to be able to get at her neck. Her neck! They have rules for this. Don't make me tie her he says, please do as I say.

Agamemnon I'll do it, Mother, the girl says and unties her dress, bares her breasts, an intake of breath from the men, hard to believe but for some of them this is a turn-on. She stands there, frail, too thin. Why so thin? Have we been starving them?

Polyxena It takes forever to untie it, my hands slick with sweat, the knot too tight, the sea of faces looking on, the drums, my mother clinging, her eyes boring into me. This is my death. Mine. Can't she be quiet? Let it be over. Just to stand here, face him, not to cry out, beg, run, takes everything I have. I've nothing left for her, nothing. And of all things I'm embarrassed. It's embarrassing to die like this in front of everyone.

Hecuba She stands there before him, alone, so alone I can't bear it, her shoulder blades curving like wings and though I know it's useless I throw myself at his feet. Have some mercy, please, or let it be me?

Agamemnon The men don't like this. Achaeans, she cries out, Achaeans have some pity,

Hecuba Achaeans! Danaans, Mycenaeans, Spartans, Hellenes, Myrmidions, Thebans, Cretans, all the countless tribes. Brave Achaeans! Show some mercy here tonight. Don't you have wives? Daughters? Sisters? You surely all have mothers. The drums pounding louder, drowning me out, deliberate, no one hears my prayer. Get up he says, and they drag me to my feet.

Agamemnon The men shift, cough, a rippling through them, as if remembering, waking, coming out of a dream. Has this war not been one terrible dream? Don't, I say to her, don't waste your breath on them. I put on the ridiculous mask. I take the girl and position her. Look at me, her mother whispers.

Hecuba Look at me, the mask is terrifying her, look at me and she does. We lock eyes. He moves her hair aside, raises the knife of obsidian, the jewelled handle glinting, he shouts something, the soldiers shout back, a deafening roar, the drums, Achilles, I hear, Achilles.

Agamemnon For the wind I say, for our triumphs, for our great high gods. For Achilles the soldiers cry out as one. For Achilles.

Odysseus He pauses. For Achilles, he spits.

Agamemnon For home. Keep looking at me, Hecuba says, keep looking at me.

Polyxena I'm looking.

Hecuba The knife slides across her throat.

Agamemnon Odysseus lifts the urn and her blood flows over it. I mustn't let her go.

Hecuba She's rasping, sweet mother divine, she's choking in front of my eyes and still she keeps looking at me.

Agamemnon It's taking too long, can feel her heart still going under my hand, hard to gauge with this mask on but I think I didn't cut deep enough, blood whistling in her throat, have I mistaken her weight, her strength?

Hecuba He cuts her again. Still she holds my gaze.

Odysseus The men go wild. Shouting, curses, shoving, we're butchering her, she won't die, a bad omen, we'll never get home.

Agamemnon She's slippery with blood, the urn falls over, the men gasp, cry out, and still I feel her heart rising and falling, she's struggling with me now, can't see in this mask, the drums have stopped. Odysseus, I call.

Odysseus One of the priests comes forward.

Hecuba One of the priests leaps on the altar, plunges a knife up under her ribs. Her face. Her little face. Her belly darkening with blood and still she continues to look at me. Her eyes flicker and then at last, at last they close.

Agamemnon Her mother falls. I wait for the screams. There are none. Give her to me she says, give her to me now. The men suddenly silent with disapproval at the botched ritual, disappointed with the spectacle and where's the wind? There's no wind. Of course there's no fucking wind.

Hecuba Polyxena. They want to drive me mad, in front of my very eyes. There's nothing they won't do. The day she was born, I wasn't young, Priam there with me through the whole ordeal, terrified I wouldn't make it or the baby would be harmed. Well, Priam, she has come to great harm, the very greatest, and where were you to stop them?

Odysseus And the men won't disperse, they were like that at Aulis too. Agamemnon still has his mask on, listening, I'm glad I can't see his face. The men are angry. This sacrifice has not satisfied. It's not enough. It is never enough and where is the promised wind? I shout at them to fall back, leave the woman with her grief, leave her with something.

Agamemnon Fall back, I say. The generals take up the command but there's cursing, shouting, fights breaking out, tribe against tribe. This is getting out of control.

Hecuba And it's not over yet, the soldiers, a swarming mass of men come in crushing us. He lifts my daughter to the skies, says something low and deep, the blood inky in the starlight dropping from her wounds on to his mask, his shoulders, flowing down his arms, the infernal drums.

Agamemnon I hold her up. I roar out into the night. The voice of Achilles speaks through me now I say. Achaeans I say, going down a register, Achaeans, I thank you for the gift of this girl, my ghost is satisfied now. All will be well. I will intercede for you here in the eternal land of the gods and the groves of the eternal dead. The wind will come soon. You will all sail home. That does it. The fuckers are satisfied or at least they're quiet. Then they cheer, stamp, howl. Achilles has heard. Achilles has spoken. Her blood seeps through the mask, down my face, into my eyes.

Odysseus Get them out of here, I tell the heralds and they run from general to general. The men take their time going, looking back, stopping, what have they just seen?

Hecuba Then the boy is there, Neoptolemus, he pulls at my sleeve, my father would never have wanted this, he says, tears in his eyes, never. But Agamemnon's men shove him aside.

Odysseus Agamemnon insists on carrying her himself to her mother's tent. She follows with her women. A brave little thing he says. Yes, I say, and I know he's thinking of Iphigenia's howls. What a waste of a beautiful girl he says. Yes I say, what a waste.

Hecuba And I'm stumbling along in the dark after them, my daughter, my daughter, and I've no funeral meats to accompany her, no oils to anoint her, no shroud to cover her and I can't believe I'm still walking this earth and she isn't.

Music. Lights.

SCENE SIX

Cassandra He comes across the sand carrying my sister. He lays her on the table and then his soldiers come and make a pyre. My mother stands, watching, speechless. Her women try to make her lie down. She ignores them. She watches as my sister is put in the flames. My mother's feet are bare, her clothes ruined, no hint of the fabled queen now. She could be one of her own servants. She doesn't insist on the proper funeral rites. No singing, no washing the corpse, no recounting the day of her birth, no stories, no paeans, no dirge, no endless panegyric, no sitting, no stroking the body, no weeping, no laughter, no three-day goodbye. No, my mother has moved somewhere beyond grief now. She wants it over. She wants it all over. I stand beside her. Polydorus, she whispers, Polydorus, all that's left to me now. I want to say you have me but I don't. I don't count in her universe, never have, the mad daughter, the oracle. I understand. It has not been easy being my mother. But I want to protect her, leave her with something, so I don't say Polydorus is dead. I don't say that I am all you have now now.

Hecuba Agamemnon and the other one, the king of Ithaca leave us. The pyre burns. More soldiers come and take Andromache. I don't protest. I don't have it in me now. I kiss the weeping girl and let them lead her away. How Hector loved her. Gone. All gone. My women have dwindled in number, some taken and some slipping away in the dark over to the Achaeans. Why shouldn't they? They're young. They've lost everything. They want a man's arms around them. I don't blame them. And I have not been a good queen. I have not protected them. My old faithfuls fuss around me. Leave me alone I say. Come to bed, Mother, Cassandra says. You go I say. I won't sleep. I won't ever sleep again. I stand there by the pyre, low now, Polyxena in ashes, Polyxena turned to smoke, her smoke in my throat. Along the beach I hear laughter from their camps, music, their songs are beautiful, why aren't they? Polydorus. If they touch a hair on your head.

Agamemnon I'm on walkabout, the beginning of the second watch, going from camp to camp, listening to their grievances, calming them, reassuring, sorting disputes, gift giving and gift taking, their endless inscrutable rituals around tribute and rank and insulted honour, none of them satisfied. I take their offered wine, I watch my back, my men guard me well and I come across her in the tide.

Hecuba I'm washing the blood from my arms and he's there with his men, his horses, his chariot of inlaid gold and ivory. Not safe for you to be here alone he says.

Agamemnon I have only the clothes on my back, she says, and they're filthy. Didn't your women pack for you?

Hecuba Your men took everything.

Agamemnon Not my men.

Hecuba Aren't you head of this army? Why don't you control your wolves?

Agamemnon I'm sorry. I didn't know. You should've told me. We'll get you clothes.

Hecuba I want my own clothes. I want my own clothes back. I want my jewels back. I want Priam back. I want my sons back, my daughter back. I want it all back, every last second of it.

Agamemnon And she sits on the sand and cries. Just a woman after all. Just a woman. They're not able for war. Not fair on them. We should've taken her out with Priam. I'm sorry, she says, I'm sorry you shouldn't see me like this, and still she cries. Well, she has plenty to cry about. I don't know what to do.

Hecuba Come, he says, and offers his hand and I'm so desperate I take it.

Agamemnon She's exhausted. I put her up on one of the horses, lead her across the sand, she sits there, straight backed, pats the horse, talks low to him, a croon, offers her hand for him to smell. She knows horses.

Hecuba He takes me to his tent, a sprawling complex of cloth and banners, braziers lit against the cold descending. Soldiers gathered, his men, they stand back, bow, not to me, to him. He sits me on cushions, gives me wine, Mycenaean he says, from his own vines, a rich purple, surprisingly good. I knock it back, rugs and tapestries in hues of green and tawny brown, bulls and lions everywhere, his emblems, Mycenaean. Spartan. His servants pour a bath for me, wash me, rub me down with olive oil, a robe materialises, sandals, undergarments, earrings, a torque, none of it mine. I let them dress me, they dry my hair, comb it through with attar of rose, coral on my lips, kohl for my eyes, essence of sandalwood on my wrists, my throat, sage for the feet. Then they bring food, a board of meats, fish, bread, many cheeses. More wine. I eat a bit. He drinks, watches me, the servants hover, some of them Trojan, all girls, afraid to look at me, their grieving queen sitting late at the enemy's table.

Agamemnon She picks, puts a bite in her mouth, forgets to chew. Her hair damp on her shoulders. You can see what she'll be like when old, gaunt, chiselled out, the paring back of time till you look like your own skeleton, no other's. Tonight maybe her final flowering. Her golden skin, they said. They said true. The long arms, the big feet, tall as any man and still so feminine.

Hecuba Eat. Eat, he says pushing more dishes towards me. He raises a hand and the servants disappear behind curtains, doorways. I'm curious about your laws he says. Our laws?

Agamemnon Yes. I'm trying to start a country, bring all the warring factions together, the fiefdoms, the small fierce kingdoms, we need a system. We have Spartan law of course, ancient, modelled on the Mycenaean, before that handed down from Crete. But the Daanans, the Hellenes, the Thebans will have none of it, not to mention all the island kingdoms.

Hecuba Are they written down?

Agamemnon Some of them.

Hecuba They must be written down otherwise it's all confusion, but you're not a literate culture, are you? You don't have an alphabet. You don't read, write.

Agamemnon We have the priests to take care of that.

Hecuba A king needs these tools.

Agamemnon Can you read? Write? She laughs, more a sneer, I've never come across a woman more arrogant though I only see it in tiny flashes. Laws are hard to land she says, takes a long time.

Hecuba Our laws were ten thousand years in the making.

Agamemnon And ten hours in the unmaking.

Hecuba Yes, lost, buried in the rubble of Troy. What a great pity he says as if he had nothing to do with it.

Agamemnon And the tears come again. She wipes them away savagely, slapping at her eyes. I'd take her in my arms but she'd read it wrong.

Hecuba He looks away. My tears irritate him. Well, let them. Is he not the cause of them? Music wafts in from the camps, celebratory. I look at him, the candles throwing his shadow behind him, a mountain of a man, his arms, face, the bull neck, covered in scars, muscles like boulders, the hands, spades. Terrifying in full battle armour. He refills my cup, his own, he smiles, take your ease he says, you're safe here.

Agamemnon We've a saying at home. At table and in bed the woman reigns.

Hecuba Is he actually wooing me? So long since I've been wooed. An unlikely suitor here opposite me, battle-scarred, soul-weary, as weary as I am. You must be longing for home?

Agamemnon I am.

Hecuba Your wife. Your children.

Agamemnon I have many wives.

Hecuba So had Priam.

Agamemnon But you were his first?

Hecuba With all the duty that entails.

Agamemnon What was he like?

Hecuba Priam?

Agamemnon As a man? As a husband?

Hecuba He was a good husband. A good man.

Agamemnon Was it a love match?

Hecuba Not in the beginning. I was very young. Were you married young?

Agamemnon Not so young. I was always warring. Was in the field at ten. Led my first army at thirteen, twenty thousand men.

Hecuba And you won?

Agamemnon Haven't lost us a war yet.

Hecuba And your queen?

Agamemnon My queen? Clytemnestra. Can hardly remember what she looks like. She refuses to speak to me, have anything to do with me now. You know what I'm talking about.

Hecuba Iphigenia, the beloved daughter taken, the altar, the wind. Yes I understand why she would be finished with you.

Agamemnon She has powerful allies so we'll have to put up with one another a while yet.

Hecuba And the other wives?

Agamemnon Pretty girls with pretty babies.

Hecuba Your heart's not in it?

Agamemnon No. And your heart?

Hecuba Do I still have one?

Agamemnon Did you love him?

Hecuba Did I love him?

Agamemnon And she laughs. Beautiful.

Hecuba Truth is he was impossible these last few years. This war wore him down, changed him completely, a new woman every week, each younger than the last, don't know what he was trying to prove. He'd come to me in the small hours, lie on top of me. Weep. What do they want from us? What is it they actually want? You baffled him. You've baffled us all. We were together for thirty-five years. Time. Endurance. All those children. How frail a king is with his crown off. If all of that's a definition of love then yeah I loved him.

Agamemnon But not as a lover, not as a man?

Hecuba Not since my last child . . . not since Polydorus.

Agamemnon Polydorus. His name hangs there between us. I can't tell her now. It'd kill her. So instead I say, and what does a Trojan queen do when her husband cools?

Hecuba She finds another. It's allowed. Discretion is needed of course but it's permitted, for all Trojan women. Society can't run if the women are unhappy. Polydorus. Will I ask him? Get down on my knees again? Seems I've been on my knees begging since Troy fell. He's definitely wooing. Well, no aphrodisiac like death they say, though this old carcass has seen better days. I hope he likes stretchmarks. Polydorus. Spare him. It's in your power, I want to say, but some instinct silences me. You do not bargain with love, you take it when it's offered, however fleetingly and from the strangest quarters, the last solace. Don't sully it. And something tells me Polydorus is gone.

Agamemnon She stands. For a second I think she's leaving. I think she thinks she is too. But no, she comes to me, leans in, kisses me, light, fleeting, a question, but strength in it. She steps back, looks at me. Lonely king she says and smiles. Come here I say, and she does. And she's all over me, starved for love, no shame in that, I am too. We go to it. We do what men and women do.

Hecuba Yes he wants me and with such quiet intensity, taking my clothes off calmly, savouring whatever's left of me to savour. He arranges me on the cushions exactly the way he wants me. Don't move he says, stay just like that, he opens a flap, stars over Thrace, that okay he says, brings a candle closer, puts it on the floor. This is a man who likes to look, he stands there, massive, trancelike, just looking.

Agamemnon She's a statue, the big legs, high horse-riding arse, God bless it, breasts that'd feed thousands, nipples cold as bronze on my tongue and she's soft, soft and lean, silk of her skin as she opens up to me, holding my gaze. Love is in the gaze, glimpsed briefly from the cradle, whole lifetime trying to find it again. And her cries, balm to this heart of stone, the milk of her all over my hands more intoxicating than any wine. It's been too long since I have loved, Troy has coarsened you, taken all the joy, the sweetness, well here is sweetness before you, under you, taste it, remember.

Hecuba I think of them. I think of them all. When I was young and Priam loved me, all my beautiful children who slipped away one by one. I give myself over to them, a sort of goodbye, how glorious they all were, how glorious it all was, we mustn't judge things by their end. And this hulk of a man, what is he remembering? His kisses smothering, the way I like them, he wants to pack all of himself inside me, rest there, give birth to himself again, a clean slate, all possibility possible, all different next time.

Agamemnon And then she's asleep, the Trojan queen is sleeping, mouth open, hair in tangles, lightly snoring. Another woman, another appalling dawn. A crime to wake her so you cover her, quench the candle, get up, don't attempt to close your own eyes. Outside stars fading, horses snorting, a flock of cranes heading for Mount Ida and beyond, the men sleeping off the wine, the revels, the excess. A breeze, faint, a pre-breeze. I wet my finger, hold it up, too light to tell. Let it come, home in three days, wherever that is now.

Hecuba I'm dreaming of our summer palace up in the high cool mountains, the children splashing in the fountain. I'm woken by one of the servants, a Trojan girl. I think her mother was one of my dressmakers. Shh she says and leads me through the many cloth rooms, a passage way, we're outside, the sea near. She points to something, what is it? I say. Your son she says, the young prince, Polydorus, and she kneels, kisses my feet. Poor queen, she says, poor queen, don't tell them it was me who showed you. And she runs off. There's a mound of them, piled like a haystack, the new dead, fresh dead since we landed here in Thrace, no smell yet, small stiff bodies, children mostly from what I can make out. Don't believe what I'm doing as I'm doing it, rummaging among them looking for Polydorus. The doomed eyes,

the ankle bones snapping, the fragile heads, some shorn
but most with the long silken tresses of our boys, how
proud we were of our sons' hair, didn't cut it to shoulder
length till they were ten. I whisper sorry, sorry as I disturb
them though I feel it is they who pity me. And there he
is, on his side looking past me, they didn't even close
your eyes. I gather him up, he resists me, doesn't want
my embrace now, will never want it again, no breath,
none. You knew you would come to this day, in you
from the start, all gone now and something akin to relief
comes flooding in, you can put aside motherhood now,
take it off like a scarf, let it swirl and flow away from
you across the shining sea. Hold his hard little body, his
lips when you touch them are ice. Who did this? Who
did this to my war baby, born in the first year of these
unimaginable times. I must bear this too it seems.

Agamemnon She comes howling, charging, her mother's
nose has smelt him out. She stumbles past me, the veins
leaping from her neck with the dead weight of him. The
howls. This. This. This. This. This. The men come to
look, the whole camp awake now. She walks blind,
stumbles, falls in the sand, no one dares to help, she
pulls herself up again, heaves the boy, half dragging him.
Polydorus, she cries.

Hecuba Polydorus. Then Cassandra is beside me, my
women, they take him from me. Is this living too? Why
did no one tell me? Am I breathing? How can I still be
here? Let me go now, you've tangled enough with me.
Let me go, down into the dark with him.

Cassandra She tears at herself, goes at her arms, neck,
face with her nails, I will put myself on my own pyre
she says, she rams a fist down her throat, bangs her head
off the ground, finds a stone, carves herself till the blood
runs in ribbons, this experiment is over, she cries, over.

We wrestle with her, she fights tooth and claw, the whole
Acheaean camp looking on. Mother?

Hecuba I am no one's mother. No one's.

Cassandra You're mine.

Hecuba You! You are my nightmare, slathering my days
in fear, making me live it twice, bringing all this to pass.

Cassandra Mother I say, I only saw, wish I hadn't,
wish I couldn't. But she doesn't listen, lies on the sand
weeping and Agamemnon comes, kneels beside her,
strokes her hair. I beg your forgiveness.

Agamemnon I beg your forgiveness for the way you
found him. He asked me not to tell you, to spare you
this.

Hecuba Well, you haven't spared me. You've spared me
nothing.

Agamemnon The voice broken, the warmth of a few
hours ago, she lies there on the sand holding her son's
leg. No, I've spared her nothing.

Hecuba Get up, he says, let my men carry him.

Cassandra He lifts her up. She goes with him, falling
against him. He has to hold her up. They could be an
old married couple. She's a ghost of herself now, haunting
herself, haunting him, all his army. They will lie about
what happened this day.

Agamemnon She's nerve and bone but still carries about
her a kind of horrific grace, death's hand is on her, fine
as dust.

Cassandra All day she sits, Polydorus at her feet,
another pyre burns, she refuses to put him on it, twines

her fingers in his long brown hair, tries to warm his feet, his hands she holds against her cheek, gathers his stiff arms around her neck, they fall away, his eyes won't close. She walks around with him, will let nothing past her lips, she's dying in front of us, nothing consoles or ever will again.

Hecuba Then Polymestor comes. Hecuba, he calls, Hecuba.

Polymestor Royal queen that lights up the Aegean. Hecuba, help me please.

Hecuba He stumbles across the sand pulling a cart behind him. They've blinded him.

Polymestor She takes my hands, touches my burning eyes.

Hecuba How could you, Polymestor? How could you have given them Polydorus? Your blood? Your wife's little brother? Priam's last living son? How could you?

Polymestor Don't judge me too harshly I say.

Hecuba I had to, he says, they ransomed my sons, they killed them anyway. And there on the cart, his little sons, Priam's grandsons, mine too, my stepdaughter Lliona's boys. Lliona, may the gods be near you when you look on this sight. May your heart not break, your spirit not be crushed. They've been tortured too.

Polymestor Culled by accident as they got on the ships at Troy, Agamemnon says. Soldiers, not Spartans, not Mycenaeans of course but the Libyans, the Danaans in a frenzy winnowing out the Trojan boys. Wrong place, wrong time, but my men retrieved the bodies. A terrible mistake but evacuating Troy was not easy, the smoke, the confusion, tempers up, the women screaming. And

the boys had tried to escape his protection, had run from
his men. A terrible, terrible mistake but this is war and
you should not have withheld Polydorus from us when
we had promised you Thrace would be untouched in
retreat he says. You played the double game, Polymestor,
and your sons paid the price. I have to face my wife. She
begged me not to take them. Then Odysseus moves in,
says I've withheld assets and tributes due to the Achaeans
as the victors. What assets? What tributes? I say. You
know well he says, ships leaving in the night from Ilion's
east pier before we took you by water, ships laden, gold,
silver, bronze, silks, spices from the east, the royal jewels,
the insignia of Priam, countless, nameless, treasure stolen
from us. And the Iberians come shouting, angry, drink
on them. Odysseus' men try to hold them back. No, they
want blood. Mine. I've killed their leader it seems, one of
their cattle raids early in the war, when we had cattle.
Yes, we killed those bandits, in a fierce battle I say, fair
and square, I lost many men. You killed our king they
roar and they push his son forward, a boy not much
older than mine, knife in his hand, they hold me down.
My eyes. He takes out my eyes. Agamemnon, Odysseus,
do not lift a hand.

Hecuba I lead him to our tent, have my women bring
sea water, there's nothing else, to wash his son's
shattered bodies, dress his ruined eyes, make him drink
a cup of wine.

Cassandra They said many things about her after, that
she killed those boys, blinded Polymestor, went mad,
howled like a dog along this shore. The Achaeans
wanted to get their stories down, their myths in stone,
their version, with them as the heroes always, noble, fair,
merciful. No. They were the wild dogs, the barbarians,
the savages who came as guests and left an entire

civilisation on its knees and in the process defiled its queen and her memory. What she did was, put her last child on the pyre, say her prayers, wait for death quietly by that pyre. And it came, grudgingly, but finally it came. And the wind came too and we sailed with it to a new and harsher world.

Music. Lights.

End.

INDIGO

Indigo came about through a series of workshops led by Mikel Murfi under the auspices of the Royal Shakespeare Company. The play was written by Marina Carr in response to those workshops and is intended to be directed by Mikel Murfi. The RSC currently hold the licence for the stage rights.

Characters

Woman

Man

Indigo Queen

Indigo King

The Morseleen

Dowager Queen

The Husband

Old Fiddler

Ghesh

Indigo Prince

The Harper's Daughter

Woman Six . . . he was six. He was golden . . . a golden child. I'm not saying that just because I was his mother.

Man You are but that's okay. If your mother doesn't think you're golden, what chance have you in this world?

Woman No, listen, he was golden. His hair, skin, a golden halo around him. Other children were drawn to him. Animals. A tiger licked his hand through the bars, everyone screaming, and he just stood there offering his hand, eyes shining.

Man Your husband is very worried about you.

Woman My husband will not grieve.

Man But there's nothing to grieve. Your son is alive, well. I assume he's at school right now.

Woman That's not him.

Man What do you mean?

Woman It's not him. I swear it isn't. I swear. My son comes to me every night in his shroud and his crown.

Man In his shroud and his crown?

Woman Please believe me.

Man Is this not a dream?

Woman No, it's real. I can touch him. He's wet. He's cold. He cries. He says, come and get me, please come and get me, I'm dying here.

Man And where is here?

Woman There.

Man But your son?

Woman That creature is not my son. He pretends in front of other people. But when he's alone with me. The things he says to me.

Man What sort of things does he say to you?

Woman That he's the king.

Man Children have huge fantasy lives.

Woman No, he is a king. A king of some sort. He can fly, change shape. He talks to other creatures that I can't see. Whispering. Whispering. There's a woman comes with long hair, hair like a waterfall and a comb. She lies on the ceiling, her hair falling to the floor. I think I'm going mad. I have to collect him from school in an hour. This creature. This king. He makes me walk behind him. He says he has come here to die. And my little son, my golden son crying in his shroud and his crown. If you saw him at the end of my bed. Pitiful.

Man I'm going to give you something to help you sleep. I'm going to give you something that will help these delusions.

Woman I don't want tablets. I don't want tranquillisers. I want my son. And if they're delusions, as you call them, then I want them too.

Blackout.

Indigo Queen (*voice out of the darkness*) Oh the dreams. The dreams. Beautiful possible dreams of languegomawrach. Stultageous, mesmerific, poweriferous drams, dreams, drapes of him. Skin of the cobalt, eye of

the sapphire, grawg of the raven. My king. My Indigo . . .
I am the last of them. The last of the fabled dynasty of
Indigo. Indigo chariots pulled by indigo horses up the
blue blue road carved out of the blue blue mountain.
It was said our roads were soft as clouds to gallop on.
And the blue gates flung wide and the sweat on his brow,
streaming down the back of his indigo neck, hands
bleeding blue from the reins and the stink of the other
world on him as he leaps and whirls and shouts greetings
to his kneeling subjects who smart and melt in his gaze.

All gone. Creeknahah.

And then he does his vanishing trick and they're all
looking, where's he gone now? Where is he? But I know
he's climbing my indigo hair as if it were the rig of one
of our ships. I feel him stealthily there, making his
progress. And then he has me by the neck.

Oh yourself is it, I say, yourself again swanking from
the wars with the other side. And he laughs in my ear
and purrs, how is my lonesome witch? My old pata?
My sancy soucy. And I say, go way with yourself and the
juice of mortal skirt flowing down your hands, for he
was ever curious. It wasn't only wars you were winning
me bronze segosha. But wasn't it you I was winning
them for? Wasn't it you I was ever thinking of? And the
scent off him, like the first snowdrop even if he is five
thousand years old. Isn't that the way of it with love,
my love, he croons on, sucking my ear. You washed the
hair, he teases, I wonder who that was for? I washed
the hair, I say, because I wash it every hundred years,
and not for you and your eyes full of them with their
little waddly legs that wouldn't fill a fairy child and their
pudgy waists and their eyes that look at you always with
the sheen of death on them. But himself likes them for
that very reason. Because they can die. Because, they say,
they can see the face of God. I believe none of it. We are
the gods here, the sixty-foot indigo giants who conjured

their land out of nothing for them. Made the trees to grow, the rivers to swell, the oceans ebbing and flowing and casting up all they can eat. We it was gave them their speech, their clothes, their music, their poems. We it was taught them all the first and most beautiful things. We the royal house of Danu. The Indigos. And they repay us by finding a new God, a harsh old boy, bitter and twisted as themselves. A god who says, do this, do that, don't look up, don't look down, don't think, don't see, don't dream. Obey. Obey. Obey and you will see my face. Obey and you will enter my stingy paradise. And the Indigos, the Blues, put aside, forgotten.

This is what I'm thinking as he's tying me to the bedpost by my hair and stripping the frock off me. The blue of his skin pulsing in the dark room. Oh, he says, falling on top of me. Oh, he says, I've missed me auld Moon. And he's riggish and meowrack and sucking and eating and swallowing like a man come through the door from a famine to an overladen table and doesn't know where to start. Dig in, says I, me fine blue hoor, but take your time because the man who made time made plenty of it and he also made plenty of me and I'm cross-eyed from the plain purl and the long stretch you were away and no one stretching me.

How long was I gone? He murmurs into my nether regions. Long enough to ruin a garden, says I. Never mind, says he, your gardener's home now with his watering can to trim your lawn and drown the foliage. And he unties my hair from the bedpost and lifts me high in the air, out through the casement, on to the turrets and beyond till he has me wedged between two comets he has ordered to halt in their travels, and my legs resting on Orion. Now, he says, now me auld navy bitch, will this take the 'b' out of your bitterness? It might, says I, if there was a trinket to go with it, to set off the stardust whirling through my hair. Trinkets no

less, he laughs, throwing his fat head back and stars
falling in and out of his mouth and dancing on his
tongue.

And then he produces him. Lifts him out of his navel.
The trinket. The changeling. The dandling. The jewel.
Here's what I found on my travels, says he, placing the
sleeping child in my palm. A mortal child. You never,
says I. A mortal boy child.

Indigo King Anything for you. Anything.

Indigo Queen Anything for you, says he, anything, as
one of the Moon's old retainers leans down to pour us
feen. Good evening, says the old retainer, eyes agog at
what lies sleeping in my palm. Be the hokey pokey pooh,
he gasps. And then he starts to cry. I never thought to
behold one of them again, says he, I thought they were
all gone. And the mortal child raises a tiny hand and
sighs, 'Ah,' and turns over in his sleep in the crook of my
palm and even the stars stop humming when they hear
his little sigh. 'Aaah. Aaah.'

Indigo King Earth years six. Found him singing to the
butterflies by a stream. He thought I was a tree, leaning
up against me, talking to himself, dreaming awake,
putting names on the flowers and the bees. I wish, says
he, to the caterpillar, I wish there was magic for real.
Enchanting. They don't deserve him. He's one of us.
And herself is besotted. Children, mortal or otherwise,
a vanished memory here. Not an indigo child born in
this kingdom for a thousand bleens. Because didn't they
stop believing in us. Them and the spells of their dark
God put a finish to us. All the Indigo playgrounds are
empty. All the Indigo cradles still. Indigo baby clothes in
flitters from moths and lack of use. No little ones. No
hope. No future. A dying race. But here's the conundrum.
Not a one of us can die. We're the immortals. You're

looking at an immortal. You're looking at the king of the
immortals.

Vanishes.

The Morseleen One minute I'm making daisy chains and
the next I'm here. It's a land of giants. Big blue giants.
And I say to her, the one who looks after me, carries me
round in her hair like I'm a ribbon. I says to her, am I
awake or asleep? You're awake, child, she answers,
you'll never be more awake than you are now. And the
blue horses are as big as houses and the blue deer glide by
like ships among the blue trees, the size of . . . I don't
know . . . the size of dreams. And they talk their own
language and they've banquets that go on for days and
all their songs are dirges. And they weep every time they
look at me. And the one who looks after me, the queen,
I think, for she has that way about her. Back off! She
says to them, because they all want to touch me and
hold me and hear me speak. And my bed is in her ear
and she's careful when she turns in her sleep not to crush
me. And at night I dream of my mother, crying out for me.
And I see my father pacing the yard. And when I ask her,
the blue queen, how long will I be here? She says, how
long is a thing we have no truck with? And when I say,
but when can I go home? she looks at me strangely and
says, you are home, little morseleen. You are home. And
they take turns listening to my heart. It seems I'm some
sort of reward. They line up in the throne room,
thousands of them, filing past me. They stand me on a
thimble on top of a table and these blue giants file past.
And they gasp and laugh and cry out. A child. A mortal
child. Who would've ever thought we'd see a child
again? A miracle, they whisper. The women stretch their
long blue fingers as if to snatch me, but she watches me,
guards me and slaps them away. And their men lead them

out as they keep looking back at me, boring into me
with their eyes the size and colour of the harvest moon.
And at night my mother comes, arms outstretched, as if
walking out of a grave. And I toss and turn in the blue
lady's ear. And she whispers, settle down, Morseleen
mine, 'tis only a dream of another time. And she lifts me
out of her ear and places me on the bridge of her lip and
breathes softly on me till I fall asleep.

Indigo Queen And despite the arrival of the Morseleen,
himself is far from happy. He's mooching round the
palace and galloping off for days. And I know he gallops
right up to the window on the mortal world and hours
he gives there, nights, watching their carry on, his nose
pressed to the gauze. And he comes home exhausted,
eyes empty of longing, and drinks himself to a stupor
sitting on his turquoise throne. And he'll take the little
manyeen, the morseleen, the child, and hold him in the
palm of his hand and look at him as if he'd eat him. And
the child gabbles on in mortal tongue, brave-hearted and
curious when he isn't crying for his mother and father
and all he knows. And I have them stitch small clothes to
fit him and mash tiny portions to feed him and have our
carpenters make him a minuscule bed, though he won't
sleep in it, preferring to be close to me. And I've grown
to love this child and fear for him as all the women are
jealous of me and would snatch him and take him for
themselves. Only their fear of himself and his terrible
spells puts a halt to them. And our numbers are dwindling.
The host reducing. Every morning word comes of
another hundred vanishing. Vanishing and no one to
come after them. Just extinguished. Us. The immortals.
The blue immortals. The Indigos. And his face is darker
and angrier with each new day.

Indigo King She's watching me like a hawk. Counting
my glasses of feen, saying, *astore, astore ma kree*, come

to sleep, come to bed now. I kiss her hand and wave her
away and she stomps off, the child swinging in her hair.
I take out my eyes because I no longer want to see. I no
longer want to look on our blue kingdom, or look at her,
or at my faithful subjects who have served me so well. I
can't bear the desperation in their faces, their barren walk,
the childless rooms. They want me to do something. But
what? I sing out all the old songs, the old spells, as if I'll
find an answer there. I call in the harpers, the fiddlers,
the poets, the storytellers. I order them to sing, to play,
to recite till they fall down exhausted at my feet and beg
to be released. And there's no joy in any of it. Because
we're here. Because they're there. And they're there because
we're here. The first law. The only one. And they've
broken it. We, their blue breath. We who invented them,
sang them into existence because we thought it would be
amusing to watch the finite world in progress. And now
they don't even hear the sound of us departing. Times I
look at that child and I want to kill him. Stamp on him
like one of their ladybirds. But herself is besotted. We
should take more of them, she whispers to me the other
night. A playmate for the little Morseleen, she croons,
one for every indigo woman, some mortal girls so they
can grow and breed here, a host of boys for the indigo
men to love as sons, because we've forgotten what that
is. Indeed and we have, says I, indeed and we have. But
what I haven't told her is this. I left a replacement in the
bed when I took the mortal boy. I left myself.

Woman No one believes me. This sixty-foot giant is not
my son. He's not my son. I walk him to school. He
towers over me, insists on putting his big blue paw in
mine, skipping along with his school bag and lunch box.
And my son's friends greet him as if he's one of them and
surround him because Johnny was always the centre of

attention, the popular one. They crowd around him in the
playground. I watch from the wall and he runs among
them, this towering blue monster, and they don't notice a
thing, shout, Johnny here, here, throw the ball here. And
sometimes he'll look back at me and smile. And I think
I'm losing my mind. And he fell the other day and cut his
knee and the blood, the blood was black, and hot, hot as
tar on a summer's day. And I looked at him and said, my
child's blood is red. Don't I know it, he answers, in a deep
gravelly voice. Don't I know it well? Who are you?, I said,
the hair standing on the back of my neck and the sweat
of fear crawling along my back, my armpits. If I told
you, he said, in the same gravelly voice, if I told you, you
wouldn't believe. And then my husband comes and lifts
him, I don't know how, and puts him on the kitchen
table and bathes the cut and I say, do you not see the
blood flowing down his leg like black milk? Do you not
see the long blue black hair? Johnny was blond. Do you
not see his head scraping the roof beams and pushing at
the tiles? And my husband looks at me and says, please,
not again, not in front of the child. And in the middle of
the night I couldn't sleep and got up for a drink of water
and he's standing in the yard, big as a crane, huge blue
head thrown back, arms outstretched, looking at the
stars. And without turning he says, you want to know
who I am mortal woman? Take your ease there in the
garden seat. Don't be afraid. Sit and I'll tell you.

Indigo King She's afraid and the glare of my skin is
blinding her so I reduce myself to the paltry proportions
of their men. There's nothing I can do about the skin.
And she's beautiful, standing there by the garden seat,
her mouth open, the teeth floating in her face like cream,
the lips pillowing, trembling. I've had plenty of them
down the long centuries since first we made them. And

I've fallen for some of them and could not bear to watch them age and die, slipping through my fingers like time. But this time. This one. The thin straps of her nightgown falling from her shoulder, the long arms, the full round body. Colour her blue and stretch her and she could be one of ours, could be my old blue queen in her prime. And for a second I feel what they must feel when confronted with dazzling beauty. The end of things. The end. That it's all fleeting and it's all now instead of this barren nightmare of forever which is only another way of saying if you have all of time then all you have is nothing. And she's looking at me, her hand pressed to her mouth, eyes brimming, you're not from here, she whispers, moving back into the trees. And for some reason I can't explain, I want this one to love me.

Woman He shrinks. He shimmers. Ribbons of silver heat coming off him. Terrifying. Awesome to behold in my own yard with my husband asleep in the bed and my son. My son. Where is he? I say What have you done with him? He's safe, he says, safe with our kind. He's adored. He's our little prince, the cynosure of all eyes.

Indigo King And her eyes fill with tears. I thought I was going mad, she says. So I was right. All along I knew you weren't him.

Woman And all the time he's talking low and backing me into the trees. And before I know it I'm on a golden bed, the moonlight turning the sheets to pewter. And the bed is floating above the trees and the clouds passing close by us and he's kissing me, kisses to die for, kisses that make you forget. And a part of me is thinking, my son, my little son, where is he? And a part of me is thinking, who is this divine devil suspended above me, whispering love and doing things I only ever dreamed of.

Indigo King We're interrupted by the husband, standing

in his birthday suit at the door, calling into the hushed yard.

Woman All I know is next thing I'm answering, yes, yes I'm here, and walking out of the trees with the sixty-foot creature by the hand. And he smiles at me and runs to my husband who lifts him up and says, Johnny, what are you doing out in the middle of the night? And I say, I heard him opening the door and followed him. And the indigo monster winks at me from my husband's arms and I follow them in. I really am going mad.

Indigo Queen And himself is stravaging the rooms and the courtyards, will hardly look me in the sool, rarely comes near me. I know I don't look as I looked a few thousand bleen ago but that never stopped him before. We all have our seasons, I tell myself, and keep busy with my duties. And the little Morseleeen goes everywhere with me and soothes my growing anger with his mortal chat and gossip. But at night I take out my rage and put it there on the table in front of me to examine it. And my rage talks back to me calmly and tells me, he has found another. Before there were dalliances which I bitterly tholed and turned the blind sool to. But this time is different. I can feel his love departing, feel it like a smoking pain that burns out my entrails and leaves me breathless. This old blue heart is breaking. We have loved each other so long. We it was gave birth to the last immortal. My tiny blue boy who vanished as he slipped from the womb, barely had time to hold him, barely time to register the stamp on his torso. The footprint of the first immortal as foretold in the prophecy.

A boy will come.

With my hoof print on his skin.

Mark this time.

Your undoing.

And we've carried him with us, that vanished infant, the blue prince, the last Indigo, and his death knell for us all. And times I look at my people, and though they profess their loyalty, secretly I know they dislike me and fear me. And times I think he resents me too, that it was me carried the sign and gave birth to it for all to see. So I go to my mother, the old Dowager Queen.

Dowager Queen I'm studying the clouds on my canopy suspended above our sapphire kingdom, my steed grazing beneath me. And like all who have lived too long and seen too much, I pray for my vanishing. And though I have the body of a young colt and skin and hair to match the best of them, I am weary with the accretion of time and welcome the interruption of my daughter galloping across our cobalt meadows, the little mortal swinging and whooping in her hair. Well, Ingin Fadah, I say, as she kneels before the canopy to kiss my jewelled hand. The little Morseleen gazes at me with those eyes of dust they all have. The mortal gaze. The gaze we crave. I stretch out a finger and he hops on and kneels and bows as my daughter has taught him. Rise up, my gallant, I say, till I have a look at you. And he stands on my finger, stretching his tiny body and puffing out his little chest. And my daughter smiles, the covetous, jealous smile of all mothers. And the little Morseleen looks to her for approval and she gives it with her eyes and the Morseleen relaxes and starts tumbling in my hand and running along the craters of my palm and climbing the steep hills to my wrist and he's gossamer in motion as he skates on my rings. And my daughter throws herself alongside me and sighs. What's ailing you now, Ingin Fadah? I say. Oh the same, says she, himself and his trousers. Well, you've known forever, says I, that he can't keep them up. But it's the places he's putting it now, says she. And where would that be? That's it, says she, I don't know. Not here for sure and they're climbing the walls in the harem and tearing the eyes out of each other for lack of it. I had to send in replacements to stop a blood fest and put the purr on their chops.

Indigo Queen And my mother throws back her massive indigo head and bares her white teeth and laughs, though I can see from the corner of her eye she is watching me close. She came out of the harem herself, wooed her way into my father's arms and affections, had him make her queen. Destroyed all round her to do it. She has curses and spells in her repertoire we don't even know about. But that was a long time ago and the aeons have softened her though you can still see flashes of that desperate vicious girl. She takes the Morseleen between her thumb and index finger and examines him. A mortal crush, she says. He's gone with a mortal. I've seen it before. Didn't I dally there myself a while, she adds, smiling at my mortal boy who smiles back, the smile of angels and innocents. And who could blame him, she finishes. There's nothing like them, the way they forget and the way they die.

The Morseleen My neck is sore looking up at them. Their nostrils are caves you could get lost in. This one now who has me on her palm, reminds me of someone but I can't remember who. And the blue queen, the one who minds me, is awful down in herself. At night when I sleep in her ear, I can hear her thoughts, wild and stormy like waves crashing over me. And I can't get used to the size of things and the hollow sounds of them as if they're all ghosts and me the only living thing among them. Though they eat, vast quantities of food I have no names for. And they drink gallons upon gallons of their blue feen. And they walk mostly though they can float and fly but it gives them no pleasure. And when they sleep they wake exhausted. And then I remember where I've seen

her before, the mother of the one who minds me. It was
in a story book, a picture of her, leaving a scorch mark
on a young man's face because he dared to look at her.
A book about fairies. The little people. But these people
aren't little. They're giants. Silver blue giants in the
evening. Indigo in the morning sun. Navy at dusk. And
I can't remember my mother's face. She's vanishing. Or
I am. Or we both are.

The Husband She was always a bit gone away in
herself, a bit addled, distracted, always saying, what?
always making me repeat myself. Even when I asked her
to marry me. Had to say it three times before she figured
out what I was asking. And I thought this scattery thing
was attractive, dreamy, girly, feminine. But now she's
making strange with the little fellah, her own son, saying
he's not who he is, ours, but some monster. Don't you
see the big blue black feet on him, she says, looking at
me like I'm the crazy one, and the eyes on him like
exploding suns. First she wouldn't go near him, cowering
in the corner as if little Johnny was a herd of wild bulls
stampeding across the kitchen floor to mow her down
and he only draping his school bag across the chair. And
at night, shivering and shaking in the bed and clinging to
me with the sweat pouring off her hands and the eyes
rolling in her head, whispering, you have to get rid of
him, you have to get rid of him and bring Johnny back
or I'm going to die of fear and grief. And then the
wailing, wailing that'd put the banshee to shame. And I
try to reason with her, comfort her. What is it, darling
mine, I whisper. And the child at the door looking at us.
Him! It's him! She shouts out, darting up in the bed and
pointing and screaming at poor Johnny in his pyjamas,
holding on to Lobby Lugs, his tattered old bear. Get
away you devil, she roars at the child and she making

the sign of the cross with her arms to ward him off. And
I say, Johnny go back to bed, your mother's just having a
bit of a turn. It's nothing, nothing to be worried about at
all. It's just something women do all the time when they
get a figary in their heads about something. And Johnny
looks unconvinced but goes away. And herself mooning
and swooning in the sheets and I have to hold on to her
till she stops thrashing and wears herself out with the
crying and the screeching. And no, she cries, exhausted,
you won't believe me but it's true, Johnny's been taken
and they've put some sort of a swop in his place. I've
heard stories about this, she sobs, I've heard stories
about this. Only auld tales, I croon, only auld bits of
rubbish come down from the old time to frighten
children in the dark. No, she says, it's happening here.
It's happening now. And I say, woman, that child in his
bed across the landing is our child. I swear it. But you
don't see what I see, she cries out. And after that she
goes quiet and I'm troubled and tired and fall asleep
though I don't mean to. And next thing I'm awake and
the bed is empty and the child's bed is empty. And I'm
the one sweating now. What if she's right? What if it is a
blue monster and not Johnny? Or worse, what if she's
doing something terrible to him right now? I race down
the stairs and into the yard and call them and there's not
a sound only the stars glittering in the puddles and
flashing off the bucket by the wall turning the world
black and silver. I call again. I'm panicking now and
about to go for help. But then she comes, calm as you
like in her slip, on her soundless feet, like some ancient
queen of the forest, a crown of leaves in her hair, the
velvet light on her, the child by the hand.

Woman After that he comes for me every night to romp
on the golden bed.

Old Fiddler Walking home in the small hours, as I often am, after playing at some dance or just wandering the lanes as I'm prone to do. Waiting for them, the vanished people, the blues. They gave me all my best tunes and the words to go with them. Gave them to my father and his father before him. I sit on the stump of a hazel. A tree sacred to them one time. Sacred to us too when we lived by the old laws, the old ways. and thought in the old style. Come and talk to me, I say, into the night. I say it every time I pass this stump, as my father said it and the grandfather before him. And they never answer any more but I say it anyway, out of habit, a sort of a prayer. For what are we without them? Only animals going from the break of day to the close of day. They're the fluff, the fluff that gives substance to a man, his sorrow and all his joy. Some are afraid of them, not me, never, nor any of mine. Not the father, not the grandfather. And didn't the great-grandmother go off with them for days at a time to polish her songs and get new ones. And they told her there was a time when we used to have banquets with them here in this very field at the edge of this wood, backing on to this lane. A sacred place. No doubt about it. And there they all were, sitting around the tables, the sky their banquet hall, suspended there, where you're looking, about ten feet above the grass. And serving women with the bodies of snakes slithering round with platters of food and jugs of wine. Their wine is blue, the great-grandmother always said, and it tastes like nothing else. And their ladies, giant butterflies, holding their lords' hands and leaning against them and kissing them between mouthfuls. And their lords, massive, massive and merry, light blasting off them. At times you could see through them, at times as solid and substantial as ourselves. Flesh and fat and bone and sinew but knitted together in a wondrous combination. They could take off their hands, arms, legs and throw them at one another and often did for sport. Mixing themselves up, a lady with her lord's head. Him, with his lady's. And they could take out their eyes and roll them along the table like marbles and pop them in their blue wine and swallow them. And with their limbs all mixed up, a leg where a head should be and an eye sticking out of a navel, they'd float in the air and join and unjoin in a dance of love, assembling and re-assembling as they pleased, swooping and diving and shimmering above the shining grass, their plates and tableware and goblets glinting in the moon. And their music? And when they sang? You'd give your life to hear it once. Such transport. Such enchantment, like listening to the first breath of the world on its first blue morning where all these things began. And their blue horses grazing beneath them, blue pelts gleaming with dew. And the ladies leaping down from their suspended table on to the horses and climbing the air just for the fun of it and just because they can and somersaulting from horse to horse and reclining with arms stretched out and backs arched as their lords drop food in their mouths. Who are they? And where have they gone?

Indigo King I'm standing right beside him. This old fiddler. If they were all like you. Even some of them. It'd be enough. Enough to keep us here. There. Everywhere. But Indigo is dying. I can't deny it any more. Five thousand of our host disappeared last night. The caterwauling around the palace walls this morning as the empty clothes and empty shoes marched towards us in the dawn. A nice night, I say, and he turns. They always start by talking about the weather.

Old Fiddler A pet of a night, I say, to this stranger walking up the lane.

Indigo King A night for hoors and wine.

Old Fiddler If there were any about. He's a young man,

well made about the shoulder with a dimple in his chin. Late to be carousing with the grass, he says. I tell him I'm coming home from a session and he reaches for my fiddle. May I? he says.

Indigo King I play a lament for him. The lament of the immortals departing. And his eyes dart greedily over my fingers and his ears out on sticks. There's no hunger like the hunger of a master fiddler for a new air. Well I never, he says, I never, and then he starts to weep. And when he recovers he plays it back to me. Perfect.

Old Fiddler It's yours, he says, it's yours now to dazzle the dazzlers. A small gift. Don't tamper with it.

Indigo King I wouldn't dare, he says, looking at me strangely.

Old Fiddler You're not from these parts? No, he says, he's not. And he continues down the lane, giving me a backward wave.

Indigo King Come back, he says, but I'm weary of them, even him, one of the good ones. And just to give him something to mull over, I vanish.

Old Fiddler I play his lament three times to get it down and to get it in. And yes, he has vanished in front of me, but that marvel comes to me second. It's the music. Their music is the first mystery. I put down my fiddle when I'm sure I have it and put my head in my hands and weep. The leaves all along the lane are with me in a dreeping chorus. What we have lost. What we have lost. He's one of them. I'd put my dead mother's eternal soul on it. I've finally met one of them.

Woman I'm shocked, shocked out of my skin. Every night I'm on the golden bed with him. Can't wait to get the dinner out of the way. Can't wait for dusk and then for night to fall. Can't wait for my husband to fall asleep. My husband that I thought I loved, that I do love, these ten years. But this is a dream, a dream, I tell myself, as I fly up in his arms to the bed of hammered gold with the sky and the stars leaning purple upon us. This is all just a dream. But if it is, dear God in your wild, unfolding heaven let me never wake from it. Let me never wake. And then Johnny. Johnny, I say, where is he? Where is my little boy? And he tells me, my blue lover, navy in the dark, don't fret my mortal girl, don't you worry, your boy is safe, and silences me with his indigo kisses.

Indigo Queen   He walks by without seeing me. He greets me absently when he has to but mostly he departs the room I enter on the pretence of some kingly business. He surrounds himself with his advisers, his council, so I can't get him alone. He has reneged my bed. And he ignores the little Morseleen and our tribe keep vanishing, their empty shoes ringing in the courtyard as they stamp their grief and outrage. We, the Indigos, the first tribe, descended from the first immortal himself. I watch him quietly. I don't know what he's planning. Ghesh, his brother and chief adviser, whispers in his ear in the long dining hall and looks at me significantly. He has always hated me, blames me for all the barren women, rumours it was I brought the curse and demise on them all. And I am heartbroken and jealous at his turning away from me.

So I follow him through the gauze.

And it hurts to enter their world. The filth of the air clogging my nostrils and searing my lungs. And the pale green fields and the stunted trees and the rivers stinking and the seas rising and heaving with sewer and marl and the cities and towns a nightmare of grey and blunted

edges and blackened pavements and the misery and
horror on all the pinched faces. I have to close some of
their eyes, finish them off there on the spot. I don't wish
to but their eyes tell me they don't want to be here and
I am bound by the old laws so I have to oblige. Some
I stand on. Some I lift in my hand and squeeze to a dull
red pulp. Others I fling into the sea, prams and all. I
didn't know it was so terrible here. So long since I last
came through the gauze. When I was a girl we used to
come through to dally with the mortal men for a few of
their soft hours but that was a long while ago now.
They've shrunk further. The vibrant colours have been
washed from sky and earth, the primary blaze muted to
sombre hue. How can they live like this? In this dull
brown nightmare with the air tearing at their lungs and
their passions the size of a pea. And he's there in front of
me, floating above them, along the river the colour of
dead dreams. I keep well behind so he doesn't smell the
blue burning off me or hear the gasp in my throat. And
he floats outside the city and turns down a deserted lane
where a heron stands in a stream and a hare stops to
look up at us before it leaps gracefully over a ditch. And
he stops before a house and transforms into . . . into the
Morseleen and goes inside as if he has always lived there.
I lean down and put one of my eyes to the window and
watch him sit at the table and eat their food and drink
their mortal milk. And the woman is beautiful, round
and smooth with sleek hair and the hands of one of
ours. And she moves around him strangely and he plays
the part without a flaw. And then a man walks in and
I can hear the air changing. He looks at his wife, goes to
touch her, kiss her, but she steps aside like a dancer and
he's left with his arms stretched out and looking like a
fool. He sighs, sits at the table, eats his food silently
without relish and pushes the plate away. He looks at
the Morseleen, my Indigo man in disguise. And my

Indigo man looks back at him brazenly and talks to him softly. Dad, he says, Dad, you want to kick ball after the tea? And I laugh at the outrageous gall of him and the window rattles and the house shakes and he turns and sees me and glares.

Indigo King She glares back, the flame of her eye wedged against the window pane like a smashed sun. Well, it was bound to happen. I carry my plate to the sink like the good Morseleen I am and run out the door and grab her by the streaming hair as she flies away from me. Let go of me or I'll put the scorch on you, she says, I'll put the scorch on you now. But I hold on tight till she has stopped struggling and bring her down in a tangle on top of an oak. And I look at her, my old queen, stretched between the branches, the silver hair falling to the grass, the lip curled in rage and defeat but trembling for all that. You've gone among them, she hisses in contempt, you're living among them, where's your pride? How could you? Because we're dying, I say. Indigo is dying. You're here for that woman, she says, I saw the way you looked at her.

Indigo Queen Yes, he says, I'm here for that woman, without a note of apology in his voice. You're replacing me.

Indigo King I don't know what I'm doing.

Indigo Queen She has you. That mortal tramp! She has you by the long blue balls. I'll do her wrong. I'll break her spell. I'll finish her. I swear to you I'll finish her.

Indigo King Do that and you finish me, I say. She raises her hand and it blazes like the first flame.

Indigo Queen I'll stretch this hand across her face. I'll sear the eyes from her sockets and barbecue them shut. I'll solder her lips to her ears and then we'll see what you love about her. And I can see the terror is on him now that I would disfigure his little woman. I've done it before.

Indigo King I grab her flaming hand, a birth gift from the old Dowager, and the pain is terrible but I don't let go.

Indigo Queen He wants me to release him first. I increase the pressure. Black tears stream from his eyes and hiss on our burning hands. This is different, he says.

Indigo King This time is different. You touch a hair on her head and I'll take the Morseleen out. She lets go.

Indigo Queen And then the husband, I take it, is at the door calling. Johnny, he calls, Johnny, come, in good lad. Johnny, I say, that's his name? The Morseleen.

Indigo King I have to go.

Indigo Queen And he walks out of the trees to the man who tousles his hair and lifts him up and strokes his neck. And he's the spit of my Morseleen. And the man says, where were you, little man? What were you doing? And he says I was only talking to an auld banshee in the trees. And he glances my way, sly, and the smirk on him full of threat and warning. And I'm afraid now, afraid for the Morseleen. Johnny. That's his name though I'll never call him by it for fear he might remember all he has nearly forgotten now. I lie there watching the lights go on in the house and I'm still there when they go out. My breath shallow as I look up at their stars, different from ours but stars all the same. And I'm desperate as I listen to the night and the small rustlings of the night creatures flying around me and scuttling below. I can hear him breathing in the house, a child's faint breath, sweet with sleep. But I know he knows I'm still here. And he knows I know he's only waiting for me to go before he can take her out and lay her across his golden

bed. I know his style. Once it was me. And though I look
no different than I did then, the soul, the soul in me is
ancient, shrivelled, the soul of a hag, an old witch of the
air and holds no mystery for him now. And I hate this
woman with a passion that surprises me. Thought I was
finished with all that but I find I am jealous, jealous as
an infant with all the rage and panic attending. And I lie
facing the silver heavens, mulling over all the ways
I could harm her and this satisfies and gives me some
comfort. I lie there until my lungs start to bleed and I
cough up globs of their gunk and welter. I give up, leave
him to his mortal dish and make my weary way home
over forest, lanes, lakes as still as mirrors that will never
reflect our kind again. Even the lakes have forgotten us.
Over the sleeping beasts and the lonely houses and the
clicking swans who glide through me in their slow heavy
climb to their feeding grounds by the mouth of the
curling river that unfurls below, a ribbon in a young
girl's hair as she runs through the pale fields to the
samphire coast and the sea who waits for her, arms open
and heaving like the first lover in the first time when all
glittered and glowed and these mortals were part of
ourselves, the most precious, time it was you could not
tell us apart. I find the gauze and slip through and
everything shimmers as I breathe in the clear giving air
of our once beautiful kingdom.

The Morseleen She takes me in her hand and blows
softly on me and I fall into the pillow of her palm. A game
she likes to play. Her huge eyes are sad. Morseleen mine,
she says, Morseleen mine, as I take a running jump and
land on one of the mountains that stick out of her chest.
She laughs as I crawl all over her face. But I hear a note
in it that isn't laughter but only its echo. What is it? I say
as I stand on the carpet of her eyes but she doesn't answer
me, only starts talking to her mother, the old dowager.

Dowager Queen She comes towards us on her blue mare with a face on her as long as a flooded field. The little Morseleen jumps up, eyes shining as he watches her gallop through the gentians. He has missed her and has me worn out asking where she is. She flings herself down beside me and empties my glass and then plays with the Morseleen a while. She has found nothing good there. I could've told her that. I can no longer bear to flit the gauze. Sing to me, woman, she says, dandling the Morseleen, sing to me to put the chambers of the heart back in kilter and align. And though I'm mad with curiosity to hear about the little people, are there any of them left even? I sing the oldest song in the oldest style that was passed down from the fish queen herself as she first came out of the sea on to dry land pirouetting on her silver-barnacled tail.

Indigo Queen She soothers me with the fish music, words and melody so ancient not even we understand them, but our ear does and the blood in our veins does and my heart lurches and shoulders itself back to its rightful groove and my lungs whistle themselves clean and the mind shuts down and I return to myself. To what I feel. And what I feel is murderous. And the Morseleen stands still and listens too and looks at me sideways clutching my thumb and shivers like a blade of grass on a barren plain as my mother's voice flows through him, telling him things, oh things, things he knows, things in their hard wiring, the same as in ours, but forgotten, refused to be remembered, discarded, the deepest, hardest enchantments of sound, shark music with the keen of the whale and the seal's wild pitched glory. And my mother pours it out well, as if she is come dripping from the sea herself for the first time and gasping her wonder at the vaults of the immortals' heaven above her and our first shore unfolding like a carpet beneath

her to the first playground, packed and tiered among the
billowing dunes with all its chosen bounty and foldedols
laid out for us with such care and such love. The best.
The best of everything. The first time, the fish queen
herself singing her thanks, a time before we learned
ingratitude, before we forgot to see, a time before we
learned to downplay awe. We knew then how miraculous
it all was. To be chosen. To be here.

Indigo King And like all the old things from the old
style. They leave you empty and they leave you full. And
though I never cared for the old woman, the Dowager,
I have to hand it to her, the crone can carry a song.
It floats across the cobalt fields and the navy pastures
where the deer graze, their antlers catching the last
sombre light of dusk. And my lady turns sensing I am
there and flashes me a look that would turn back the
very night coming down. And I fear for my mortal
woman and for myself.

Dowager Queen Prancing he comes, the big bull neck on
the mottled blue shoulders. For a long time, a very long
time, he was a good and faithful king. He bows, pays me
my due homage. I wave him away with my hand. My
daughter snorts, and do you bow to your mortal trollop
like that, my gallant knave?

Indigo King I ignore the barb and greet the Morseleen.
He answers me shyly with the long lashed glance of his
mother a world away. I stretch out my hand for the child
to jump on but she closes hers and turns away. The old
dowager looks straight at me.

Dowager Queen So it's begun.

Indigo King What has begun?

Dowager Queen The exodus.

Indigo King What exodus?

Dowager Queen There'll be none of us left at the finish.

Old Fiddler I'm at the fire after the bit of dinner when
I see a light passing beyond the ditch in the lane. I walk
out thinking maybe it's one of the neighbours calling or
someone looking for help with a cow calving. And
coming towards me is this . . . this thing in blue, skirts
swishing, legs the size of trees, feet that gouge clumps
out of the lane, the eyes swivelling in great yellow arcs as
she scans the place. She stops right beside me as I creep
into the foliage praying to the Lord God she hasn't
clapped them eyes on me. Behind her rattles a carriage,
drawn by four horses with not a head between them.
And on the carriage is a coffin. Black. Lucifer black and
pulsing evil. Her hair streams behind her, impossibly
long, no end to it, a live thing, spreading like fog over
the fields and ditches. You could plant wheat on it. Her
hands are talons of flame. You, she says.

Indigo Queen You.

Old Fiddler Not looking at me. Her foot beside me. She
could crush me like a beetle. Forgive me, I say, falling
on my knees, forgive my intruding on your procession.
And in desperation I kiss her foot. Who are you,
stranger, she says.

Indigo Queen Who are you, stranger?

Old Fiddler Leaning down and taking me up in her coal
red hand. I'm only an old fiddler, I whisper, only an old
fiddler who should be asleep in his bed. She laughs,
throwing her head back, the big blue throat on her, the
veins knotted like the boles of an oak.

Indigo Queen A fiddler? Well, if you're a fiddler let's hear you fiddle.

Old Fiddler And a fiddle appears in front of me and then a bow.

Indigo Queen And he plays and I listen till he finishes.

Old Fiddler She looks at me a long time. And then the verdict. Useless, she says.

Indigo Queen Useless. Where's your heart, man? Where's the old soul in it? You're wasting my time.

Old Fiddler And the headless horses snort and stamp the ground with their mighty hooves and the hair whirls round her face in the wind and the coffin creaks as the lid opens slowly and I know it's for me.

Indigo Queen I have another tune, he says, and he shaking with the fright and the fear. I have a tune that might please you and before I can stop him he's playing it. One of our laments. The sacred one. The lament of our immortals departing. He gets most of it but he's too nervy and his touch is too heavy and his tone is just the smidgeen off. Exhilarating to watch, someone fiddling for their life.

Old Fiddler Not bad, she says, and not good either. You've been talking to one of ours. But have you heard this one? And she takes the coffin in one hand from the carriage and puts it against the collar of her bone and strings appear on it and a bow materialises and on each of the bowstrings is a head, wailing heads everywhere that she plays across the strings of the coffin. And I gawp and gape, perched there on her bowing hand that moves like lightening. I'd kill for a bowing hand like that, the fluid in the wrist like salmon jumping up the weir and battling the tide. And in the tune, all the sorrows of our race since the gates of Eden closed softly on our naked backs and we learned what it is to lose and we learned what it is to die. Now you play it, she says, handing me the coffin.

Indigo Queen I have to go over it with him three times, there in the lane, till he gets it right. When did they get so slow? Then I let him go. It's not for him I've come tonight.

Old Fiddler The coffin returns to a coffin there on the carriage. The horses still. The flaming hand puts me back in the ditch. Thank you for the gift, I falter.

Indigo Queen What gift?

Old Fiddler The tune.

Indigo Queen We've libraries of them, countless, gathering dust. Make sure you pass it on. You're welcome.

Old Fiddler You're welcome, she says, and almost bows and then continues down the lane. And when the sheen of her is gone and the hooves can no longer be heard, I realise I'm holding her fiddle in my hand and the bow with all the wailing faces is now dripping blood on the leaves. But nothing will do me but play her tune over and over till dawn.

The Husband Hooves in the yard. I go to the window and see a creature leaping off one of them. She squats, cat like, looking around, sniffing the air, and then stands slowly to her full height. Her hair floats around her bare feet. The curtain trembles. Like lightning she locks me in her searing gaze, though it's pitch dark in the room I know she can see me. My heart thumps in my chest. I'm a bowl of sweat. Watch me, her eyes say, and she goes to the carriage drawn by the horses so still, unmoving they could be carved from stone. She opens the lid of the coffin and lifts from it . . . my son. She carries him to the window. I see his chest rise and fall softly through his light shirt. Not dead. Just sleeping. I nearly cry out with relief. His hair, long like hers, how can this be? It hangs like a bronze sheet over her arm, plays in the breeze. His lips are open. She looks at me the whole time to make sure I clock what she's showing me. Then in one leap she's on the stone horse with Johnny still in her arms and the hooves are galloping out of the yard.

When I recover, it seems a long time after but it may have been just a second, I run to Johnny's room. He's there in his bed, eyes open. Go back to sleep, Dad, he says, it was only her and her silly games. Who? I say, who's her? But his eyelids flicker and he goes back to sleep if he was ever awake.

Indigo King I hear her miles away so I'm waiting for her when she comes clattering the yard with her entourage to spook the small creatures of the earth. I stand in the trees watching. She knows I'm there but ignores me. I want to see how far she dares to go. This is a test of wills, a battle for precedence. She does her coffin trick. I laugh loud enough for her to hear. She stands there holding the Morseleen. She's made herself vulnerable bringing him here. She knows this. I whisper, where's your basin of blood, woman, or are you losing your style? You'll be a basin of blood before long, she hisses back. Go home, I say, you're only making a fool of yourself. And she stands there at the window holding the Morseleen and cries, not her usual bloodcurdling banshee shriek but the slow black tears of our kind when we are wounded to the deeps. I've shamed her. She leaps on to the horses. That was only a taster, she says, as she passes me on the velvet grass, there's still the main course and then there's the gravy. Her voice shakes. I've never seen her so angry or so broken. A close call. I check my mortal woman. She's sleeping peacefully, has slept through the whole thing, a smooth round arm covering her eyes. But the husband is stuck to the wall, eyes frozen to the ceiling. I put the calm on him and he crawls between the sheets and drifts off. With a bit of luck he'll wake and think it was just a terrible dream. I look at them a long time. I've grown protective of these two. What am I doing here pretending to be human? And my old blue queen. Indigo, I'm making you suffer. I go back to bed with my teddy bear, arch deceiver, charlatan that I am.

Woman The days pass in agony. I make the changeling his breakfast. He eats quietly. I brush his hair and put his lunch box in his hand, his school bag on his back. He looks at me gently, gratefully. I am keeping our secret. And yet when I see him run along the lane in front of me, Johnny's run, my heart stops. This is like no story I've ever read or heard and my throat floods with fear and loss. And the way my husband looks at me across the room, something has gone and it will never return. We're only going through the motions of what we were. And I can't talk about it. How can you talk about something like that? Where to start? But the nights. The nights. Intoxicating navy nights where the breeze is always warm and the stars are always leaning, dripping molten on our skin above in the golden bed. I am fucking a ghost. My son's ghost. While my son lives and moves through his days among the immortals. The blood rebels as the soul succumbs, Nightly. Nightly. The world has become one glorious night. The day has become impossible. He runs to me from the school yard. Why can no one else see? The mind collapses with

the strain. I'm not equipped for this. I want my son.
I want my son back. And I want the ghost. My blue
ghost. My lover.

Dowager Queen He is in so deep. He's haunting himself.
My daughter's lips are pressed tightly. The Morseleen
plays, eats, grows. I teach him the old songs to keep him
entertained. He picks up our language. He dances like
one of us and gets all the poems effortlessly. My daughter
lies beside me, a gentian in her teeth that she sucks on
gravely, savagely, crushing it to a pulp that stains her lips
and teeth. And we're vanishing, vanishing. Every morning,
another army of empty dresses, empty coats, empty shoes,
hollow in the courtyards of the keep. Indigo is emptying
and the din of their vanishing is deafening, polluting the
once calm air.

Indigo Queen I have to confront her. But I'm afraid. I
have much to lose. The Morseleen. I live in fear he'll be
taken from me. I never knew what it was to love a child.
A mortal child. Turns out it's mostly pain and terror, of
course the odd dollop of joy but never enough to stave
off the growling fear. That he will die is certain. It's the
natural end for all their kind. And himself has not
returned from beyond the gauze. He's angry with me
and stays away to put me in my place. He is tearing the
heart out of me. And I'm ashamed, ashamed I used the
Morseleen like that, conjuring him out of the coffin to
put the heart skaaways in his father. The look on his
face, thought he was going to drop dead in front of me.
It was her my tableau was meant for but didn't the
Jezebel snore through the whole thing, snoozing there in
the bed, sated with my Indigo. And then it comes to me.
I know what I will do.

Woman I'm walking the lanes, wringing my hands,
because I don't know what to do with myself, wondering
am I in this world or the next. And the air changes, an
arctic blast on this summer's morning. And there she is.
Standing. Eyes on her like cracked frost or stars in a
bog hole, cold, full of mystery and hate. And I'm walking
towards her as if she's reeling me in on a line of yarn
though I'm struggling to flee in the other direction, her
big moon face fierce with concentration. Her skin as blue
as his, her fingertips the burning yellow of the gorse.

Indigo Queen His little woman. The little brown feet.
She loses a sandal as she struggles with me. Her toenails
are painted the colour of rust.

Woman Her hair coils like a bucket of eels around her
feet. Her gown, many coloured, floats around her navy
legs as I walk towards her in spite of myself. Am I never
to stop seeing these things? Am I never to be let alone?

Indigo Queen Her face, terrified now. Always surprised
how I terrify them. The high forehead. The big mouth, the
uneven teeth glimpsed as she whispers to herself, Jesus,
Mary and St Joseph protect me, whoever they are.
Jesus, Mary and St Joseph she keeps muttering, their
new savage gods is it? Her skin is smooth with hardly a
trace of time on it yet, the lines so delicate on the white
cheeks, barely around the eyes, blue as the sky's cerulean
gaze on a cloudless day. The hair, thin, but plenty of it.
The body, like one of our statues in miniature, like one
of the dolls our children used to play with, when we had
children, rotting now in our museums behind dusty
glass. My king, besotted with this. My old paramour
risking it all for one of her sly glances. What is it?
What does she have except the grave beckoning and a
few of their years that we'd flitter away in an Indigo
morning.

Woman Then she's changing, shifting, the air hot and smoking, and then I'm looking at myself, a replica of myself that is talking to me.

Indigo Queen I get her imprint down. Down to the tiny mole above her left nostril. I watch with amusement her disbelief. They all think they're unique, irreplaceable, whoever told them that.

Woman She laughs with my laugh. I see my own tongue clicking against my own teeth, see my own heart rising and falling beneath my light summer dress.

Indigo Queen She screams. I put my hand over her mouth.

Woman Don't be afraid, little woman, she says, I'll do you no harm. And when I can bear to look again, she is back to herself, smiling cynically, triumphantly as if she has got ten out of ten in her spelling test. I check myself, slap my legs, arms, make sure that I'm still here.

Indigo Queen Now, the Morseleen, I say. She looks at me in terror. Johnny, I say, the child.

Woman Johnny? Where is he? What have you done with him? But she turns and starts walking away, starts dissolving before my eyes. Johnny!

Indigo Queen Johnny, she cries, please, please, please, she begs, running after me. And this old heart of bronze swings in its chains. She loves my little Morseleen with all the hopeless love of mortal women. I raise my hand and beckon her. I have her now.

Woman I follow the hand. I follow the voice across, I don't know where. Is that the river? Trees that pierce the heavens and keep climbing. And I feel that I'm dying, dying. The hand beckons. The voice says, not much farther now, a sweet musical voice, all the notes of the flute in it, and something else, something so old in it, you ache to hear it. And she's taking me to Johnny, whoever she is, wherever he is.

Indigo King I find my queen in the banquet hall, the Morseleen singing for the guests, standing in her hair. Everyone is enchanted, holding their breath as the young voice spills out our old repertoire, giving it dimension and feeling, making it new and to hear our poets on the mortal tongue gives us courage, reminds us of better times when the traffic between us was constant. A time it was they worshipped us, prayed to us, begged us on their knees for benediction and beauty. And we gave those things willingly and more. We knelt at their altars too. And my lady greets me and makes room for me beside her and her humours seem yielding enough, her colour high purple as she pours for me and orders them to set a place for me, the Morseleen singing deep into and behind the meaning and the sense. The old dowager has taught him well. He has all the trills and curlicues and ancient ornamentation that she brought with her from those long ago days in the harem's school. She fixes me with her ancient eye, eye of the first crow, and raises her jewelled goblet. I raise my own in deference and appreciation. And my queen smiles. So we're having a party. I wonder, I say, what it is we're celebrating? The End of course, my blue queen answers. The End. And she kisses me and the whole hall cheers and the Morseleen sings on, the way they were born to sing before they forgot. I take him in my hand from out of my lady's hair and say to him, little ladeen of the two worlds, precious morsel that calls up the Age of Gold, you golden child, may you always be like this whatever comes to pass. May you always be as you are this night and may you carry it with you always. The Mystery. And

its answer. More Mystery. And then they call from down
the table to pass him along. And my lady does, guarding
him like the jewel he is as he goes from hand to hand
and they marvel and bless him as he walks lightly on
their palms, smiling at them, the prince we dreamed of
and will never have. But this night we pretend that he
is him. And I see something in the eyes of my people
I haven't seen in centuries. Love. Mortal love.

Woman She wears me on her ear inside one of her
diamonds. I dangle and sway through her days and
nights. I call out but no one can hear me. She takes me
out to feed me when all is quiet and dark and then locks
me in a silk casket that reminds me of an emperor's
coffin. My fingers bleed trying to force a way out. It's
useless. You said you were taking me to Johnny, I say, as
she feeds me soup. I hit the bowl away. It splashes and
scalds my arm. She lays a finger on the burn and the
pain is instantly gone. And I will, she says, I will, be
patient, little woman, don't be upsetting yourself over
things you've no control of. Where am I?, I say, you're in
Paradise she answers and laughs, showing teeth grained
and ridged as boulders. You're in Paradise. And she
shuts the casket and turns the key.

Indigo Queen I lay my head on the mortal woman's
pillow, in the mortal woman's guise, her nightdress on
my small round body and feel what it must be like to be
a flea. Her husband lies beside me, space between us for
an army to sleep. Is this how they go to bed? My blue
gallant, for all our difficulties, sleeps tangled in me. I
miss my hair. I reach across and lay a hand on him. He
jumps as if I've stabbed him. Aroon, I say, Aroon, and he
freezes. Have I got her voice wrong? Have I used a word
she doesn't use? But he comes to me, kisses me, the
sweet mortal kisses of dust and he is pleasing and keeps
me awake for hours. She's had him on rations. Eat your

fill, I say, now is the time of plenty. He laughs and covers me again. I cry out as loud as I can so himself can hear me across the landing. And sure enough he comes to the door, the Morseleen for all the world, though I know it's my own blue king pretending. And he stands there, glaring, jealous. I watch him through the crack of my eye. Come, he says, stretching out his hand. No, I say, turning to the husband, putting my arm on his sleeping back. No, not tonight, I'm sated. I see the shock on his big navy face. The rejection. The insult. Is this his first refusal? Two can play this game me bould blue segosha. I have to duck under the covers so he doesn't see me laugh at the consternation on his face.

The Morseleen I dream I'm in a silk-lined casket with my mother and she holds me and weeps and kisses me and wrings her hands and says, Johnny, Johnny, we have to get out of here. And I say, who are you, and I don't want to go anywhere. And then I wake in the Indigo Queen's hair and she's striding along, singing. And she takes me and tosses me up, up to the high chandeliers and catches me as I fall for what seems like forever.

Indigo Queen The little woman pines among my rubies and gold. Himself mopes about the pastures, training horses, but his heart's not in it. He sits at council and doesn't hear a thing, his thoughts in the other world. You seem too happy, he says, as I pass him in the corridor with the Morseleen napping on the bridge of my nose. If I am it's no thanks to your attentions, I answer and keep walking lest he starts divining me. No, come here, he says, running after me and pulling me by the hair. He examines me closely. What are you scheming? he says, you're planning something. I turn on him. We're vanishing, I say, vanishing. Give me a scheme that'll reverse that. There isn't one, he says. Our time is done. I almost long for it. You may long for it, I say, but

our people do not. They're angry, desperate, depressed.
They want to rip the gauze and take out your precious
mortals, our betrayers. I'm telling you they won't go
quietly. I know it, he says, with such wonder and
awfulness and almost willed treachery in his eyes. All
he cares for now is her, her I've locked away among
my jewels.

Indigo King What are you even doing here? she says,
why aren't you ensconced beyond the gauze with your
girly for the grave, with her streel's hair, hair with
strands of grey already in it, she stammers, knowing
she has thousands of their years on her.

Indigo Queen I do love honesty, he snorts in that ironic
tone that makes me want to put the scorch on him, I do
love honesty in the matter of grey hairs and lines on the
body and the visage. You with your peerless skin are
unknowable.

Indigo King Unknowable? she hisses, her face darkening
to bottle black rage. Me? Unknowable? she growls, and
the Morseleen jumps in fright on her nose. May the first
immortals rue the pink morning I first clapped eyes on
you, she says slowly, her voice coiled with hate. You and
your horse, it was all you had. Indigo gave you everything!
I gave you everything!

Indigo Queen You gave me a stillborn prince with the
immortal's hoof print of the end on his torso. That
terrible prophecy written on his skin. Yes, you gave me
everything, he says.

Indigo King And she falls at my feet and weeps. And the
Morseleen falls too. I catch him in his sleep. He lies in
my palm like a kernel. And I don't know why it is, my
queen weeping, the child sleeping on, innocent, in my
sweaty hand, but I am full of some wild hope. Indigo,
I say, raising her up.

Indigo Queen He forces me from my knees, the
Morseleen safe in his palm. Indigo, he says softly, indulge
me, indulge me a little while. You I love but her I want.

Indigo King And I think of my mortal woman waiting
for me, stretched out on her golden bed.

Indigo Queen I can hear her moving through his
sapphire veins, can hear the old heart in him churning at
the mere thought of her. Her. Locked away. He wants
her. I'll give him her.

Old Fiddler You see I heard an old story about them.
The mother got it from this old man before he died, who
had it from his grandmother, who got it from her uncle's
great-grandfather and it goes even further back than
that, all the way back to one of the earls of the Ely
O'Carrol baronies. It was always said that his mother
was from the other side, what with the way he could
turn himself to a bird or a butterfly or a towering blue
statue of a man. I don't know if there's any truth in it
but they all had the yellow eyes with the flecks of green
and brilliant white like the harvest sun departing for
another year. And some it was said shattered like stars if
you said the wrong thing and you saw the blue entrails
flow over the glass like ink on snow. And their entrails
smelled of honey and new leaves when you crushed them
in your hand. But the gist of the old story is this. A child,
a boy, his name forgotten, let's call him Johnny. But
wasn't he taken to the other side and didn't his mother
nearly die with the weeping and the grief and the loss of
him. And didn't the crowd from the other side take pity
on her and didn't he return. But when he came back, he
was different, and no one would believe her when she
told them what had happened except this old fiddler,
who heard the lad singing one day in a field of crows.

And the crows standing round him and the sheep with
their mouths open full of cud and the very trees not
rustling for fear they'd miss a note. And the old fiddler
sat on the stone wall and listened to the end and then
called the boy to him. And the boy ambled over, a blade
of grass in his teeth. And the fiddler says, You never
learned that song here, if you learned that song here then
I'm the son of God and all his angels. No, says the boy,
indeed and I never learned that song here. Didn't I learn
it in Indigo at the dowager's feet. Indigo, says the old
fiddler, and where would that be now? It's away off in
over after beyond behind within the gauze below the
lake, says the boy, but why do you want to know? I'd
like to go there and learn their tunes, says the old fiddler,
for he was covetous of the old music and airs and fierce
stingy with them when he got them. Then come with me
this night, says the boy, wait by the white thorn over
there in the corner and I'll bring you to Indigo. So that
night the old fiddler waits with his fiddle. And the moon
comes up and he sees striding towards him, not the boy,
but a man as wide as the field he's crossing, his face as
blue as a summer sky and hands swinging that could
hold the whole parish in them and still have room to
spare. And the old fiddler quakes when this mighty
vision stops before him. Well, are you ready? says he. I
expected the boy, says the old fiddler in a whisper. And
here I am as promised, says the royal blue apparition.
And you'll hear tunes tonight that'll crack new pathways
to your heart and the hearts of all you come from. But
hush, says the cobalt giant and he turns and across the
field comes running a young woman, her feet slapping
the dewy grass and he's running towards her and
shrinking as he runs and when he catches her and swings
her around, he's the size of a mortal man but with still
the blue sheen off him there under the moon. And they
whisper hot words in the quiet of the night and only the

corncrake for company and me, that they've forgotten about, says the old fiddler. And he holds her and they rise up in the air and swirl and twirl, dancing under the never ending vaults of the heaven, clothes falling into the field. Surely I'm looking at a god, the old fiddler thinks to himself as he marvels at their sky reel and the way she falls through the air and the way he catches her. And time stops and it goes on and on and the old fiddler has to look away to catch his breath and clutch his heart to make sure it's still beating and has to take glimpses because to watch it full on is too shocking for the earthly eye. But the woman, he realises, the woman he sees through his fingers, prancing the air, dazzling the sky, the trees, the fields, the blue god, this woman in none other than his own wife. This knowledge comes to him slow. Because hasn't he just left his old wife asleep and snoring in the bed a short while ago. But here she is above him, in her pelt, having a moon bath with her lover. And she's young, impossibly young, as young as the day he took her to the altar. And when he glances again isn't she kissing the blue god and then he feels her lips on his and suddenly he's up there with her and it is he who is dancing and swirling and loving her as he never did, never knew how to, refused to, on the ground. And just when he is about to make sense of it all, he falls to the earth, dead. The last thing he sees as his eyes close on the black grass, the last thing he sees is his wife as he has never seen her, as he has never allowed her to show herself and he knows now he has committed a great crime against the music, against her and against himself. And the blue god floats down and says as he closes the old fiddler's eyes, there's the tune you wanted, there's the music you hungered for all your life. You've seen Indigo now and you've heard her, safe journey old fiddler, safe home, get it right next time.

Indigo Queen This samphire coast, the brown shadows that trail to black as I weave my way above their lakes, the rushes swaying like a thousand wands, the breeze balmy on my face. The grass is burnt to ash, the corn ripens and dances like many crowned girls. My lungs are getting used to this. The mucky air doesn't bother me as it used. I put on my mortal shimmer and slide in the window. Where were you? he says, the husband. I push my hair behind my ears, a habit of hers, I lick my lips, my tongue feels tiny between my teeth. I couldn't sleep, I say, so I took a gander. I get in beside him. He is already reaching for me.

Indigo King I take my mortal woman to our golden bed above the trees, the smell of pine on her skin as the day's heat releases it up, up to the vaults of their heaven. She is slow and languorous, heavy with the sweltering night air.

Indigo Queen He moves like a panther over me, I, his willing prey. I have to hold back a bit, do it all differently so he will not recognise the familiar touch of these ancient hands. We have done this a million times but this night he is new. Tell me about her, I say, tell me about your Indigo, your blue queen.

Indigo King Her eyes dazzle in the light that falls lemon from their stars as she lies quietly under me, waiting, just waiting above the rustling trees, her hair spread out on the pillow. She reminds me of her.

Indigo Queen You remind me of her, he whispers in my ear and kisses me to silence me. But I won't be silenced now. My curiosity is up.

Indigo King How so? she says, leaning up on an elbow, breasts colliding like orbs, a flash of silk on my lips. How so? she murmurs, How do I remind you of her?

Indigo Queen When I first knew her, he says, when the world was new and the first immortals supped with us in the sapphire halls of Indigo. And tears come to my eyes and I have to turn away for I remember that time well too. A time of love, a time of art and beauty. Days with nothing else in it but their vanished poetry and song and the thereness of there and the nowness of it and the crystal light and the lips spilling waterfalls of wonder and the ease of it all. We were blessed and we didn't know it. In our ignorance we assumed it would always be thus.

Indigo King And she's quiet and the sky wrapped round us like a scarf of pewter as we hang there, nothing to hold us but the air. I can't get enough of her. But you haven't told me about your queen, she says.

Indigo Queen And he laughs and says curiosity killed the cat and changes into a swan thinking to distract and amuse me. He beats his wings over me and wraps his neck around my thighs. Obviously this gets her going. I'm tempted to match him, to grow my wings, to wrestle him, to see our feathers float down in the star burn, to draw blood. But I restrain myself, lie meekly like the little mortal I'm supposed to be, laugh, pretend surprise, astonishment even. Thou, I say, thou, pulling his wings around me.

The Husband She's too happy. She's too in love with me. She's too yielding. I was always the one who gave. Knew this from the start. I was the lover, she the taker, taking what was her due. But now, she sings all the time, her eyes are bright, she follows me from room to room, waits on me hand and foot. It's perfect. From indifference to adoration. There's something not right. Something voracious in her navy gaze. And she disappears every night. She's there and she's not there, like holding on to a cloud. I don't trust her. I look at her and God forgive me but I see coffins, coffins everywhere. I'm beginning to hate her. And Johnny? His eyes. They're cold. He watches me while I sleep. I begin to think he's a copy of himself. He does all the things a child does, but he does them formally, coolly, his reactions are a few seconds behind themselves, his laugh is hollow. He smells strange, not his smell at all. He hums tunes I've never heard. Only last night, this melody, unearthly, from his bedroom, in no language I've ever come across. I go in and he's standing on the window ledge, the window wide open, singing. He looked like he was about to take flight. I called his name and he turned like a cobra, rage on his face, which he masked quickly. But I saw it there, prideful anger and disdain, eyes flashing. And then it was gone. I said, Johnny what're you doing? He didn't answer for an age and then he whispers, I don't know, Dad, I don't know, lift me down. And of course I lifted him so he didn't fall out the window and crack his head on the flags of the yard below. But I had the sense he was only acting and knew precisely what he was doing. And though he's just a little fella, I had the feeling he was looking down on me from a great height and judging me by some inscrutable code of his own. And the thought went through me, my son doesn't like me. This is mad I know. But it's what I felt. It's what I feel and it's what I saw and it cuts me.

Dowager Queen The thrones are empty. The great hall quiet. The Morseleen downhearted and crying for my daughter. Where is she? he says every few seconds, will she never come? I try to take his mind off her but he's not having it. He won't eat, won't dance, won't sing, just lies in my hand wasting, staring off into the nowhere.

How can she forget him like this? What is she doing there? The days pass, dark vermillion days in this eternal navy prison. I'm afraid the Morseleen will die. Ghesh hovers. He wishes the Morseleen wrong, hates the mortal world and all things temporal with an unbridled hate, on account of his wife falling for a harper in the long ago and turning herself into a swallow when Ghesh came thundering after her through the gauze and shot her down with his poisoned spear from his blue stallion. If we are wounded there we die there. And I wonder now as I look at the grieving Morseleen, is this what my daughter wants. I'm afraid to close my eyes so I take them out and place them in front of the sleeping Morseleen on my palm to keep him from harm. But my immortal soul will not lighten and slide into the first glorious soup so I take down the Indigo annals and quietly retrieve one of my eyes and pass the night perusing the beauty of our first time when we were new, new as the mortals beyond the gauze. And the Morseleen sobs in his sleep and I blow on him to comfort him and turn the enchanting pages that I know by heart but could read forever, these sagas in the old red ink. They wrote then with the blood from the arteries of their heart, would crack open their breast till the blood spilled into the inkwell in a gushing arc. And their signature at the foot of every page, a damask thumbprint, the metallic smell of it still there on the cracked parchment. And the old annals were signed off then by the queen. A smaller thumbprint, silver, licked and flattened by the stars, liquid, tiny. Indelible. There they thought for all of eternity. The future of yesterday. The past of tomorrow.

Woman I howl and smother in this velvet dark, her rings, her diamonds, leaning treacherously towards me, glinting and lethal. Then the lid of this coffin opens. I must've fallen asleep. A giant finger, navy, places Johnny against my chest. And then the lid closes. Johnny, I say. Aaah, he sighs and continues sleeping, Where are we? What is happening? I hold him to me, feel his heart rising and falling, the hot sweet breath mingling with my own, the sticky hair plastered to his neck. I feel his limbs. He's all there, real as me in this unreal place we have come to. I whisper prayers of thanks in this glinting coffin and cling on to him as tight as I can.

Ghesh My little brother, the one they call the Indigo King, lord of these tiered lands and cobalt purlieu, has grown weak and foolish. The mortal sickness is on him, flitting the gauze like a moth to the flame. When we first rode in here, the immortals' footprints still visible on the sand, it was I who was going to rule. It was I who was going to be king. But the dowager's heir, the blue queen, had eyes only for him. And so it passed and so I let it happen. Let the little brother have it all. And for a time I was happy. Who wouldn't be happy here? The verdant sweep of these immaculate lands, the kingdom flowing effortlessly down to the sea, the pink dunes, the crenellated towers that float high above the fluid buildings of turquoise and gold built by the first race of them. And in time, I took a wife. Dreac. One of the minor cousins to the dowager but the pick of them all. How I loved that woman. And thought that it was returned. But no, wasn't she nightly vaulting the gauze, her heart, for we do have hearts, bronze, but hearts nevertheless and hers was soldered to a harper from the other world. I followed her to her love nest, a canopy she'd devised on their southern shore, a lonely place of rock and seagull, and watched her dance on that bed as he played her. And before you know it, isn't she with child. She's carrying the harper's child in her big blue belly. Something I couldn't do in five thousand years. And I gave her many opportunities to come clean, but no, she denied it with her cool faithless eyes. Right, I said to myself, you want to play it that way? I can play it that way too. So I waited, waited and watched, nightly followed her through the gauze and watched from the foot of the bed as she cavorted with her harper. Heard all their whispered plans, how he was making a cradle, how he was having the house painted, how he was going to have her measured for silk dresses and hats. And how she cooed along in agreement. And I felt sorry for the harper. The poor fool hadn't a clue who he was dealing with. He even put a ring on her finger, a paltry band of diluted gold when I had showered the plundered riches of archangels upon her. But this she treasured. This she kissed. This she wore on a diamond ribbon between her breasts. This piece of tin. Once I grabbed her in one of our liquid halls and said, what is it? What is it he has that I don't? What is it who has? she answered, ice in her eyes, brazen as they come. Then explain to me what this is, I said, putting a hand on her swelling stomach. I could see the growing child through her dress, a tiny girl, sucking her thumb, nestling like a pearl in a shell that will never open. But she pushed me away. I'll tell you what he has, she said, I'll tell you what he has that you don't have. He has Death, he has music, he has mystery. But mostly he has Death which is three parts of love and may I perish with him.

Indigo Queen I come back reluctantly, sated, my mind full of the mortal world, my head full of her memories. I grow to love her husband. The oddness of him. The attentiveness. The sweetness and gentleness. The way he holds me in his sleep. And my Indigo gallant and those wild hours on his golden bed. The centuries roll off me

there. I can live and be. I begin to understand his need
for his mortal girl. I enjoy taking on her mantle, slipping
into her skin. But the Morseleen. The Morseleen. My
mother comes flying towards me across the navy maze
that skirts the gauze and before she opens her mouth
I know there's something wrong. The Morseleen, I say,
as calmly as I can, scanning her for sign of him. He's
gone, she says and black tears fall out of her ancient eyes
and black blood gushes from her heart and stains the
bodice of her dress. She throws herself at my feet. I woke,
she says, and he was gone.

Dowager Queen When, she says, when did you last see
him?

Indigo Queen On my palm, she says, sleeping, my eyes
were watching him, I must've nodded off and when I
woke he wasn't there.

Dowager Queen How could you? she wails. Didn't I tell
you? Didn't I warn you? You were too long away, I say,
I'm exhausted. She stands there, hands shaking, panic on
her face, her chin trembling, the eyes smoking lamps as
she flicks through the list of ours who would wish her
harm. The list is long, endless, resentment against her
here brewing down the ages. Ghesh, she whispers.

Indigo Queen Ghesh.

Dowager Queen And she soars up into our cobalt sky,
a monstrous crow, and vanishes.

Indigo King My mortal love sleeps. I carry her down
from the treetops and place her beside the husband. I
leave my copy in the Morseleen's room and depart. I take
a moment to watch her from the door. She's on her side,
the covers thrown back, a shapely leg flung out. The

husband is on his back. Their hearts rise in unison,
sleeping breath perfuming the room, earthly breath that
fills my nostrils, breath of the clay, mineral, silt and
salt of their fragile bloodstreams. I lean closer to read
their dreams. He is dreaming of a woman in snow boots.
She dreams of me. Me coming towards her with the
Morseleen in my palm. And now the picture changes,
she's dreaming of our vanished prince. And he's alive.
No hoofprint on his torso. He's alive and galloping
through our forests of mossy jade. How can she dream
such a thing? How can she know about our vanished
hope, our little prince, the last of the Indigos? I never
told her of those things.

The Morseleen I wake to the sound of hooves. I'm held
tight in a gnarled palm that I don't recognise. I call out,
in their language. *Vreema tuat mayma?* Where are you
taking me? *Melneesyom*, he says. *Melneesyom*. And
where is that, I say. *Tuata rend hoon ano*, he answers.
It's Ghesh. The Indigo King's brother. My blue queen,
my blue mother fears him and hates him and has never
allowed me on his palm. We gallop through the night
and are still galloping as dawn comes in. Have I ever
told you what an Indigo dawn is like? First the stars
whoosh down and dance and sing us goodbye and depart
looking over their shoulders as if they'll never see us
again. Then the sun bleeds slowly up from the caverns
of the deep, flooding and blinding till you can't see, the
indigo chariots straining with the weight of him and the
slingers pinion him to the sky. He fights, he grumbles,
like a baby just awake until he is coaxed out of his black
cloak and stretches and prances and tumbles, molten
sparks angling off and shooting into the sea. Then he
yawns, his powerful breath blowing the night away.
Sometimes he and the moon do battle, clashing like

314

monsters, tearing chunks out of each other that roll
across the dome and make the ground tremble. But this
dawn is lazy, floating above us in muted umber. They
won't fight this morning. The moon contents herself with
one derisive spit and departs. It singes his chest, sending
off tendrils of green and orange steam. Ghesh's horse
announces he is tired and throws us off. I fly through
the air but he catches me. I'm weary of being so small.
I would have thought by now they'd treat me as one of
them. Give us one of those mortal laughs, Ghesh says,
and I tinkle out a false guffaw and his eyes turn inward
with longing and he tickles me with a blade of grass to
hear me laugh again, for real this time in spite of myself.

Woman It's hot and close here, the air stale and rancid.
I'm going to die. Am I dead already? I remember Johnny
was here or did I make that up? I'm weak with hunger.
They've forgotten me. I scrape at the lock until my fingers
bleed. I call out, scream till my throat is raw and my
voice a cracked whisper. I pass out. And come to. I've
wet myself. This is where the dream has taken me, this
velvet coffin, lined with her rings and bracelets. I will
ossify to a brooch of white bone that she'll wear in her
long witchy hair. I pass out again.

Old Fiddler The blue gull they called her or so the great-
grandmother's uncle said. It was one of his grandfather's
brother's sister's cousin's son's nephew's that had the
dealings with her. The famous harper. Him. And nightly
she'd swoop in to shore and lay out her stall, a bed of
star sheets, pillows of the dead angels' down, and she'd
lie there singing in a voice that'd put the mermaids to
shame in their jealous swoons, till she drew him to her
and he walking out of his bed somewhere between wake

and sleep. And some say her name was Dreac and Ghesh was her fairy prince. And through the cornfield he came, down through the lavender beds, the seaweed crackling under his bare feet as he strode the shore towards her. A man in desperate love. A man under the enchantment. The harper. And there on the sand he'd plant his harp and conjure notes for her song and they say even the waves stopped breaking to listen, so strange and full of beauty was their combined music. But didn't she have a jealous man beyond the gauze. Ghesh. And didn't he follow her and didn't he watch and wait, his bronze heart smouldering in his breast with revenge. Nightly he planned their penalty. Nightly he watched their love making and it was a spear through him to watch them moaning and groaning on her silver bed. And as he listened and watched he planned the most terrible revenge, for Dreac was carrying the harper's child, her belly ripening with it, a girl, they say. And come the night on the bed of star sheets and the pillow of dead angels' hair, come the night when the child would be born. And the harper there in a panic and Dreac as cool and calm as a summer's breeze, her eyes full of the joy and mystery of the new creature about to come among us. And just as the last heave shook her body that would wrench the child into the world, didn't Ghesh tower over them at the foot of the bed. Now my lovely streel, now my fairy tramp, now my immortal strumpet and jade, now don't I have you? And he threw a flame from his eye that left the harper in a pile of ashes that flew away on the wind coming in from the sea. Dreac screamed and changed herself into the blue gull that was her emblem and disguise. But if she did, didn't Ghesh fly up after her and hurl his spear at her throat. And as she fell heavily on to the foam didn't the child slip out of her, a fairy child with a mane of hair the colour of leaves in autumn and eyes like lamps that swept over the waves on to her

mother's body and her father's ashes. And before she fell
between them didn't Ghesh catch her and swoop her
away to their kingdom beyond the gauze. I've always
wondered what happened to that child, how she could
survive in the blue, for she was one of us and must've
carried in her the imprint of here. But that was a long
time ago, when we believed differently, when the heart
was more open and we didn't doubt the dream.
And believed in the night and measured time not by
minutes and seconds but by moments of blood-stopping
wonder and tracked our soul's trajectory with a vanished
pride and hunger. All lost. All gone.

Indigo Queen Ghesh's steed is missing from his stable.
I circle our phosphorescent skies, the light sinister in the
navy dusk. My eyes telescope the pink mountains, the
tiered fields, the bottomless valleys. I can see no sign of
him. My Morseleen. What has he done with him? Where
has Ghesh taken him? Is he dead already? I shout his
name. Morseleen! Morseleen mine! Where are you?
Come back to me? Come back to your old blue mother.
My voice bounces off the silver, cracks and melts the
rivulets of gold that thread our dazzling hills. I hold my
wings out, fall on my knees and pray to the first
immortals. Keep him safe. Keep him safe. The moon
sidles down and catches me by the throat in her claws of
steel. Think those boys will come to succour you in your
hour of need? she hisses, malevolent, spewing curses on
my bowed head. I fight her off and fly for cover to my
room, fall in a heap on the casement, exhausted. I have
to get beyond the gauze and pretend to be the mortal
woman. I check the casket. She has passed out, close to
death it seems. I scoop her up, put her under my tongue
and flee for the mortal world and all the fallen.

The Morseleen It's a graveyard but a graveyard like
I've never seen before. A yellow field stretching away
to nowhere, boundless, vast, hordes of children sitting,
playing, running, jumping off tombstones, their voices
high and light, so long since I've heard the sound of
another child. They crowd around me, touch my clothes,
my hair, their eyes are huge violet lamps that swivel over
me. Ghesh holds me aloft so they don't tear me limb
from limb. Where is your prince? he says in their language,
Oh fana durasna nei? And they babble and shout and
fall away like the waves on the shore of another world
that I've forgotten mostly. And he walks towards us, a
towering child, the hoofprint on his naked torso and the
hieroglyphic writing of the immortals tattooed down his
back and front to his navel. He stretches out a smooth
blue hand. Welcome, boy, he says, welcome home. And
the thing is, it feels as if I am home or rather it feels as
if I am him. I can't describe it, only a shock in the blood,
my heart racing, recognition that defies reason. I am
looking at myself, or he is looking at himself in miniature.
I feel the scorch of the hoofmark on his torso. I recoil as
they tattoo the hieroglyphics on my back, my skin. Who
are you?, I say, who are we? He smiles, his mother's
smile, my mother's smile. My blue queen. Where is she?
Will I ever see her again?

Indigo Prince He's tiny. His skin is a pasty white, his
eyes the transparent blue of still light on clear still water.
His curls are plastered to his neck, his hands tremble. So
insubstantial, but for all that, he is there, completely
there, my usurper.

Ghesh I want my mother, he whispers, the Morseleen,
I want my Indigo mother. And his lip goes and the
invisible tears of mortals pour down his face. I lick them

greedily as they pour. The Morseleen jumps, stumbles,
falls. All our Indigo children, born and unborn, rush in
to watch shrieking and shoving. I roar at them to stop, to
get back. The Morseleen lies on the ground, a stranded
beetle. It's time, I say to the prince, it's time.

Indigo Prince This is a day I thought would never come.
Three thousand years I've spent in this playground, this
graveyard of vanished children. I call my bride. She
stumbles from her tomb, the children scatter and shriek.
I take her mottled claw to guide her as she lifts her
leathery face and toothless mouth towards the light.
Long ago she lost her sight.

Ghesh The harper's daughter, I say. She knows me. Ghesh,
she spits. Are you still here?, I say. She tosses her head.
I brought her here the night I put a spear in her mother
and turned her father to a fistful of ash. When was that?
Every breath a torture, she growls, every breath of these
yellow pastures agony. Will no one let me go? And the
Indigo Prince takes the harp from her back and begins to
play and she slowly takes the shape of the girl she was,
the beauty in her prime. Half us. Half them. No blood
mix like mortal and immortal meshed. She dazzles, the
air throbs around her as once it did around her mother,
Dreac, my faithless wife. The veins in her temple pulse
royal purple, the hair yellow as this field we stand upon.
The children rush in again to kiss her feet and stroke her
hair. You're leaving me, you're leaving me, my lord, she
says to the Indigo Prince, who will play my harp now?

Harper's Daughter He takes me in his arms. I know he is
torn and I know I have to let him go. I ask only one thing.
Ask it, he says.

Indigo Prince Bury me in the other world, she says, in
their clabar and muck, in their wet, seething clay. I'm not
made for this eternal clamour and din of the vanished,

this shrieking field of blue children who have never lived and never died.

Harper's Daughter When I have the courage to break my harp, remember to do this.

The Morseleen Ghesh lifts me from the ground and opens my shirt and with the nail of his little finger prods around my heart. The shrieking children fall silent. Their bowed heads will not meet my gaze. The prince with the hoofprint on his torso and the hieroglyphs tattooed on his skin comes close. You mean to harm me, I say.

Indigo Prince You mean to harm me, he says. The harper's daughter gasps. No, she whispers, no. Do it, Ghesh says, do it quickly now.

The Morseleen Little mortal, he says, little man of clay, little boy of the finite world and all things fleeting, I ask your understanding of what you cannot understand. He moves quickly, a slash along my chest, the blood pours, dark red down my stomach. I have been opened, ribs stretched wide like a creaking gate. He pulls my heart from my body in a sucking lurch. The shooting pain. My legs buckle. He holds it aloft between forefinger and thumb. And then he eats it. I watch in . . . dis . . .

Ghesh Dark ribbons flow down his clothes pooling in my palm, this bonsai creature, the life draining from him. And then he's still, a husk in my palm.

Harper's Daughter My ghost groom stands there, the hoofmark on his torso fades and disappears, the immortal hieroglyphs unravel and fly upwards like a flock of starlings. He is lost to me now, mortal blood on his lips, he is Indigo again, unvarnished, substantial, the last hope of his kind.

Indigo Prince Ghesh laughs. Throws back his boulder of a head and laughs, his eyes sinister, wild. The little mortal already cold in his hand. My bride, the harper's daughter, takes him gently and croons words of benediction to the dead child, innocent creature of earth and sky, you're still now. You're quiet. Let me string you to my harp and when the time comes, I'll take you with me, I'll take you home. I'll return you to where you came from. And she looks at me and I know I am changed though I feel nothing, no difference between here and there when it comes right down to it. They fade in front of me, the little one, the one they called the Morseleen, all the vanished children, my companions of aeons, my harper's daughter, my bride, my bedfellow, my playmate, as if they were never here. The yellow field is empty. Voices that have yet to be are no longer heard.

Ghesh He jumps up behind me on my steed, this glowing blue youth, the Morseleen's heart vital within him. We head for the hills. My proof and my revenge. Their Earth is over and all the little people in it. Their great mottled skies will know silence again. We will take them, each and every one. The third great age of Indigo will begin. Me at the helm this time.

Dowager Queen Malice. That's what I smell in the air around me. Malice of intent. Our people colludering and hatching in groups, falling silent as I pass, many of them regarding me with open hostile stares. He comes striding through them, weary, with the dust of the earth on his clothes. Where is my queen? he says, she's not in any of her usual haunts. The Morseleen is missing, I say. No, he says, not the Morseleen, how can that be? He shouts for his stallion and thunders away across the purple valley towards the gauze.

Indigo Queen I'm waiting for him in the bed, my human shape on. His little woman. The real one. The real little woman he's losing his mind over I've left asleep in the forest. I gave her water, some berries that she couldn't eat. Johnny, she whispered, my son, you promised, where is he? I don't answer. I tell her to drink. She tries but the cup falls from her hand. I try my healing on her but it won't work. She's fading. I leave her there and make my way to her husband, put on her nightdress and slip in beside him. He grabs me by the hair, you changeling, you witch, who are you? I try to speak calmly in her voice but he has me pinned beneath him. Where is my wife? he says, shaking me till the teeth rattle in my head. Where is she? What have you done to her? And he has me by the throat. He's going to kill me. There's nothing for it but the scorching hand on his face. The room fills with smoke, his skin melts and slides down his bones. I've used too much pressure in my fright. He lies there on the burning sheets, a heap of charred bones, his vitals smouldering. I didn't mean to kill him. I can't undo it now. And I'm about to flee but there he suddenly is, my Indigo King, at the door in the guise of the Morseleen. He looks in disbelief at the heap of bones. His eyes change. You, he says, you.

Indigo King I didn't mean to take him out, she says, stretching into her true self, as I stretch too. The roof comes off the house, slate and beam falling into the yard. I take the bones of the husband and stuff them in her mouth, eat them, you immortal reel, I say, eat them. She gags on the flames, spits, struggles but I hold her fast. He never did us a moment's harm.

Indigo Queen Don't I know it, I say, but he was choking the life out of me. Where is she? he says, slow and deadly.

Indigo King Who? she says, spewing thigh bones and flashing me a stare of jealous rage. And I'm afraid now. Afraid for my mortal woman.

Indigo Queen Where? he hisses, what have you done to her?

Indigo King What have you done to the Morseleen, she shoots back. I've done nothing with him, I say, I swear to you I have done nothing to him or with him. Well, he's gone, she says, and great black tears brim and roll from her eyes and down her bodice as the rivers of her ancient heart erupt, rusty and foul smelling. My Morseleen is gone, she wails and I can see she's murderous with the loss of him.

Indigo Queen I swear, he says, gently, but calculation in it too, I swear I have not harmed your Morseleen, now where is my mortal girl?

Indigo King And as I speak, she comes stumbling from the trees. She stands gaping at the two of us with our heads poking from her roof and the walls in rubble around us.

Woman He comes towards me, bricks and mortar falling from him that he brushes aside as if they're only leaves. He reaches down and lifts me up in his hand.

Indigo Queen I want Johnny, she cries, her voice thin and high, where is he? What have you done with him?

Indigo King We'll find him, I say.

Woman Find him? Is he lost? My eyes scan the ruins of my house. My husband? What have you done?

Indigo King And she shrieks and wails there in my palm. Calm, girl, calm, I say. I'm taking you to Indigo. I'm taking you through the gauze.

Woman No! Not there! Not there! Not that navy coffin.

Indigo Queen Johnny, she wails, Johnny, and I join her. Our cries echo in the yard. My little Morseleen, where have you gone? My Indigo King soars up with his love, his mortal love held fast in his hand. He doesn't deign to look at me. I follow them, heartsore and ashamed at the scene of carnage I'm leaving after me. Ghesh then has my Morseleen. He's always hated me. Finally we'll have our showdown. We cruise over their valleys and their cities, the lights winking where they huddle and swarm, never knowing we pass above them. I hear him whispering, sweet sootherings that once were whispered to me and I burn with jealousy and grief. He never looks back though I am right behind him.

Indigo Prince We ride through many lands. Ghesh points out for me the ruined towers and desolate fields where the first immortals played. Not even the rivers flow, the sea is a frozen blue plate to our right as we gallop across the grey sand. Our horse leaves no footprints. I sleep and wake, each time, marvelling that I am here. I thank the mortal boy whose heart I have taken. My blood is warm. My skin is real. I never thought to be here again.

Ghesh The horse announces he is tired and throws us off. We land roughly on the packed sand. Your first bruise, I say to the Indigo Prince and heir and he laughs and dusts himself down. We rest in the ruins of an ancient palace, pillars of dirty Saturn gold glinting dully around us. I lay out our provisions and he looks at me for guidance on how to eat. And once he gets the hang of it, it's hard to get him to stop. What's this? he says. And this? And this? cramming it into his mouth. And this? That's a napkin, I say for wiping away the sauce and the crumbs. Oh, he says, blushing and puts it down. He's an innocent. One could do with him whatever one liked. He has the easy manner of my brother, his father, no sign of the white scorch of his mother or the old dowager.

Indigo Prince His eyes are on me. My bride, the harper's daughter, feared him. He was married to her mother, Dreac the betrayer. I miss my bride. I've known her since she was a helpless babe first come to the yellow field of children. How long ago was that? Will I ever see her again? Thick-hearted, was her pronouncement on this man who examines me closely with his hooded eyes. Thick-hearted. He tells me he is my uncle, that he was there in the birthing chamber as I slipped from my mother's womb. He tells me of the horror when they saw the imprint of the immortal's hoof on my chest, the studded prophecy tattooed on my body and my vanishing before their very eyes. He tells me how my parents have soured with the long swathes of time in their childless kingdom. I hear my bride's voice in my ear. Thick-hearted. Not to be trusted. I bow my head and listen. I keep my expression blank. He tidies and packs as I feed the horse from my hand. He accepts the food reluctantly. Nothing good will come of this, he says when he has cleaned my hand. Why so? I say. Because you cut the heart from a child and ate it. It was only a mortal child, I say. Tell that to his mother and father, says the horse and snorts and tosses his mane and moves away.

Dowager Queen It's dawn when I see Ghesh approach Indigo's border. He canters by, not deigning to greet me, a young man sleeping behind him. A boy really. An Indigo boy. My heart creaks, my voice quakes, who have you there? I say.

Ghesh Your grandson.

Dowager Queen Your grandson, he says, swaggering triumph in his voice and eyes. I have no grandson, I say, not in this world nor in any other.

Ghesh You have now, I say. She looks at me in amazement. It's worth it for this alone, shock the old shaking witch. What have you done? she says, her eyes devouring the sleeping boy.

Dowager Queen I've done the impossible, he says, and throws back his big boastful head and laughs. The boy wakes, film of death clouding his sleepy eyes. He regards me coldly.

Indigo Prince Your grandmother, Ghesh says, your mother's mother, the old dowager. High in her saddle, her elegant fingers holding the reins, sits a woman of incomparable beauty. It is customary to kiss her feet. I get off the horse and take the long blue foot in my hand and press my lips to it.

Ghesh What have you done with the Morseleen? she says, her voice lethally calm.

Dowager Queen My daughter is beside herself. What have you done with him? Where is he?

Ghesh He's where all his kind go sooner or later and good riddance to them.

Indigo Prince Tears spring to her eyes, they flow from her orbs in a river of black. You killed him? she says. You killed the little Morseleen, her voice cracking with sorrow. Why? What did he ever do to harm you? He brought us nothing but joy. My daughter will vanish you. Both of you. You and this wraith! And she spits at my feet and flames of carmine leap from her fingertips as she goes for me but Ghesh intercepts her and they roll and wrestle across the samphire fields hurling incantations and blows and then their horses go at it biting and hoofing and rearing and then they come galloping, the Indigo King and Queen, their crowns flashing in the sun, my father, my mother. I fall to the ground. Forgive me,

I say, I killed him, I didn't know you loved him. I am
your son.

Indigo King The boy on the ground. His face in the
dust. I am your son, he says. I killed him, he says. Stand
up, boy, I say, and he stands to his full height. An Indigo
child. A sight I never thought to see again. He looks at
me with fear in his eyes. I have no son, I say. Do you
dare to mock me?

Indigo Queen I'm the prince you had in the long ago, he
says. But this cannot be. The one with the hoofmark on
his torso, he says, the one who carried the prophecy of
our tribe's end. Then where are those marks now, says
my lord, gaping in wonder, show us them.

Indigo Prince They vanished when I ate the heart of the
mortal boy that Ghesh brought.

Indigo King You ate the heart of the Morseleen, my
queen says, and buckles in her saddle. No, she cries, no,
not my Morseleen, anyone but the Morseleen. I have to
hold her up.

Indigo Prince Was that his name? Yes, I ate it, I say, and
now I'm here, the prophecy reversed. A sound pierces the
air, high and thin.

Indigo Queen His mortal woman screams and writhes
in his palm. He croons to her. No, she cries, where is he?
Where is his body? Where is his small helpless body? She
tries to escape my lord's hand. My boy, my child, my son,
she weeps, what have you done? What have you done?

Woman The Indigo Queen looks at me and bows her
head. Is it shame? Her towering body shakes in the
saddle as the black tears of her grief flow from her
breast. The giant youth, the murderer, looks at us all in
consternation. They've eaten my son's heart. My mind

swoons with the knowledge. My son's heart is inside this monster with the lantern eyes swivelling from face to face. They alight on me.

Indigo Queen My mother has reduced Ghesh to a heaving pulp. She has scorched one of his eyes shut, the skin drips from his face like wax. She has severed his left hand from his wrist with her magenta flames. She is moving in for the kill, for the vanishing when my lord intervenes.

Indigo King I pull her from him by the witchy hair. My brother lies there laughing, taunting. This is the thanks I get for bringing your son safe from the yellow field of children. I'm tempted to finish him off but my queen stops me. My mortal woman weeps in my palm. Her cries rend us, we burn with shame, we have not taken good care of the Morseleen, forgive us, I say, forgive us, but she shakes and weeps on, who would have thought they could feel so much. They're like us. They're exactly like us. In miniature.

Dowager Queen My daughter leaps from her horse and circles the Indigo boy, the self-announced prince and heir. She touches him wonderingly, as if her long blue fingers would go through him, as if he will slip away from her again. The boy is quiet, fearful. You killed my Morseleen, she says quietly. I often dreamed of you returning, I never thought it would happen. And never, never like this. I would swap you in a heartbeat to have the Morseleen again in my palm but those days are gone. And then she does something extraordinary. She kneels. She kneels and takes his hand and kisses it. Welcome, my vanished beloved, she says, welcome back to the fold.

Indigo Queen Let him ride in triumph before us across our pavilions and tiered pastures. Let all of Indigo see. Their prince has returned.

Ghesh She offers me her hand. A truce. Have your
witch mater unsever and unblind me first, I say. And
the dowager reluctantly and in bad faith mutters the
incantations as if they're choking her. She puts my hand
on backwards. A reminder, she says, and on this point
she will not budge, the wicked old crone.

Dowager Queen My daughter puts her son . . . am I
actually saying these words? Her son? The prince? Up he
goes on her horse. She runs her hands over him and he is
transformed from pale waif to shimmering heir in silk
shirt and raiments. She winds her pearls and rubies in his
long purple hair. She puts kohl on his eyelids and crimson
on his white lips. She walks beside him as he sits in the
saddle, stunned, a drowned statue hauled up from the
deep. She has dreamed of this day, haven't we all? This
triumph, this magical return that will leave them gaping,
her tormentors, her detractors, the prophecy reversed, the
stain on her removed. Her eyes shine though her hand
trembles on the bridle. There is an Indigo child in Indigo
once more. And if we are still doomed, never again can
she be blamed. Never again can our desperate fate be
laid at her feet.

Indigo King And they come to stare, from their pavilions
and hunting grounds and down the crenellated valleys
and the high cobalt crags. They come in droves.
Swooping. The men gasp, the women stretch out their
hands and shriek and weep. I look at my brother Ghesh.
He nods slyly, his withered hand hidden in his pocket.
What sorcery has he achieved? What opaque art is
involved here? The women rush forward to touch this
apparition that calls himself my son. But he's real. He
stretches out his hand to clasp theirs, his back is straight,
he moves among them like a dream, a little guidance and
he will play this part to perfection. He has his mother's
fineness. Her cold proud gaze. My mortal woman is

stretched on my palm, eyes red with grief, but if they are,
she can still manage hot smoking glares of hatred and
rage at me, at my queen, at my newly returned son. I
close my palm over her. Not now, I whisper, not now.
I feel her scrawbing at my palm, her teeth biting into
my flesh. Not now, my broken enchantress, not now.

Old Fiddler Then the horses came in on the waves,
hooves hurling the sand behind them and cutting
swathes through the breeze. But I need to go back first
to something the grandmother spoke about around the
fire, in winter, the wind prowling the house looking for
a way in. And the grandmother was only a girl when this
happened, a girl sitting on her own grandmother's knee.
On a night of stars, a clear summer night, dusk coming
down like gossamer on the trees and the mountain
behind and the moon swelling over the tide and there's a
sound at the door. Not a scratch. Not a knock, more like
a string breaking. And the grandmother's grandmother
goes to the door and opens it and standing there is a
woman with hair as yellow as the buttercup and skin
white as the virgin's soul, and over her shoulder a harp
and in her arms a dead boy-child of six or seven years.
And the grandmother's grandmother reels back in fright
and says, what world blew you in? And the woman
answers, all of them, in a voice like a new opened tomb.
And how can I assist you? says the grandmother's
grandmother, shaking in her shoes.

Harper's Daughter (*carrying the dead Morseleen*) And
I can see I'm terrifying the poor old woman who has the
eyes of one who has never done deliberate harm. I'm in
a quandary, I say.

Old Fiddler I need sacred ground to bury this mortal
child, she says, and I don't rightly know the lie of your
land and purlieu, your earth and sky being all novel to
my doomed eyes. And the child is heavy in her arms and

her lips cracked with the dust and mire of the journey wherever she's come from. And the grandmother's grandmother is afraid to invite her in but her generous heart and the old decency of the old style in the rules of hospitality to wounded strangers gets the better of her and she widens the door and steps aside and the woman with the yellow hair and the dead boy in her arms and the harp on her back floats over the threshold. Take the weight of your weary feet, says the grandmother's grandmother and the grandmother, only a child herself, runs to the pail to get the woman a cup of water and a slice of oatmeal cake and the bit of mackerel left over from the supper. And the woman flings the harp from her shoulder and lays the dead ladeen at her feet and drinks and eats with the relish of a body that has just discovered taste. So that's what they call food, she says, always wondered what it was. And the dead child at her feet is the hue of alabaster or one of those marble angels with the sightless eyes, his lips pressed together in horror and his clothes as flimsy as the wings of a dragonfly.

Harper's Daughter Is the child yours? the old woman asks. Indeed and he isn't, I say, only I've carried him on my harp for the longest time and longer than that again.

Old Fiddler He's one of your kind, says the woman with the hair the colour of the honey bee's stripe and eyes the mother of all blues, cornflowers opening and fireflies darting from them when she turned her gaze on you, or so the grandmother said. And then she took up her harp.

Harper's Daughter It's better if I sing it. Everything comes truer when it's sung. This is a song I learned in the yellow field of children.

Old Fiddler And her voice floods the room, a voice of such sweetness and beauty, with its high and low tones

and its quicksilver moods and phrasing to die for, a voice
before the Ark of the Covenant, a voice of the seraphim
and all the lost repertoire, a voice with the echo of God
himself in it. The aristocracy of sound, the curling notes
and tones of eternity, all its bounty and superfluity. You
could die happy after you'd heard it. You could rest in
your grave and go peacefully down as you watched her
and listened as she leaned over her harp. And the hours
pass and still she sings on and she changes all the time,
old, young, young, old, a shrivelled crow, a skeleton
whose bones move deftly across the strings, a butterfly,
a dog, a gull, she shapeshifts to all of these creatures and
into others the grandmother had no names for. And the
night goes on and her song is endless and the boy a
statue at her feet in his shroud and his crown. And the
grandmother falls asleep in her grandmother's arms and
when she wakes the woman is still singing and plucking
at her harp.

Harper's Daughter I come to the part about the mortal
boy at my feet. The Morseleen they called him. Johnny
I believe his name was on this earth and under these
haunted skies.

Old Fiddler And it's a fearful song of illicit love and
child-stealing and murder and hearts ripped out and
women weeping this side of the gauze and the other. And
prophecies of wonder and hoofprints on the torso of her
lover, some Indigo Prince of the long ago who forsook
her for the cobalt meadows of his prime. And between
the jigs and the reels the gist of it is she took it upon
herself to come through and put the boy back into the
clay he came from, and herself with him because she has
lived too long and no longer has the courage to witness
and sing of what has yet to come.

Harper's Daughter I pluck the last string for the last time and stand and lift the dead boy, some mortal woman's child.

Old Fiddler And the grandmother's grandmother leads her to the old graveyard, the harvest moon lighting their way. And with her harp the woman with the yellow hair scoops out the clay until she has space enough for herself and the child. She throws the harp in first, then falls backwards upon it in a swoon, the child in her arms as the grandmother and the grandmother's grandmother look on with their mouths open wide. And as they watch the clay slides back in on top of them covering the dead child and the living woman and grass grows over them and then the weeds come, the wild flowers, the brambles, and finally the hazel tree that looks as if it has been there three thousand years if its been there a day. And the grandmother's grandmother runs for safety to the house with the grandmother by the hand and she locks and bolts the door behind them. And they doubt what they have just witnessed but the cup that the woman with the yellow hair drank from is there on the table and the mackerel bones and the crumbs from her cake and the sound of her harp and her song still echoes around the room.

Indigo King My Indigo smiles. My mortal woman weeps. Won't eat, won't speak, won't look at me. I put her in my navel and let her mourn because I don't know what else to do. She lies there immobile, a pearl in an oyster weeping for the Morseleen, tears that run down my stomach in a never-ending stream and this ancient heart of bronze cracks in its groove. I thought I had seen everything by now, felt everything there was to feel. My Indigo Queen struts, her head high, her Indigo Prince by her side. She watches him jealously, fearfully as if he will be snatched from her again. And my people are buoyant, hopeful, eyes shining with it. They smile conspiratorially. Something's afoot but I can't figure out what.

Indigo Prince My mother gets the whole story out of me. Her eyes fill as I describe the death of the Morseleen and my second birth. One precious for another, she says and kisses my hand and runs her fingers through my hair. Indigo has its prince again, she croons, Indigo has its prince.

Ghesh I gather eighty of the finest warriors we have and we gallop to the gauze and rip through it as one. We scoop them up like butterflies wherever we find them, from their sleeping cots, their playgrounds, from their green rolling meadows, their beaches, buckets and spades still in their hands. They scream and cry but we have them fast in our saddlebags, under our tongues, clinging to our hair as we flee into the waves and back through the gauze. And the long, long gallop to the yellow field of vanished children. And a day of high butchery, their hearts in our palms, Indigo children out of the invisible as they swallow the precious meat and elixir, the harper's daughter screaming as she gathers the husks of the mortals we have flung aside so fast are we working. Murderers, she cries, murderers, as she puts them in neat piles and strings them to her necklace. Blood-spattered, exhausted, we come away with upwards of a thousand Indigo children as shocked and stunned as we are. It worked. It worked. Tears on these hard men's faces. They never thought to see the like. And the women, the women go wild when we march in. They run, they shriek, they tear at themselves, they sit on the ground and weep as Indigo's children come home, tall, blue, forever graceful, mortal hearts locked in immortal frames, a bit weary and dusty now from the journey but here at last. The prophecy reversed. Denied. But instead of reward I'm shunned, feared, given dark looks when the details of this miracle get around. What did they expect? That there would be no cost? The miraculous does not come cheap.

Dowager Queen These Indigo wraiths crowd the chambers, eat voraciously, the kitchens strain with effort to feed them. Nothing satisfies. They devour every morsel put in front of them and shout for more. They fight over scraps, clawing each other, ice in their eyes, death in their borrowed hearts.

Indigo Prince I'm sent in to talk to them, reason with them, explain etiquette and codes. They crowd around, leering, fantastical. Is this it? they shriek, is this all living is? Hunger and despair? You told us Indigo was everything. It is nothing but rules and suspicion. Where is the love promised? The easy days of verdure? The shore? A mother and father's patience and worship? These people hate us. And it's true, after the first exciting days the Indigos have withdrawn fearfully from their new returned children. Afraid of our eyes that watch coldly, afraid of our sudden inexplicable rages, of our ferocity to live, of our confusion, our eyes don't close, we are unable to smile, no childish laughter is heard. Only howls, howls of terror and fear. Some die within days, sitting in corners, unable to understand. Some are killed by their companions. They go at one another with ferocious intent. Their strength is formidable. Their passions way beyond the passions of children, dark, perverse things they inflict on all and sundry. I know their turmoil, every cell aches for their abandon. I'm afraid to unleash my self, my real self. I say to them, be patient, be calm. No, they roar in unison.

Indigo Queen The kingdom is in uproar. Ghesh is hauled in. My Indigo King seethes. The mortal woman looks at me, triumph in her eyes, bitterness. Our torment pleases her. We live in fear of these monsters we have mistaken for our vanished children.

Woman They build a fortress, erected overnight, double-walled, reinforced stone imported from the old abandoned territories and ruins of the immortals. They herd the monsters in. They fight tooth and claw. Many are the fallen. I watch from his shoulder as the black blood flows. Ghesh stands guard at the entrance. The old dowager has cast him in bronze. He leers there at the mouth of the tunnel, a gargoyle, stunned, one hand backwards, the eyes wild with horror. It brings no comfort. It will not return my son.

Indigo Prince It's a nightmare. These my soft companions of centuries. These my playmates from the yellow field. How gentle we all were when we were nothing. And my harper's daughter? I say to the group of little girls who were her handmaidens in the long ago. Your who? they say, blank-eyed, they have no memory of her. The yellow field, I say, and they look at me in consternation. The yellow field? What yellow field? And they're herded in like horses, nostrils flaring, bodies straining, kicking, biting in fury, boiling and frothing from their cobalt lips.

Indigo King The sounds that come from the fortress rending our once-peaceful skies. The sounds of those children dying, a second death, needless. Take me home, my mortal woman says, take me back through the gauze. Take me back to the other side.

Old Fiddler And then the horses came in on the waves, hooves flying over the sand, leaving no foot prints. This time it was the women they were after. They lined up like juggernauts, monstrous silhouettes on our midnight hills, dwarfing the gorse and the old oaks that grow there. And then they started to sing, a tune of ache and enchantment and the women walked out of their houses, from their beds, from sleeping husbands and nursing babes and ran for the hills where the demons sat still on their horses, nothing moving except their lips and their eyes roaming over the approaching women like searchlights where they pinned them and they froze and they plucked them like blackberries off the black ditches and grass. And the women and girls swooned in their hands, drunk on the fairy music that was written to drive us mad. And then the horses pawed the air and as one they turned and rose and hurled back into the blue they came out of. Or so they say. This story so old, hard to tell if it ever happened or maybe it is a tale of things to come. Others claim there was no song of enchantment but a bloodbath on that hill. Women and girls hunted down like deer, blood pouring from wounds and blows of the chase, clothes ripped and flung away, dragged screaming and flailing on to the horses by creatures with the faces of devils, roaring through black lips that they'll never see the face of God so all eternity must be for the having here, as they dragged the weeping women pleading for their lives. And the harper's daughter twanged in her grave and the hazel tree shook with the vibrations and leaked tears of blood from its leaves. We're dealing with fragments here and I can only pass on what has been passed down, the old stories, the old time, when there was mighty traffic between all the worlds. Their defence, it was told, was because we had stopped believing in them, stopped praying to them, were deliberately wiping them out. I can understand this, respect it even. There's only the gauze and which of us is the right side of it, the real side, is a momentous question, the answer to it beyond my venturing. But this much I know. It's a dream. A dream. Space, time, memory, these creatures, whoever they are, us, whoever we are, an ever-enfolding, always unfolding unstoppable dream, invented by time and the one who made plenty of it.

Indigo Queen The Indigo children break out of the triple-ringed fortress and go on a spree of carnage before they empty my king's stables of all the horses, thoroughbreds with blood lines going back to the first immortals. And they head for the gauze, Ghesh at their helm. The Indigo Prince looks on with those eyes of his that never close. And then he comes to me this morning and tells me he is sickened and weary of Indigo and that he is journeying back to the yellow field of children, the yellow field where he came from and should never have forsaken. I'm going back, he says, to fulfil a wish and a promise I made to my bride, the harper's daughter, my cousin Dreac's child that she had by a mortal back in the mists of time.

Indigo Prince The hoofmark reappears on my torso. The prophecy is again studded on my skin in the old hieroglyphics of the first time. My mother teaches me her lore, her spells and incantations. The dowager looks on in disapproval. She leads the exodus out of Indigo, back, she says, to the abandoned territories of the first age. My mother refuses to go with her. Their parting is terrible, but my mother wants to wait for my Indigo father who has gone through the gauze with the mortal woman hanging from his beard. I follow the dowager across the ancient territories and beyond that will take me to the harper's daughter. I want to be nothing again and I want to be it with her.

Dowager Queen My daughter watches us from the casement of her tower, a lonely figure, mouth open in grief, it is killing me to leave her but there is no reasoning with her. She is waiting for her Indigo King to return. She will wait forever. I tell her the gauze is shifting, the gauze is diminishing. Soon the gauze will be sealed. She says, that's the risk she will take. I lead my people out on foot, they have taken all the horses. Our numbers are greatly reduced. They bow their heads and water the blue meadows with their tears as the dazzling towers of Indigo vanish and the deer and the trees kneel down as we pass. I come from the abandoned territories, I tell them, I come from there. We'll start from scratch, I say, we'll start again. I've done it before.

Indigo King Once more through the gauze. I'm taking my mortal woman home. My Indigo Queen is waiting for me on her steed, pawing the air above the navy maze. When will you return to me? she says. I'll return to you, I say, when this woman in my palm is no more. And we gallop through the rent and I hear her call after me, my Indigo Queen, I'll wait, she says, I'll wait. I lost the Morseleen too.

Woman He takes me to a remote glen and we live peacefully there for a time. He sings for me, plays, hunts, our table overflowing with the bounty of the forest and the rivers. At night there is the golden bed, my blue man whose dalliance has cost me so dear. And the years pass and I grow old as he stays the same. And he nurses me as I sicken and whispers not to be afraid, that it is only like opening a door and stepping into another field. And the last thing I see as breath departs is his shining blue face hanging over me and my son in his shroud and his crown, in the arms of a woman with hair the yellow of the gorse and eyes the mother of all blues.

Indigo Prince Excuse me, kind stranger.

Old Fiddler A soft night.

Indigo Prince It is and I believe you're sitting on the grave of my bride.

Old Fiddler This stump of an old hazel?

Indigo Prince That's no stump of the hazel. That's her harp and her emblem. I'd know it in any world.

Old Fiddler And this young man, this stranger, wrenches the stump from its roots as if he's plucking a daisy and there's the sound of strings and he pauses and looks around with such yearning, as if he is drinking up the world for the last time and then he tips his hat to me and walks down into the clay to meet her.

Music. Lights.

End.